BASTIONS ON THE BORDER

BASTIONS ON THE BORDER

The Great Stone Forts at
Rouses Point on Lake Champlain

James P. Millard

AHL
America's Historic Lakes
P.O. Box 262
South Hero, Vermont 05486

For Lynn

My friend, my wife, my love

CONTENTS

ACKNOWLEDGEMENTS

This book would never have been possible without the assistance and generosity of many individuals and organizations. My task here is to mention them all and somehow find the words to express my gratitude and to let the reader know how vital their contributions were to this work. I sincerely hope I can do that in suitable fashion.

First and foremost, this book never would have happened without the love, patience, support, and good-humor of my wife Lynn. Lynn has helped me through the last decade in so many ways, not the least of which was her role as my research assistant at National Archives.

After Lynn I owe the most to my friends Roger Harwood and Charlie Barney. Roger was the first to motivate me to take on this task; it was he who first put me in touch with the owners of Fort Montgomery. It was he who supplied me with the wonderful photos from the archives of the Clinton County Historical Association. Roger, who accompanied me on one trip after another to the fort. Roger, the retired industrial arts teacher who studied the plans and details of the ruins to help me understand so much. And it was Roger Harwood who works with me to this day to share the story of the fort as I finish this book.

Charlie Barney is one of the major photo contributors to this book. A Rouses Point native, now living in Buffalo with his wonderful family, Charlie's father, Charles Senior, was an accomplished photographer during the Second World War in Europe. Before going overseas Mr. Barney spent his time as many locals did, at the fort. Fortunately for us, however, Charles Barney Sr. often took his camera with him. His son, my friend, has shared those wonderful images with me. They can be seen in this book and the one that preceded it. Charlie has also supported me through the years with encouragement and his wonderful off beat sense of humor.

Others, many others, have generously shared their photos and plans with me. Some of the most wonderful photos in this book came from Raymond Seguin. Ray, born in Rouses Point eighty-nine years ago, experienced the fort in a way not many today could have. His vintage photos are gems and they add so much to this book. His son, Brian graciously assisted by digitizing some of these photos.

Quebec historian and author André Charbonneau has kindly allowed me the privilege of quoting from his excellent book, "The Fortifications of Île aux Noix." I am grateful to have had the book as a resource and highly recommend it for further reading.

Liz Clark and the family of the last Fort Keeper, Sgt. Thomas Bourke generously donated photos and the memoirs of Thomas's son, Harold. They grace this book and add so much to it.

Other photo and document contributions came from the collection of the late Victor Podd through the generosity of Stephen and Victor Podd and the efforts of Ann Thurber. Long-time Rouses Point resident Ben Arno has shared many wonderful photos from his collection. I am grateful to Ben for the photos and for securing the rights for me to publish them. I owe a debt of gratitude to the Clinton County Historical Society, my friend Geri Favreau of the Rouses Point/Champlain Historical Society, the owners of Fort Montgomery, Stephen and Victor Podd and their hard-working and dedicated representative, Ann Thurber. The Podds have allowed me access to their property over the last decade. Ann is the one who has made it happen.

Other people who have shared photos with me are Tia Hollowood, Ralph Gilpin, Addie Shields, Gordon F. Lemnah and Robert Fraser Farnsworth. Not all of their photos made it into this book. All of them, however, contributed to my knowledge and insight into the fort.

An individual who was of much assistance early on was Harold E. Nelson of Maine. Mr. Nelson generously provided me with much useful information regarding the 45th parallel and the Border Controversy.

Noted Third-System Fortification authority John Weaver provided much to me in the way of support and information. His generosity and expertise are much appreciated.

Former Rouses Point Mayor and military enthusiast Tom Batha kindly provided me with much useful information about the disposition of the fort's guns.

I am grateful to the staff of National Archives in College Park, Maryland, Library and Archives Canada, Special Collections at Feinberg Library, Clinton County Historical Association, and the good people who set up and maintain the remarkable resource at Northern New York Historical Newspapers- Northern New York Library Network.

And of course, I learned much from the work of the Reverend Daniel Taylor and John Ross, individuals who loved the fort during their time on this earth and whose writings about it contributed much to my knowledge and understanding.

Finally, I would like to thank the hundreds of people who came to my presentations and tours of the fort over the years. It is your interest in Fort Montgomery that helped keep me motivated and devoted to finishing this book.

INTRODUCTION

The mysterious ruins north of the bridge

Few places along the beautiful and historic waterway we know as Lake Champlain have been the source of more mystery, misinformation and controversy as the stone ruins at the border in Rouses Point, New York. Situated as they are at the very entrance to the lake, the ruins of Fort Montgomery have beckoned to travelers on land and lake for generations.

There are many reasons for the confusion. Early on, local newspaper accounts merged the two separate and distinct fortifications built here into one, an unfortunate situation that occurs to this day. Other issues have arisen because much of the property that became Fort Montgomery Military Reservation was previously known as the "Commons," property that local residents had use of and felt should always be so.

Some know a massive stone fortification was constructed here on a small sand island but believe it was a mistake, a foolish example of government waste, a "blunder." They point to our long history of friendship with Canada as the reason for their belief. Why build a fort to defend the nation from Canada of all places, they ask. And, why especially, would we build it after the War of 1812?

I hope to answer these questions in this volume. When I first started my research into the fortifications at Rouses Point, I had only a vague idea of the history of these forts. I knew what I had been told; I understood what I had read. Old Fort "Blunder," built by the US Army on Canadian soil! The butt of jokes, an embarrassment to the nation, no wonder they tore the thing down! These are the things I thought I knew about the fort at the border.

The truth is much more complicated and very much more interesting. Those who love the Fort "Blunder" story need not fear. There was a fort constructed here on the wrong side of the border. Yet, we are not served well by misinformation and half-truths. The true story of the great stone forts at Rouses Point is fascinating. I have endeavored to share those truths in this book. They enhance rather than diminish the tale.

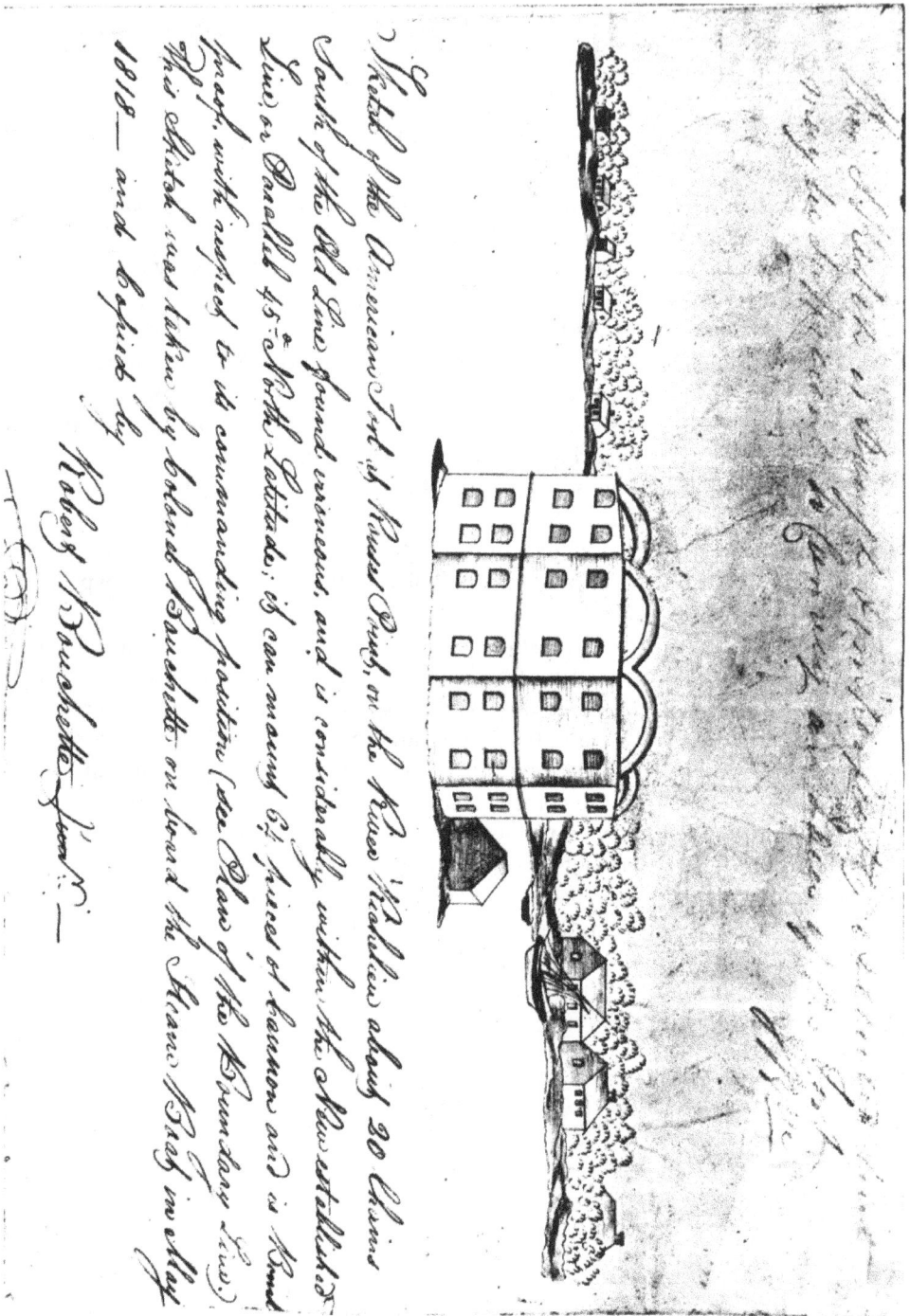

Sketch of the American Fort at Rouses Point on the River Richelieu about 20 chains south of the Old Line found erroneous, and is considerably within the New established Line or Parallel 45 North Latitude; it can mount 64 pieces of cannon and is Bomb proof with respect to its commanding position (see Plan of the Boundary Line.) This sketch was taken by Colonel Bouchette on board the Steam Boat in May 1818 - and copied by Robert Bouchette. Courtesy: Library and Archives Canada/Bouchette Family collection/1992-584

PART ONE: HISTORY
CHAPTER I

The First Fort: Fort "Blunder"

Lake Champlain has long been an important transportation corridor from the mighty Saint Lawrence to the Hudson. From the earliest of times, Native Americans had used the water route to travel from what we now know as Quebec along the Richelieu River south along Lake Champlain to Lake George and points south. These waterways now bear the names given them by the Europeans; it is they who ended up settling these places, using the great transportation corridor for their commerce and their wars.

It was shortly after the War of 1812 that the tiny sand island in Rouses Point was fortified for the first time. Repeatedly mighty armies and massive naval flotillas had traversed the narrow reaches of the river between what is now New York and Vermont. The small islands to the north, Hospital Island, Ash Island and Isle aux Noix had been the scene of frantic military activity and unspeakable suffering as these powerful forces drove north and south along the river. The sand spit called Island Point was fortified in an attempt to prevent invasion from the north yet again.

It is not known why the island itself was chosen as the site for the fort. Original plans called for a much larger, multi-bastioned fort to be built to the west just beyond the shoreline. In 1817 the newly appointed General Simon Bernard drew up a proposed trace for this massive fortification.[1]

Immediately to the west of Island Point, between the shoreline and the island, was a long, narrow peninsula pointing north. The northern tip of this narrow strip of land was known as Province Point because it extended beyond what was understood to be the 45th parallel, into Canada. To the peninsula's west, separating it from the mainland proper was a marsh that became open water during the spring. It was along this narrow strip that some of the region's first settlers built their homes.[2]

On October 17, 1817, the state of New York ceded lots 62-66 of the former Canada-Nova Scotia Refugee Tract (some 400 acres) to the United States government for use as a Military Reservation. It had "been deemed requisite by the President of the United States that fortifications should be erected" here at this strategic location.[3]

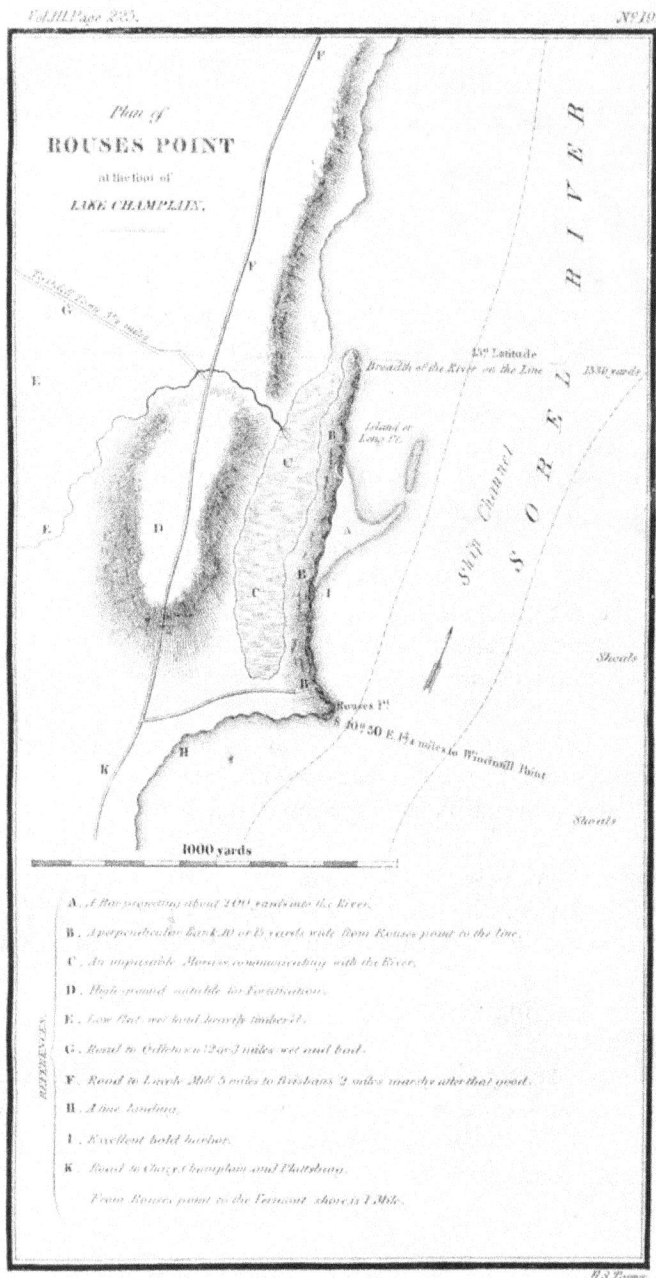

Vol.III.Page 233.   *No 19*

Plan of
ROUSES POINT
at the foot of
LAKE CHAMPLAIN.

1000 yards

A . *A flat projecting about 400 yards into the River.*

B . *A perpendicular Bank 40 or 45 yards wide from Rouses point to the line.*

C . *An impassable Morass communicating with the River.*

D . *High ground suitable for Fortification.*

E . *Low flat wet land heavily timbered.*

G . *Road to Odletown 2 or 3 miles wet and bad.*

F . *Road to Luch Mill 5 miles to Brisbans 2 miles marshy after that good.*

H . *A fine landing.*

I . *Excellent bold harbor.*

K . *Road to Chazy Champlain and Plattsburg.*

From Rouses point to the Vermont shore is 1 Mile.

H.S. Tanner map of Rouses Point circa 1814. Courtesy: Clinton County Historical Association.

This grant did not include Island Point, the small island where the battery was to be constructed. Interestingly enough, the land was officially turned over to the federal government well after work had begun on the fort. It was not until May 15, 1818 that Island Point itself was ceded to the US government. [4]

A contract was signed on November 1, 1816.[5] Brevet Lt. Col. Joseph G. Totten represented the US Government. The contractors were three Scots- Malcomb McMartin, James McIntyre, and John Stewart. McMartin and McIntyre were from Keene, NY, Stewart was from Albany. The families were related and all were prominent local businessmen.

These masonry contractors were to have the walls completed within two years- by November 1, 1818.

For their efforts they would be paid "Two Dollars and twelve and an half cents [sic] for each Perch[6] of Straight wall consisting of sixteen and an half cubic feet" and "Three dollars and Twelve and an half cents [sic] for each perch consisting of Sixteen and an half cubic feet of Masonry, actually laid by them in Arches."

BRICKS & LIME.

LT. COL. TOTTEN will receive *proposals* at Plattsburgh, during the current month, for furnishing 500,000 *BRICKS*; to be delivered at the Battery begun near the Line, in the months of May, June, July, August and September.

Proposals for a supply of 20,000 bushels of *UNSLACKED LIME*; to be delivered at the same place, in the months of April, May, and June, will also be received.

March 7, 1817.

☞ *The Printers of the Northern Sentinel, National Standard, Rutland Herald, Vermont Republican, and American Register, in the State of Vermont, are requested to insert the above notice in their respective papers for 3 weeks, and transmit their Bills to Lt. Col. TOTTEN for payment.*

LUMBER.

PROPOSALS will be received by Lt. Col. TOTTEN, at Plattsburgh, until the 15th April next, for the supply of the following descriptions and quantities of *LUMBER*, viz:

300 pine joists, each 22 feet long, 1 foot broad and 5 inches thick—amounting, in board measure to	33,000 ft.
63 do. 24 1-2 feet long, 1 foot broad and 5 inches thick—amounting, in board measure to	7,718 ft.
120 do. 16 feet long, 1 foot broad & 5 inches thick—amounting, in board measure to	9,600 ft.
45,000 feet, board measure, of pine plank, each plank 12 feet long and 3 inches thick	45,000 ft.
50,000 feet, of inch boards	50,000 ft.
	145,318 ft.

All the Lumber to be perfectly free from rots, rotten knots, splits, wain, or worms; and the Planks and Joists to have the stub-shods taken off.

Thirty Thousand feet of Boards to be delivered in May—the remainder of the lumber, during the months of June and July, 1817, at Rouse's Point, near the Line. *Plattsburgh, March 13, 1817.*

☞ The Printers of the *Northern Sentinel* and *National Standard*, in the State of Vermont, are requested to insert the above notice in their respective papers until the 15th of April next, and transmit their bills to Lt. Col. TOTTEN for payment.

Above and right: Ads placed by Col. Totten in March and April, 1817 soliciting building materials for the "Battery begun near the line" at Rouses Point.

The contract with McMartin, McIntyre and Stewart was for "all the mason work of the said Battery excepting Brick work of all kinds, Flues, Chimneys and fire places, Wells, Drains, Gutters, Sewers, Furnaces, [six words are illegible], projections of any kind from the Body of the wall, Cut or chiseled stone work, Plastering, Slating…" We do not know how much of this 'finish' work was to be completed by other contractors.

The structure, referred to in the contract as a "Battery, Fort or Castle," was to be erected on a 'grating or grillage of Timbers and Planks' built by the Army. In a clause that Totten would come to regret, the Army promised to have the grillage completed by November 15th, a mere 15 days away! Totten also agreed that the Army would build "a convenient wharf… upon which wharf vessels may unload their stones" and a "good & sufficient house" to store the lime and sand which would be provided by the government.

Construction in earnest began the first week of March 1817 with the arrival in Rouses Point of Totten. Beginning on March 15, 1817 Totten advertised for large quantities of lumber in New York and Vermont newspapers. The following month ads were placed for 500,000 bricks and 20,000 bushels of unslacked lime.[7] Work was progressing nicely; these large contracts were a boon to the local economy.

On March 21, Totten wrote his superior, General Joseph G. Swift at Plattsburgh that "contractors are busy drawing stone on the ice".[8]

On Friday morning, July 25, 1817 an auspicious event occurred at Island Point. President James Monroe, on a tour of the northern frontier, visited the site accompanied by Lt. Colonel Totten. The Press Republican made note of the event:

> "The President's visit to Rouses Point, where important works for the defense of this frontier having been commenced under the supervision of Lt. Col. Totten was not mentioned in our last paper...He arrived at the line at 4 o'clock AM and landed at 6. After having inspected the work which is erecting on a small island north of the point, the President, attended by his suite and Col. Totten, who had by special order joined him at Burlington, proceeded on horseback, to view the site for the principal work on the mainland [At this time there were still plans to erect the much larger fortification on the mainland to the west]. The position selected by Col. Totten is justly regarded as the key to one of the most important inlets to the heart of our country; and it will be favorable to our defence that the chief magistrate has made himself personally acquainted with its importance."[9]

On October 5, 1817 Totten reported "work goes well...to my perfect satisfaction...just throwing the arches over a 2nd tier of embrasures. The large piers are at the height for springing the great arches... the small piers are 8 ft. above the 2nd platform and all parts of the work in a state of forwardness." [10]

This "castle," as it is referred to in Engineering Dept. plans of 1816[11], was not large; about 150 feet by 200 feet. Octagonal in shape, it consisted of nine sides; four were 45 feet long, four were 80 feet long, and the western face measured 195 feet from salient to salient. There were 36 casemates, 18 on each of two tiers, 20 appear to be for gun batteries. The gun casemates were about 36 feet deep from scarp wall to parade. There was to be a third or barbette tier at the top of the 32 foot high wall. The fort appears to have had embrasures for 48 guns *en casemate* with another 16 mounted *en barbette*.

The small parade was only some 70 feet x 100 feet in size. The wall facing the west, or land side, referred to in military parlance as the 'gorge,' enclosed six rooms, three on each side of the entrance or 'postern'. There was a large earth and masonry 'cover face' also known as a 'counterguard', along the western face that protected the gorge walls from bombardment from siege guns on shore. It appears that this cover face was to have been heavily armed with cannon also.[12]

An integral part of the defense strategy consisted of erecting a large V-shaped earthwork, or redan, just south of the island on the point. This ancillary work is sometimes referred to in contemporary accounts as a second fort. Altogether the works at Rouses Point were to mount almost 300 cannon. [13]

The swamp, referred to as "an impassable morass" on Tanner's map, had to be contended with. Access from the west, known as the "Commons," was addressed by constructing a long bridge across the swamp to the peninsula. It is clearly shown on the Bruyeres map of 1818.[14] The octagonal fort proper (on the island) was to be surrounded by water except during periods of very low water.

On November 18, 1817 the final piece of property was handed over to the Army. John and Mary Warford sold lot number 60 to the United States of America. This lot was important in that it included the actual "point" of Rouses Point. Here was to be sited the large earthen redan. [15]

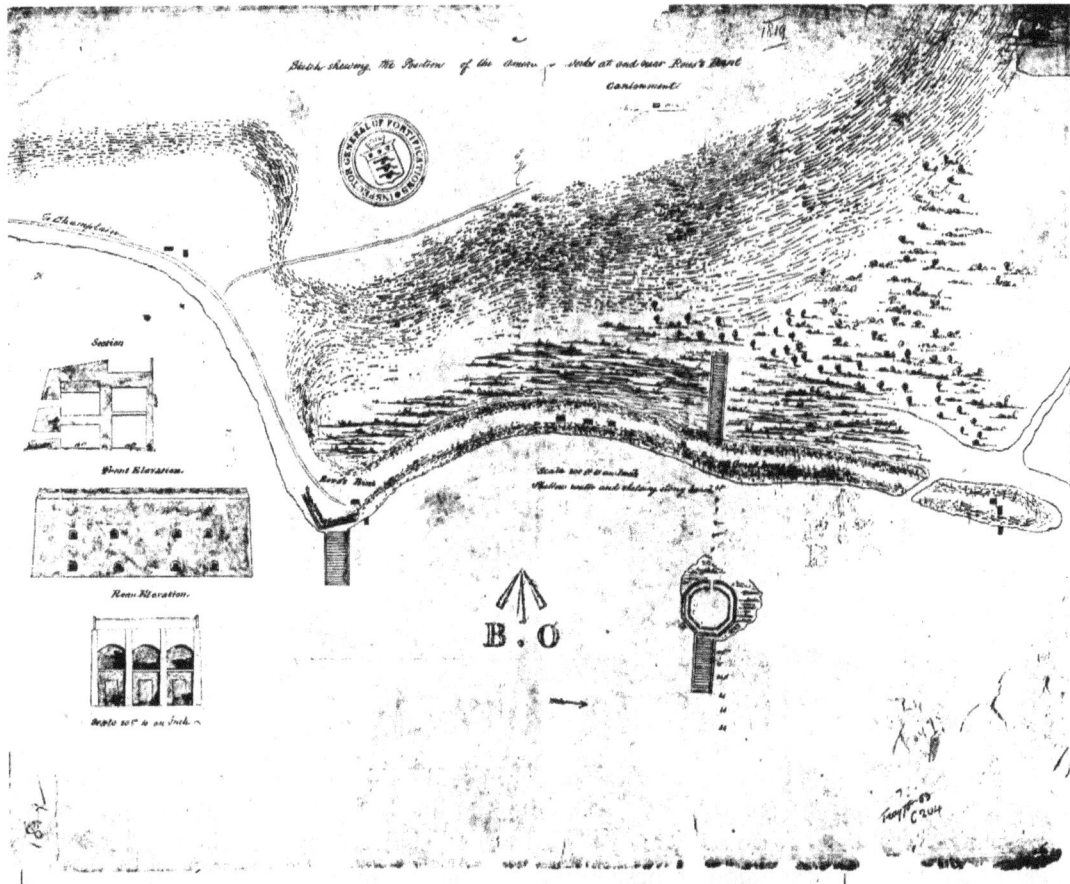

H.P. Bruyeres: Sketch showing the Position of the American Works at and near Rous's Point Cantonment. 1818. Library and Archives Canada/ NMC 7722. Note the structures along the narrow, snake-like peninsula to the west of the fort and the bridge across the swamp. A structure at the east end of the bridge is identified as a "Guardhouse."

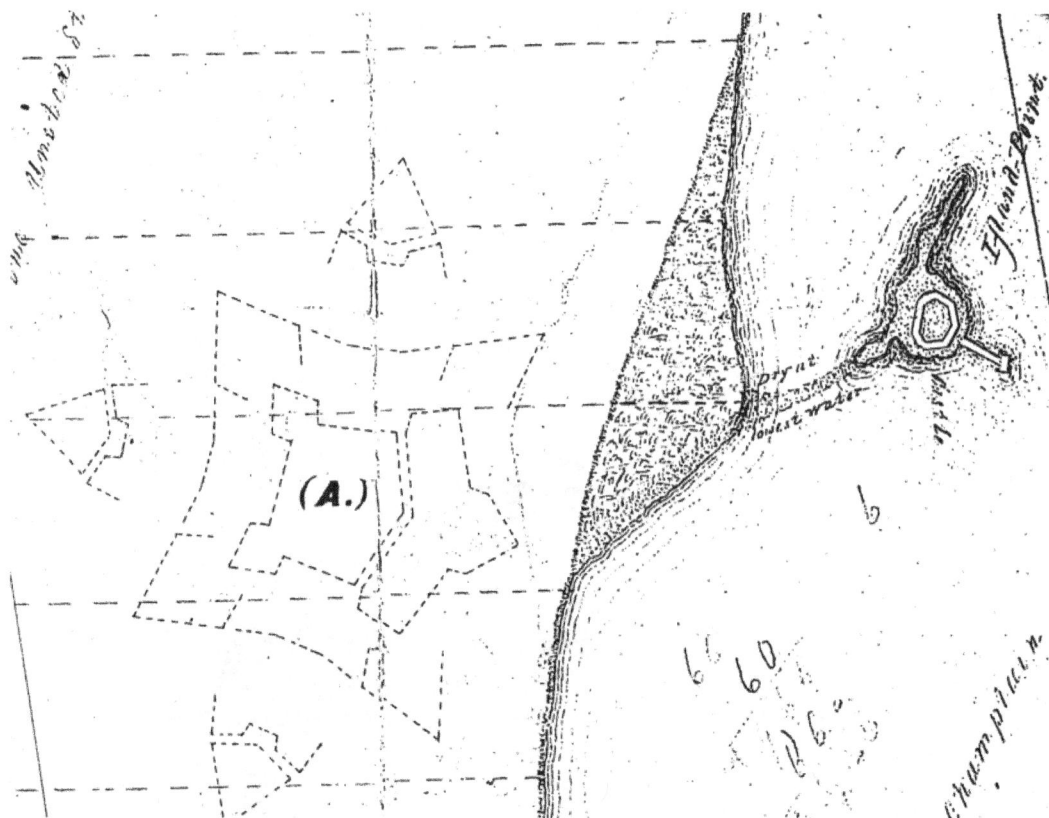

Detail of National Archives, Drawer 7, Sheet 20. This document shows the "Trace proposed by Genl. Bernard" drawn on a map of the original "Metes and Bounds…" document of 1817. It also clearly shows the fort constructed at Island Point. Note the remarkable differences in size.

These works at Rouses Point caused much consternation north of the border. Genuine fear was aroused in some quarters, much of it among the prominent and influential. Governor Drummond, never one to trust the Americans, had stated in 1815 that the United States' "dearest object is the possession of these Provinces." These concerns were shared by his successor, Governor Richmond.[16]

Certainly, the construction of a large fort at the border so soon after the signing of the Treaty of Ghent did nothing to alleviate those fears. André Charbonneau tells us that "the initiative of the Americans in the spring of 1816…sowed panic among the officers of the colony." This fear of American intentions led to the construction of Fort Lennox at Île aux Noix.[17]

In June, 1818 several companies of the U.S. 6th Infantry were posted at Rouses Point to assist with construction and security. Totten was concerned about sabotage from Canada.

The previous fall he had heard rumors of plans to "set fire to the combustible material" consisting of "great quantities of timber collected within the walls".[18] The regulars were there but a few weeks. On August 22, the Plattsburgh Republican reported that "frequent desertions from the regiment since it has been stationed on the line rendered a removal desirable… more desertions have taken place in the few weeks that the troops have been stationed at Rouse's Point than in any one year since the regiment has been on this station." The paper went on to state that "The removal of the troops will not, we understand, retard the progress of the works at Rouse's Point; labourers will be employed on the fortifications."[19]

By late summer 1818 more significant problems were becoming apparent. Despite its supervision by the soon-to-be prominent Totten, the fort was built upon a weak and unstable foundation consisting largely of debris brought up from the demolished ruins of Plattsburgh batteries and outworks. A 'grillage of timbers' worked fine when built upon piles driven deep into the lake bed. It does not appear that this aspect of the work was properly done. Within a short time, Totten had an unstable structure on his hands with walls that were sinking into the sandy soil. Had the most significant blow of all not come down in the autumn of 1818, Totten would have had to spend considerable time and resources shoring up the structure.[20]

As serious as this was, it really did not matter. With the cold winds and brilliant colors of autumn came dramatic news that would cause all construction to halt immediately. The new fort was being constructed on Canadian soil.

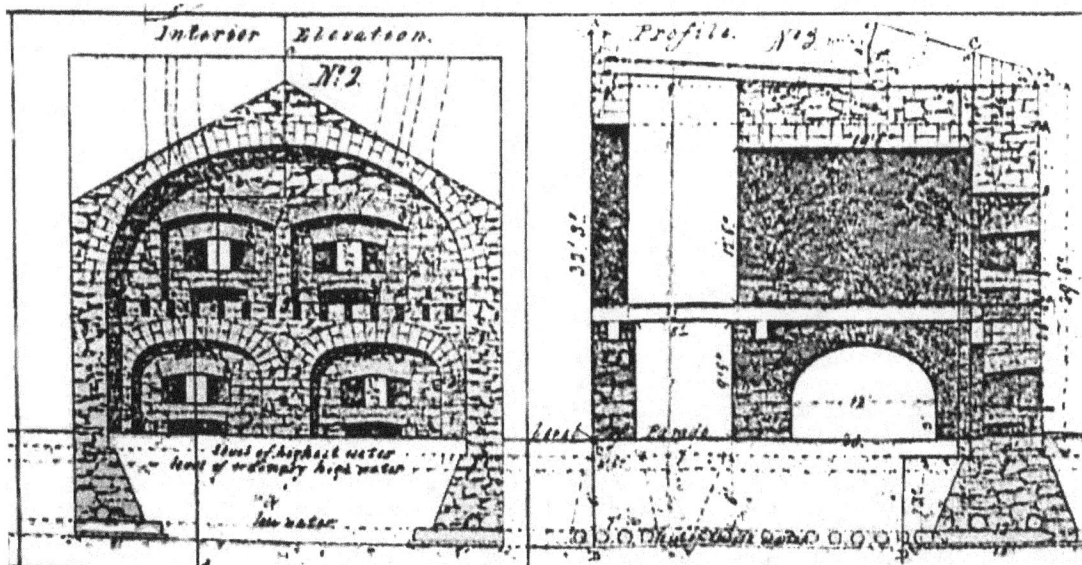

Detail: Profile and Elevations for a Castle for Island Point. Rouse's Point, Lake Champlain. NARA, Records of the Chief of Engineers, Fortification File, Drawer, 7, Sheet 5. Undated, probably 1816. This drawing features the casemates of the first fort at Island Point, Fort "Blunder." Digitally enhanced for legibility.

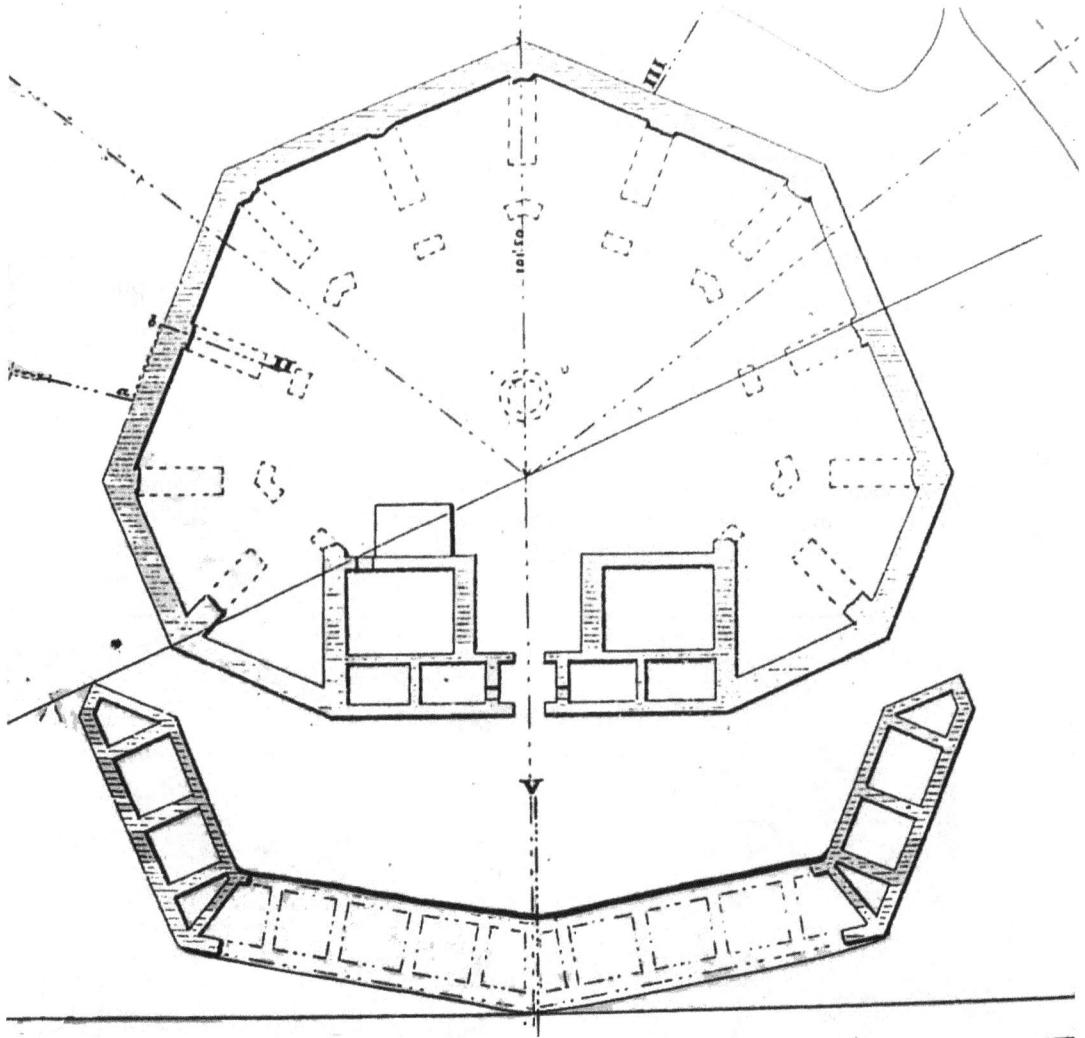

Detail: Plan and Sections of Fort _____, Rouse's Point; exhibiting the condition of the work on the 30th of September 1844. NARA Records of the Chief of Engineers. Record Group 77, Drawer 7, sheet 15. This document was prepared to show the progress of the new fort (still unnamed). The full plan shows the grillage of timbers being laid upon piles. It also shows, as pictured above, a plan of the earlier work, constructed by Totten in 1816-17- Fort "Blunder." What was left of the old fort was being demolished as the new fort was being erected around it.

CHAPTER II

The Border Controversy:
The United States constructs a fort on Canadian soil

Few stories in northern lore hold such appeal as those regarding the great fort that was built by an inept American army on Canadian soil. Unfortunately, many of those accounts, while fascinating, are rife with inaccuracies. The truth is actually less of an indictment of Totten and the Engineers than a testimony to some startling realities about the United States-Canada border.

In order to really understand how it was that the works at Island Point came to be built upon the soil of another sovereign nation, we must go back to shortly after the French and Indian War. In 1763 The Royal Proclamation set the boundary between New York and Lower Canada (Quebec) as the 45th parallel. In 1772 John Collins, Deputy Surveyor-General of Quebec and Joseph Smith of New York surveyed the line of 45th parallel some 22 miles east from the shore of Lake Champlain. By September 1772, the survey was completed by Collins and one of Smith's successors, Thomas Valentine, as far as the Connecticut River. The survey was completed from the St. Lawrence to the Connecticut in 1774.[1] This line was accepted as an accurate and true survey of the 45th parallel. The 45th parallel was again accepted as the boundary between the United States and British Canada in the Treaty of Paris, which effectively ended the American Revolution in 1783.

By 1796 some had begun to question the accuracy of the survey done by Valentine and Collins. Burlington, Vermont resident William Coit informed the Vermont Assembly that the line was actually south of the accepted 45th parallel. Nothing was done until 1804 when Governor Isaac Tichenor insisted that the Assembly investigate the matter. Rev. Samuel Williams of Rutland was hired to ascertain the actual location of the line. The results were inconclusive and William's report left much to be desired.[2]

On February 17, 1815 the Treaty of Ghent was ratified; officially ending the War of 1812. "By Article V of the treaty of Ghent it was provided that since the northwest angle of Nova Scotia had not been determined nor any portion of the international boundary between the source of the River St Croix and the St. Lawrence River surveyed or marked, two commissioners should be appointed to determine this portion of the boundary in conformity with the provisions of the treaty of 1783; *that they should cause the boundary to be surveyed and marked, and that they should have a map made of the boundary to which they should annex a declaration, certifying it to be a true map*"[3]

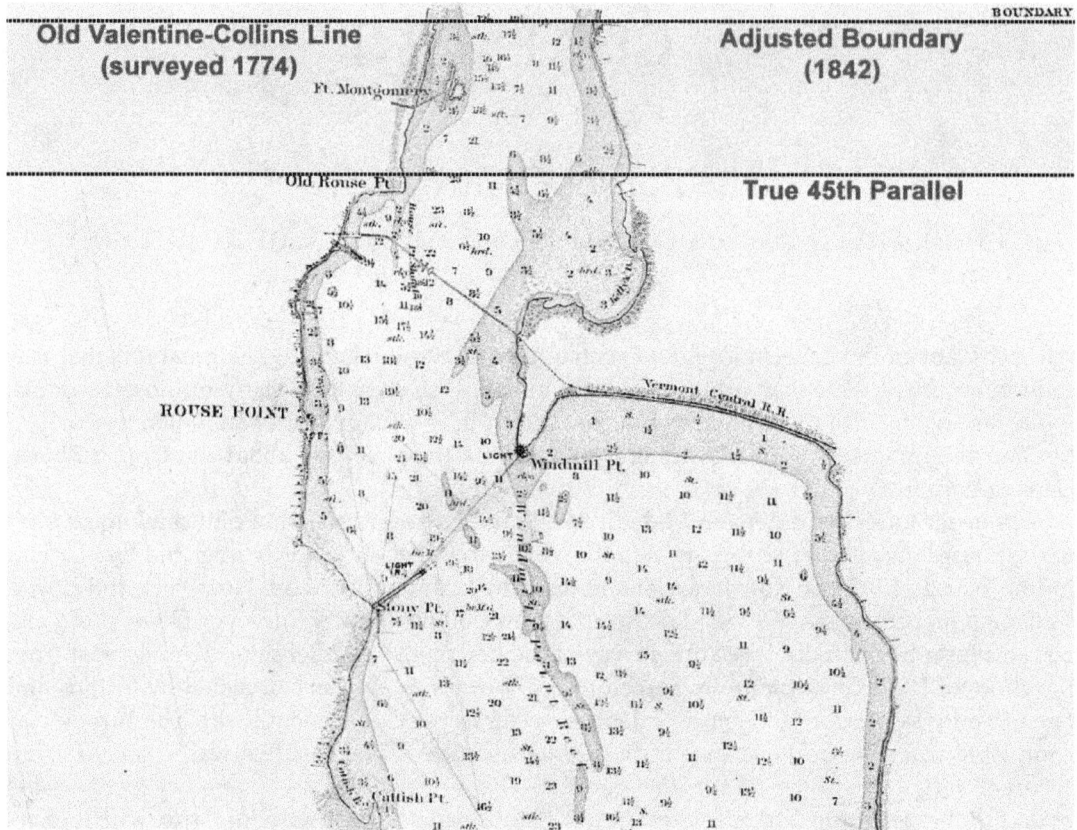

This map, after a US Coast and Geodetic survey map of 1879, shows the adjusted border and the actual line of 45°
as corrected in 1818.

So, in 1816 another survey, this one under the supervision of David Thompson, was begun in order to clarify the border between Canada and the United States, as stipulated by
Article V, Treaty of Ghent.[4] Unfortunately, this is the same year that the contract was signed
to construct fortifications at Rouses Point.

In October 1818, a remarkable discovery was made. The survey team led by J.C. Tiarks, a
British astronomer, and F.R. Hassler, first superintendent of the US Coast and Geodetic Survey, determined that the old line of 45th parallel, known as the Valentine and Collins line,
was incorrect.[5] The actual line was found to be some three-quarters of a mile south. The implications of this error were profound for the new fort under construction at Island Point. The
new survey effectively placed the structure in Canada. On November 21, 1818 the Montreal
Herald announced the news:

"We have just now been favoured with accounts from Lake Champlain by which it
appears that the *Great Fort* built at Rous's Point by the Americans since the peace,

and completed last summer, is on the *Canada side of line 45°* as laid down by the Commissioners appointed for that purpose. In this case the Fort is built on British Territory, and little doubt can be ascertained to whom it belongs." [6]

On December 19, 1818, the War Department reported to Congress "Orders have been given to suspend the works at Rouse's Point until the line between the United States and Lower Canada shall be determined. The [additional] sum of $200,000, which was estimated for it, will probably not be required, and may be omitted in the appropriation for fortifications."[7] All construction stopped at Rouses Point, $113,106.21 had already been spent, a huge amount in 1818 dollars.[8] Work was never resumed on this first fort, construction halted before it received its first guns. The fort was never officially named. Disgruntled workers would give it a moniker that would echo through history- Fort "Blunder."

Not everyone south of the new border was unhappy with the new situation, however. Maine actually stood to benefit from the new arrangement; witness this gleeful report from the Portland Argus of October 1819:

"It appears probable that the fort which our government had begun to erect on Lake Champlain, falls within the British lines. This is to be regretted, but if it fairly belongs to them, let them have it. – If we loose Rouse's Point, it is said we shall receive a compensation in the District of Maine. Our Northeastern boundary it is said will be many miles further north than has heretofore been supposed…It will extend so far as to completely cut off the communication between the provinces, and will embrace within our limits a considerable French settlement, which has formerly been under the Jurisdiction of Canada.[9]

It would be the summer of 1821 before representatives of the two governments met at New York to present their arguments to the commissioners regarding the proper border. As expected each country advocated the line furthest south or north, respectively. The commissioners failed to agree and [ten years later 1831][10] the matter was brought to arbitration by the King of the Netherlands, a neutral party. The King recommended the line be the actual (astronomical) parallel, with a provision that the United States be left in possession of territory within a circle of 1 kilometer from the fort at Island Point. Britain accepted this but the US, largely as a result of protests from Maine and Massachusetts, did not. [11]

The consequences for the fortifications at Rouses Point were obvious. The fort, now effectively on Canadian soil, was abandoned. Even though it was now sited on British territory, construction was not resumed by its new owners. This was probably due to the ongoing negotiations and continuing controversy. The British engineers may also have been aware of the structural weaknesses of the fort. Detailed plans of the works were drawn up and presented to the Board of Ordnance.[12] Instead; work began on a new fort, further up the Richelieu at Isle aux Noix.

The abandoned works at Island Point were subject to predation by enterprising local citizens. The locals carried off much of its materials for use in their own homes, stores and places of worship. Fort "Blunder," as it came to be known, lives on in the walls of some of the more ancient and prominent buildings in the Rouses Point area.[13]

The Ezra Thurber home in Rouses Point, believed to have been constructed in 1818 with brick from Fort "Blunder."[1] Photo courtesy of Charles Barney.

CHAPTER III

Mutual distrust leads to new fortifications

The relocation of the border in 1819 did not lead to an easing of tensions between Britain and the United States. Rather quite the opposite occurred. Always suspicious of American intentions and never sure they would keep the new swath of territory north of the line of 45, the Crown set to building Fort Lennox at Isle aux Noix. The north-south waterway had played too important a role in previous conflicts to be ignored.

The United States also felt an urgent need for protection along this great gateway to its heart. As still happens today, one weapons system often led to the construction of a "defensive" system on the part of a potential adversary. Construction of Fort Lennox was begun largely as a result of Canadian fears aroused by the works at Rouses Point. [1]

Fort Lennox was constructed over a period of ten years. Situated on the site of earlier French and British works, the fort spread over the entire southern end of Isle aux Noix.

Above: Aerial photo of Fort Lennox at Isle aux Noix. Photo courtesy of Roger and Doug Harwood.

Consisting of five earthen bastions surrounded by a moat, this fort was not a brick and masonry fort like the one to the south. It did share one remarkable similarity with the American-built structure, however. The massive limestone barracks and storehouses at Fort Lennox were built entirely of stone from the United States! Quarried, as was the stone at Rouses Point, from the ancient reefs at Isle La Motte, Vermont, this beautiful limestone known locally as "Black Marble," rich in fossils, was shipped down the lake and along the Richelieu in merchant vessels. If modern-day visitors to the impressive Fort Lennox National Historic Site miss the interpretive displays that point out this interesting fact, the knowledgeable tour guides do not hesitate to point out that "money knows no boundaries."

Above: The Soldier's barracks at Fort Lennox. Author photo.

By 1836 the unprotected entrance to the lake was still giving American defense strategists pause. Col. Joseph G. Totten, architect of the first fort at Rouses Point, sounded the alarm. The builder of the defenses at Plattsburgh in 1814 still feared an invasion south along Lake Champlain. In a lengthy report to Congress that April, Totten laid out his concerns, the remedy, and some interesting insight into strategy should war break out:

"...The lake frontier, indeed, presents some peculiar considerations; and I think the views submitted by the Engineer department respecting Lake Champlain are entitled to much weight. This long, narrow sheet of navigable water opens a direct communication into the States of New York and Vermont, while its outlet is in a foreign country, and is commanded by a position of great natural strength. It is also within a few miles of the most powerful and populous portion of Canada, and open to all its resources and energies. With a view, perhaps, to possible rather than probable events, it may be deemed expedient to construct a work at some proper site within our boundary, which shall close the entrance of the lake to all vessels ascending its outlet. As such a work, however, would be an advanced post, and, from circumstances, peculiarly liable to attack, its extent and defences should be in proportion to its exposure… Lake Champlain penetrates the territory in such a way that an enemy, having the naval mastery, might make a deep inroad and greatly harass the country along the shores, although no enterprise, even in the present state of population, could be carried far into the interior. Were it only to relieve a long line of frontier from predatory incursions, access to this lake from the north should be denied. But there are other very strong reasons for this exclusion. By closing the lake at its northern extremity, an expensive and uncertain strife for naval superiority on this lake would be avoided, and the whole lake would remain in our possession, serving as the best possible military line of communication in case the United States should assume offensive operations against the weakest point of the Canadian frontier. From the northern end of this lake the forces of the United States should march into Canada and intercept the communication of the St. Lawrence, either at or near the mouth of the Richelieu river, at Montreal island, at some point where the ship channel of the river could be commanded, intermediate between these places, or at any two or at all of these places, according to the circumstances. Maintaining any or all of these positions would limit the defence in the province above to the consumption of the means then in store, and would completely paralyze its offensive power. Although no other object were in view than the defence of the frontier upon the upper lakes, no effort necessary to secure and maintain this position should be spared, because it is only thus that the contest for naval superiority on the lakes (which, if once suffered to begin, is both exhausting and interminable) can be avoided. Without aid from abroad Canada cannot contest such a question with the United States, and, so long as the United States posses that superiority, the defence of the upper portion of the frontier will be complete… it would appear that the peace and safety of the parts of the frontier extending along the River St. Lawrence, Lakes Ontario, Erie, Huron, and Superior might be made to flow from military operations carried on against Canada by the line of Lake Champlain and the river Richelieu; and in order to this military operation being always practicable, and to be taken up at pleasure, nothing more is necessary than the fortification of the outlet of Lake Champlain. The military consequences of the occupation of the outlet of Lake Champlain are so obvious, that it must not be supposed they are not perfectly understood by our neighbor across the border. A position for closing the lake, selected during the last war, and of which the fortification was begun soon after the peace, was found, after some progress had been made, not to lie within our territory, and was abandoned. There is, however, a position equally good close at hand, and in all respects admirably adapted to the object in view. The fortification of this outlet will probably cost about $600,000. [2]

Totten was suggesting that a new fort be constructed south of Rouses Point village, directly opposite Vermont's Windmill Point, on the slight promontory of Stony Point.

Within a year tensions flared yet again as rebellion took root in Upper and Lower Canada. The Canadian Rebellions of 1837-39 caused a significant deterioration in relations between the two nations as American agitators and Canadian rebels crossed the border seemingly at will to raid. Much effort was made to provoke war between the US and Great Britain. The "Caroline Affair" strained U.S.-British relations when a group of Canadian loyalists crossed the border into the U.S. to capture and burn a rebel supply ship. Albert B. Corey, in his important work, "The Crisis of 1830-1842 in Canadian-American Relations" wrote- "...war between Great Britain and the United States was universally expected...," [Ref. National Intelligencer, Jan. 19, 1838]. In Lower Canada, Sir John Colborne, the governor, expected "serious consequences" to result from continued violations of neutrality, and in Washington, Henry Fox, the British minister, asserted that "war might occur at any time due to events on the frontier."[3] Canadian rebels and American sympathizers established an arms depot at Rouses Point in 1838. On November 5, 1838 some 400 Canadian rebels crossed the border at Rouses Point and Alburgh, Vermont with a cannon and muskets from their Rouses Point arsenal. They attacked the militia based at Lacolle and were repulsed but not before eleven men were killed. Many others were wounded.

These incidents and others contributed to a belief by many on both sides of the border that war with Great Britain must surely come.

A new low point in Anglo-American relations was reached in 1838-39 over disputes concerning the Maine border. The Aroostook War ended up a bloodless conflict but only barely so. British troops were marched to the border in large numbers and Congress authorized $10,000,000 and 50,000 men to prepare for war. President Van Buren sent General Winfield Scott to Maine. Eventually an uneasy truce was declared and war narrowly averted.[4] The military readied itself for what seemed inevitable. Appropriations were requested for fortifications at the outlet of the Lake. On November 30, 1839 Secretary of War Joel R. Poinsett lamented that Congress had struck out funding for new fortifications on Lake Champlain- "This work is deemed of essential importance...Hopes are entertained that Congress will not again withhold the necessary appropriations to enable the Department to commence these works...with as little delay as practicable. The disturbed state of the Canada frontier, and the absolute necessity which exists to keep upon that line as large a force as can be spared from other points, will require the erection of permanent and comfortable barracks..."[5]

In 1840 plans were drawn up for an enormous fort to be constructed at Stony Point.[6] The British already knew of these plans and were troubled. The peace was uneasy; an arms race of sorts was underway.[7]

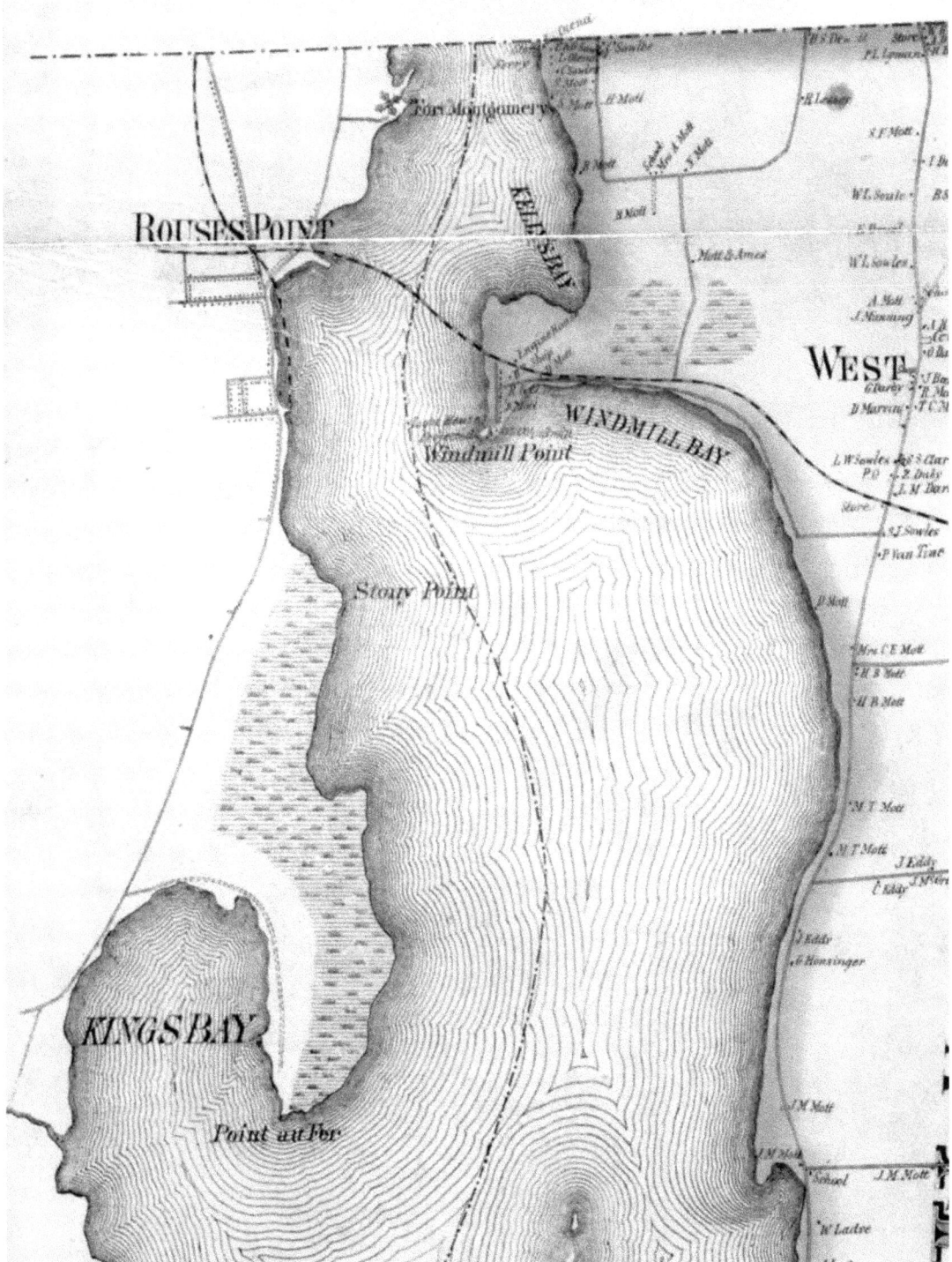

Detail of 1857 H.F. Walling map showing Rouses Point, Stony Point and Windmill Point. Library of Congress.

CHAPTER IV

We will protect the lake:
The massive new fort at Stony Point

Totten's recommendation to Congress in 1836 was taken seriously even if it did take time for Congress to approve appropriations. The Richelieu River and Lake Champlain remained a threat, pointed like an arrow deep into the heart of the eastern states. Navigation had become easier and faster, steam could easily propel hostile vessels deep into the heart of the nation at speeds unimagined even a few years before.

The Rush-Bagot Agreement of 1817 stipulated that Britain and the US were limited to no more than one vessel on the lake, and that limited to no larger than 100 tons and one 18-pounder cannon. Both sides knew however, that this simple agreement's hold on each nation was tenuous at best, each side had constructed warships in record time in the past, it could always happen again. The border regions festered with controversy; armed bands crossed back and forth as a result of the Canadian Rebellions of 1837 and 1838.[1] Many Americans, particularly those along the border, sympathized with the Canadian rebels. Rouses Point had become a hotspot of rebel activity, with insurgents retreating to the homes of American sympathizers at will. Fort Lennox had been completed in 1829 and, largely as a result of the unrest in the country during 1836-37, was garrisoned by some 500 troops.[2]

In addition, many Americans believed that Canada should be annexed to the United States. Most Canadians were aware of this, and it was disconcerting to many, particularly the military and the politicians. There was also lingering resentment about the border controversy and the results of the survey of 1818. The waterway had simply played too crucial a role in military planning in the past, too many expeditions had traveled up and down this waterway; yet another fort would be constructed. On April 18, 1836 the United States Senate passed a resolution directing a survey of "the most eligible site for Fortifications on Lake Champlain, near the Province of Lower Canada, suitable for the defence of the commerce of said lake within the United States." In 1836 the most logical place was Stony Point. The drawings of the preliminary survey were completed in March, 1839.

Windmill Point (foreground) and Stony Point. Photo courtesy of Roger and Doug Harwood.

In 1840 the site was surveyed again and soundings were made of the channel between Stony Point and Windmill Point. Joseph G. Totten, now Chief Engineer, made the following recommendation to the Secretary of War:

> "...it is recommended that a fort be first established at Stony Point, on the western side of Lake Champlain, a short distance within the parallel of 45°. The estimated cost of constructing the fort is $268,000. It is to mount 75 guns *en barbette* — say 24 pounders, the cost of which could be furnished by the Ordnance Department.
>
> Although a work on the opposite shore [Windmill Point] will be necessary to the complete defence of the outlet of the lake, the work now projected will exercise a powerful control over the passage, and serve, moreover, as a most important point of support for military operations on that frontier."[3]

Plans were drawn up. Negotiations were undertaken to purchase 264 acres from six individuals- John W. Bailey, Solomon Fitch, Daniel T. Taylor, Ezra Thurber, Benjamin F. Wood and Moses Yale. The owners were to be paid a total of $9,792, roughly $40 an acre. Considering the property was ill-suited for most purposes, it was an attractive offer for the six.[4]

There were problems with the Stony Point site. The point is a wetland, very marshy. Though not an obstacle that would prevent construction, this wet land would significantly increase time and cost of construction. Also, the lake is wider here than at the old site. In order to sufficiently cover all of the approaches to the lake and prevent vessels from navigating along the Vermont side, Windmill Point would need to have a battery also.

The fort planned for Stony Point was unusual in several respects. Two slightly different "projects" were drawn by Montgomery C. Meigs. Hugging the shoreline of the slight promontory just south of Rouses Point proper, plans for Project One show an octagonal five-bastioned structure, complete with a substantial citadel and an additional, very long and unusual hornwork that extended south of the fort proper along the lakeshore an additional one thousand two hundred feet. Three of the fronts were to be four hundred twenty feet in length, with the remaining two fronts approximately 310 feet in length. Also, though casemated, this fort would not have guns placed inside masonry walls; these plans show emplacements for 75 fore-pintle mounted guns atop the barbette tier. Project Two differed primarily in that there was no citadel and there were four full bastions and two demi-bastions.[5]

More interesting details regarding this fort were featured in the January 30, 1841 of the Plattsburgh Republican. Quoting Totten's Dec. 17th letter to Secretary of War Poinsett:

"…The estimated cost of constructing the fort is $268,000. It is to mount 75 guns en barbette— say 24 pounders, the cost of which could be furnished by the Ordnance Department. Although a work on the opposite shore will be necessary to the complete defence of the outlet of the lake, the work now projected will exercise a powerful control over the passage, and serve, moreover as a most important point of support for military operations on that frontier.

The newspaper also quoted letters from the Ordnance Department:
"… such fortifications as are called for… will require an armament of 75 24-pounders mounted *en barbette*, I have the honor respectfully to report as to the cost of the armament:

75 24-pounder guns —	$24,948
75 24-pounder barbette carriages, with implements and equipments complete —	$24,375
Total cost of armament	$49,323

G. Bomford
Col. of Ordnance

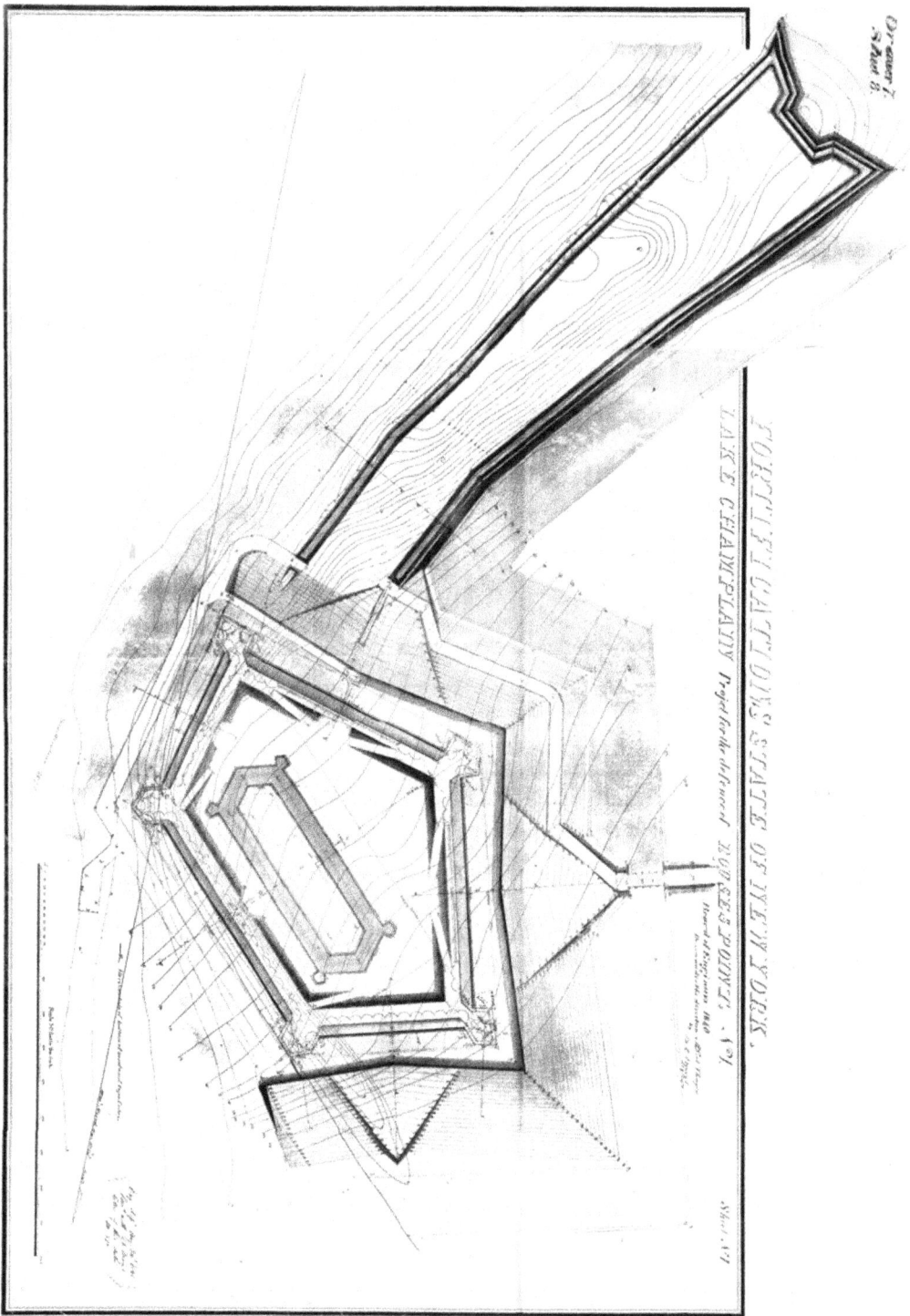

Stony Point Project No. 1: Project for the Defense of Rouse's Point. Drawn under the direction of Lt. Col. Thayer by M.C. Meigs. Sheet 1, General Plan of Work. NARA: Records of the Chief of Engineers, Fortification File: Drawer 7, Sheet 8. 1840

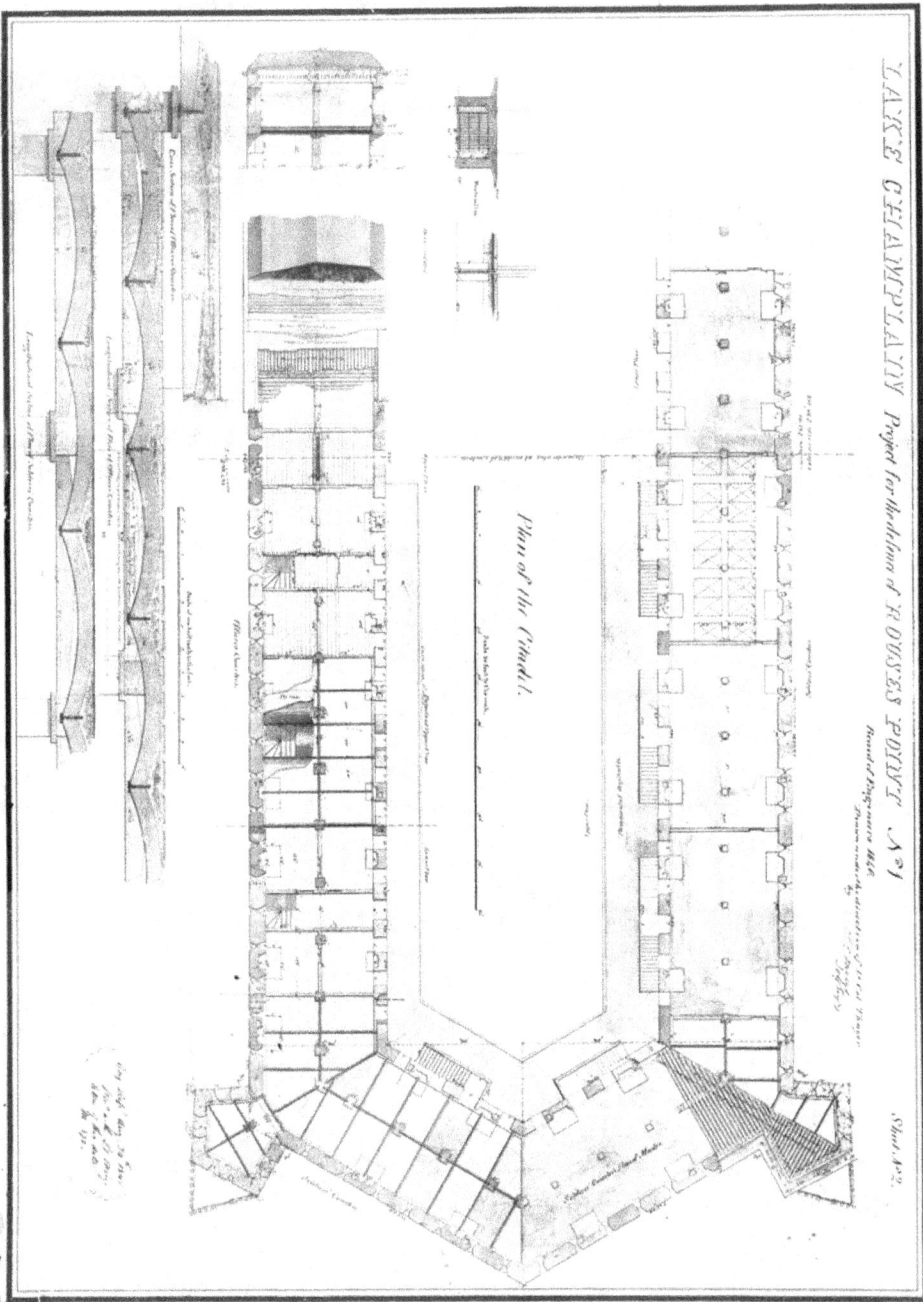

Stony Point Project No. 1: Project for the Defense of Rouse's Point. Drawn under the direction of Lt. Col. Thayer by M.C. Meigs. Sheet 2, Plan of the Citadel. NARA: Records of the Chief of Engineers, Fortification File: Drawer 7, Sheet 9. 1840

The citadel, an uncommon feature on Third-System fortifications, was oblong in shape and was to have four bastions. Salient to salient, the citadel would have been 350 feet long. One front was to house the officer's quarters, the other the soldier's barracks. Each would have been two stories high.

The citadel was never constructed. Stony Point and Windmill Point were never fortified. The military had not given up on a fort at Rouses Point; rather a dramatic new turn of events had occurred with respect to Island Point and the border.

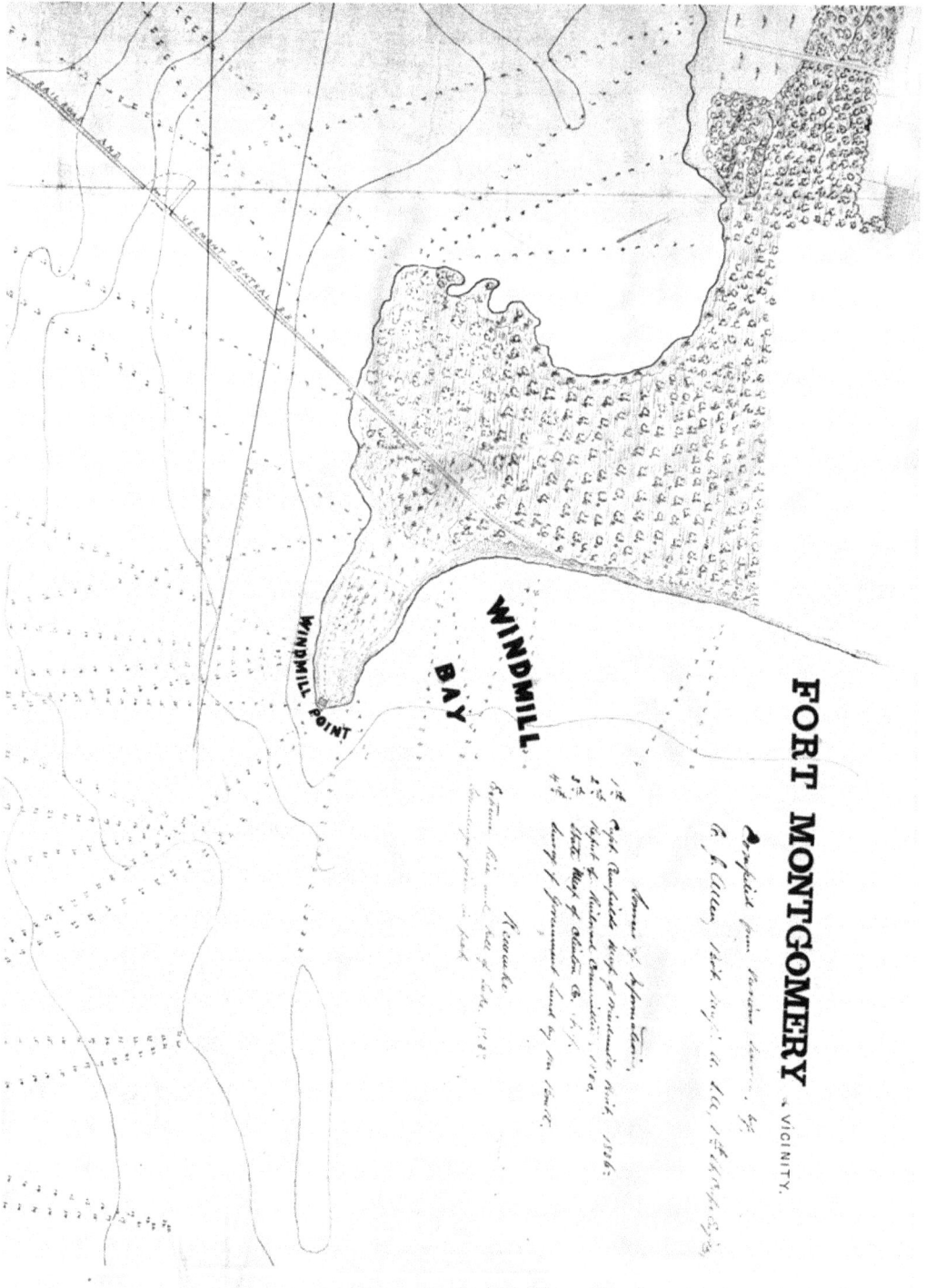

FORT MONTGOMERY & VICINITY.

WINDMILL BAY

WINDMILL POINT

Windmill Point. Had the United States not recovered Island Point and been forced to build the fort at Stony Point instead, an ancillary work would have been necessary here. This drawing dates to 1867. NARA: Records of the Chief of Engineers, Fortification File, Drawer 7, Sheet 65.

CHAPTER V

The Design, Construction and Armament of
Fort Montgomery

The Webster-Ashburton Treaty of 1842 changed everything. The treaty redefined the boundary north of Rouses Point to the former line, the old Valentine-Collins line, above the actual 45th parallel. Island Point reverted to United States ownership. Plans for works at Stony and Windmill Points were abandoned in favor of rebuilding on the old site.

At first, there was some question about whether to construct the new fort on the island itself or the shore. Prominent members of the Fortifications Board had proposed that the fort be built on what is known as the "Commons" years earlier. As late as 1850, well after work on the new fort had begun, Lt. Montgomery Meigs had sent a copy of plans for the entire 640 acre military reservation to headquarters. This document, originally drawn in 1817, showed the superimposed trace of an impressive five-bastioned fort well inland from the site of the old fort on Island Point (see page 10). This fort was noted as being the "Trace proposed by Genl. Bernard..."[1]

Despite Simon Bernard's original plan, this fort would be built on Island Point. Plans were drawn up for a substantial octagonal shaped, 5-bastioned fort. The fort was well-designed and constructed, a good example of what is known as a "Permanent" or "Third-System" fortification.[2] These forts, the product of contemporary military thinking shortly after the War of 1812, were notable for certain design and construction features. Based upon the ideas of noted French engineer Vauban, Third-System forts were the brainchild of Bernard, a Brigadier in the French Army hired by the US government to design a network of fortifications to protect the nation's vulnerable ports. One of the most important influences on Third-System fortification design was Joseph G. Totten himself. This capable engineer, who we recall was also involved the construction of the ill-fated first fort on the island, was one of the leading military minds of his time. Totten was no stranger to the region; he had a unique perspective on the strategic value of Lake Champlain. Assigned to help Alexander Macomb with the defense of Plattsburgh in 1814, it was Totten who designed the network of earthen forts that protected the south side of the Saranac River. He was brevetted Lieutenant Colonel for gallantry. His influence is unmistakable at Fort Montgomery.

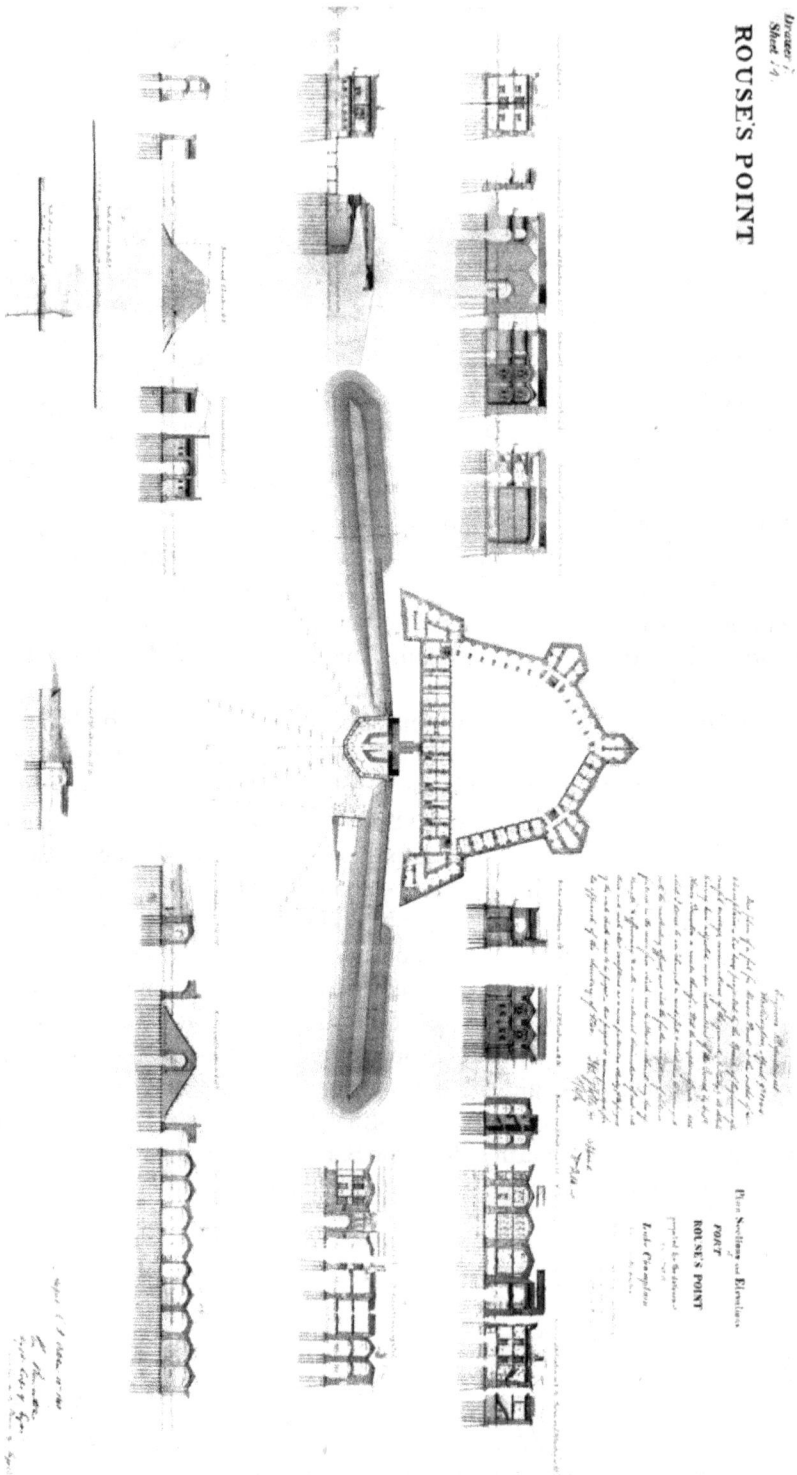

ROUSE'S POINT

Drawer 7, sheet 14, 1843. Plans, sections and elevations of Fort _____, Rouse's Point. Projected for the defense of the outlet of Lake Champlain.

This new fort would dwarf the earlier work. Fort "Blunder" fit on the island itself. There were even structures constructed outside the walls, still on the island. This new fort was so large (approximately 2.5 acres) that the island would be enlarged artificially with the fort walls surrounded by water on all sides. A causeway would connect the fort with the shore.[3]

Unlike the old octagonal work constructed without bastions, this modern new fort would have five bastions and an enormous earthen cover face. Early plans show a redoubt or block house (referred to as a guard house on some plans) complete with a multiple gun battery on the cover face before the postern or main entrance to the fort.[4] This feature was started but never finished.

Construction began on July 13, 1844 under the direction of US Civil Engineer Henry Brewster and superintended by Capt. Henry Brewerton.[5] The work was to be done by private contractors under the close supervision of the Engineers. The stone would come from a number of sources, a small quarry at King's Bay in New York, Gilman's quarry and the Fisk quarry in Isle la Motte, Vermont. A Rouses Point firm, Webb and Rawdon contracted to provide brick and other building materials.[6]

Fisk Quarry at Isle la Motte, Vermont. Most of the stone used at Fort Montgomery came from here. Photo courtesy of Doug and Roger Harwood.

The quarry at King's Bay. This small quarry supplied stone used during the earliest stages of construction. Photo courtesy of Doug and Roger Harwood.

Among the first tasks to be undertaken was the erection of cofferdams and driving of piles for the "grillage of timbers". This was to be completed well before stone arrived from the quarries. Also needed early on was a substantial wharf for unloading of stone and supplies. This first summer was a busy one; for the first time the sounds of a steam pile driver were heard on Lake Champlain, materials were arriving regularly by boat and team.

Two pile drivers were employed at the site; one of six horsepower requiring an engineer and three laborers to operate it, and a second, larger eight horsepower unit requiring a crew of five. These units were expensive- Brevet Lt. Col. (then Lieutenant) James L. Mason reported that "The original cost of engines was $4388.71; — the consumption of oil and rope, together with the repairs applied to them, has amounted to $1982.21; — making the total expended on the engines $6370.92...". A total of 4383 piles were driven into the lake bed in 1844-1846. Most were spruce, hemlock and tamarack but a few were beech and ash. Each pile was 29-32 feet long and roughly 9" at the point and 15" at the butt in diameter. Each of these piles was to support an astonishing 34,125 pounds, "in addition to its own weight and that of the grillage." Mason was even able to break down the "total cost of piles and driving, — $17017.67 or $3.88 pr. pile." [7]

Mason also shared much information about the grillage upon which the actual stone would be laid:

> "The grillage was laid in two courses; the lower of timber 1'3"wide and one foot thick, was generally laid perpendicular to the scarp, thus connecting together two rows of piles parallel to the scarp. It was notched down four inches on to the piles and pinned... The materials for the grillage, consisting of 45610 running feet of timber of the sizes, 12"x8", 12"x12" and 12"x15", and of
> | | |
> |---|---|
> | 12147 hard wood pins cost, | $2277.45 |
> | The cost of measuring hauling and securing this timber for the winter was − − | |
> | | 235.80 |
> | The cost of preparing, laying and pinning it | 2318.02 |
> | The cost of machinery, − − − | 70.00 |
> | The cost of contingent services and contingencies | |
> | Belonging to this part of the work, was − | 612.16 |
> | Making the total cost of the grillage, − − | $5513.93 |

Mason's remarkable account goes on to detail "The cost of the coffer dam and dyke", pumping, excavating, and more "contingent services and contingencies." I will not venture to share those numbers here. Of interest, however, might be the total cost of preparing the timber foundation of the fort— $27,580.61. Also of interest are Mason's remarks about water level and preservation of the timber grillage:

> "The difference of level between the highest and lowest water in this part of Lake Champlain, is nearly 8 feet: according to our memoranda 7'10". To prevent the decay of wood, it was necessary to place the top of the grillage at least as low as the lowest level of the surface of the water; − the piles had to be accurately leveled 1'4" below the top of the grillage. It thus became necessary, let the stage of water be what it would, to enclose the area with a coffer dam and dyke and to pump out the water."[8]

Engineer Mason did his work well. At low water ends of these well-preserved grillage timbers can still be seen protruding from what is left of bastion A.

Original timbers of the grillage extending from beneath bastion A. The white objects are Zebra Mussels, an invasive species that ironically serve to clarify the water so that the timbers can be seen. Photo by the author.

Unfortunately, with the work that first summer came the first accidental deaths. Rouses Point resident Thomas Hammond perished while working at the site, as did "two others subsequently, a Frenchman and an Irishman."[9]

On September 30th, a report was filed accompanied by a detailed plan showing the extent of work accomplished. This plan is one of the most interesting documents this writer has yet to discover regarding the fort. Entitled *"Fortifications _____ New-York, Outlet of Lake Champlain", and subtitled "Plan and Sections of Fort _____, Rouse's Point; exhibiting the condition of the work on the 30th of September 1844";* [10] the plans show, first of all, that the fort was yet unnamed. This is important since a popular (and widely published) misconception is that the *first* fort was named *Montgomery* and the second fort simply assumed the name. The plan also clearly shows the old fort and its unique earth and masonry coverface located squarely in the center of the trace of the new fort. The plans show in detail the piles and grillage placed by September 30th, and the location of the cofferdams. Also of interest is the fact that the temporary wharf had not been constructed yet, nor was work started on the wet-ditch (moat) or massive coverface to the west. A footbridge ran from the south end of the island to the shore. A report to Congress detailed the progress shown on the plan:

"A survey of the site to be occupied by the work was begun in May last. After determining the position of the shoal forming the site, with respect to prominent points of the lake shore, careful soundings were made, to ascertain the depth of water, and the bottom penetrated to various depths by boring, in order to determine the nature of the substrata.

A portion of the machinery required for driving piles was received by the officer in charge of these operations in June last, and soon afterwards the driving of piles was commenced. This work has continued, with but little interruption, throughout the season.

Up to the 30th of September last, the work done was as follows: completing the piling of the two curtains and one stairway, and that of one of the flanks, nearly; laying about one-half of the grillage of curtain No. 4; removing the greater portion of the foundations of the piers and cover-face of the old work; constructing an embankment of earth around a part of the foundations, and coffer dams around other portions, in order to facilitate the operation of driving piles; erecting a small temporary building for an office and for the use of a fort keeper, and executing various details of small extent.

The labor of the year will he continued as late as the season will permit, and it is expected that a considerable extent of the piling and grillage will be completed before the close of operations. Early next spring the work will be recommenced, and it is proposed to apply the funds now available, and the appropriation asked for, to the following objects: the construction of a temporary wharf and the necessary machinery; the completion of the piling and grillages; the laying of the foundations and building of the superstructure to the level of eight feet above the lowest water; giving additional security to the foundations by means of an enrockment; forming the parade, and raising the embankment of the coverface eight feet above lowest water, together with other necessary details."[11]

Construction in earnest began with ice out in 1845. The first piece of limestone, probably from the quarry at King's Bay, was laid for Curtain IV by stone cutter and mason John Sweeney. Sweeney was only one of a number of craftsmen who would continue to work on the fort for the next 30 years. At his side was fellow mason Joseph Hamelin. Hamelin (1823-1908) will work at the site until 1870.[12]

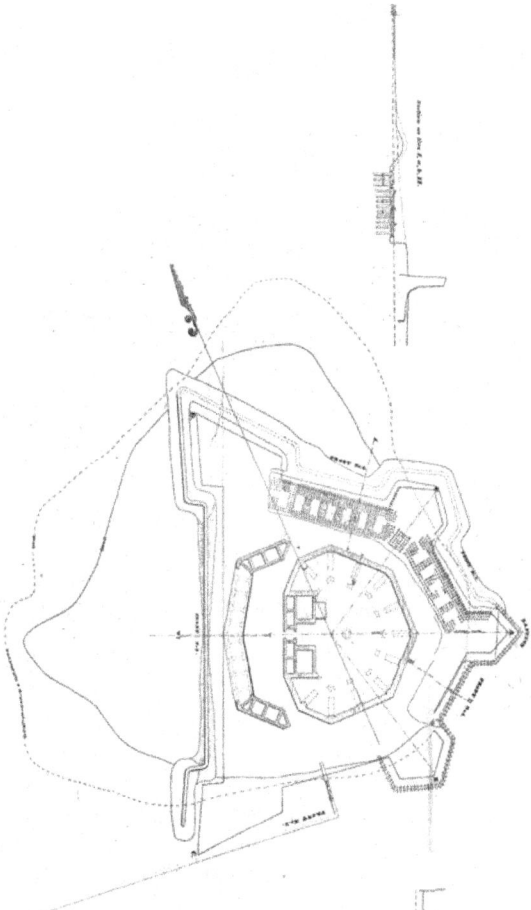

NARA Records of the Chief of Engineers. Record Group 77. Fortifications _____ New-York, Outlet of Lake Champlain", and subtitled "Plan and Sections of Fort _____, Rouse's Point; exhibiting the condition of the work on the 30th of September 1844 Drawer 7, Sheet15.

Early this first year, Capt. Brewerton was replaced by Lieut. James L. Mason as Engineer Supervisor of the work.[13]

On January 13, 1846 the United States went to war with Mexico. Lieut. Mason was ordered into action where he was severely wounded at the Battle of Molino del Ray.[14] Mason was but one of a number of Engineers associated with Fort Montgomery to serve with distinction in Mexico and the Civil War.

Although most construction work at Island Point was suspended during the hostilities with Mexico, we know at least one quarry- Gilman's, continued to cut and ship stone during the war. On September 2, 1846 a sloop carrying stone from the quarry to the fort sunk off Isle la Motte. Daniel Hall, one of the vessel's hands was drowned in the incident.[15] During the winter of 1845-46 upwards of 175 men were at work at the King's Bay quarry excavating and cutting stone.[16] We also know work continued at the site into the autumn of 1846. Col. James Mason wrote "Bastion A, the bastion nearest the channel, was finished in the fall of 1846 with the exception of the parapet wall surmounting the scarp."[17]

Montgomery C. Meigs served as Engineer Officer at Fort Montgomery from 1848-1854. This photo was taken during later life after he attained prominence as Quartermaster General. Library of Congress Prints and Photographs Division

By the time hostilities in Mexico finally came to a close on February 2, 1848, a large amount of Vermont and New York limestone was on site. A significant number of local craftsmen anxiously awaited the arrival of the Engineer's officer and resumption of construction. By late spring, Mason, recovered from his wounds, was back in Rouses Point. Work began anew under his supervision. Capt. Mason was only on site for a short time before he was replaced by another Corps of Engineers officer- Capt. Montgomery C. Meigs. Meigs would continue in command until the fall of 1854.

From resumption of construction in 1846 through the summer of 1851 attention was focused on the fronts facing north, IV and V, along with bastion E. Work was not progressing rapidly, however, despite the fact that these walls faced the Richelieu River, from which direction an enemy would come. A little-known fact about these forts is that they were armed well before the entire fort was completed, thus providing some level of defense well early on.[18] Once these north-facing fronts were finished, guns would be brought in and mounted. These walls, more properly referred to as ramparts, were built mostly with old-style brick embrasures on both tiers. An interesting annotation on fort plans from August 26, 1851 sheds some light on when the newer technology of masonry embrasures strengthened by thick iron bands was introduced:

"The lower story of the curtain parade wall is finished. The scarp of the curtain is carried up to 34.66 feet. The embrasures are not constructed, except No. VII which was built by Col. Mason of brick."[19]

It appears that this was the last casemate tier embrasure constructed of hardened brick; the note and later photographs show the balance of embrasures on curtain IV are iron-reinforced masonry.

One of the advantages of the fort being constructed over such a long period of time was that newer technologies were incorporated as they became available. The iron-reinforced embrasure is a good example.

Bastion E and a section of Curtain V at very low water. This was the first part of the fort constructed. Curtain V is the only curtain constructed with old-style brick embrasures on the second tier. Since bastions A and E were the first built they have the brick embrasures on both tiers. Note also the wooden embrasure covers installed in the early 1880's. Courtesy Clinton County Historical Association.

The two types of embrasures at Fort Montgomery. At top left is a flank howitzer embrasure with its pintle intact. At top right is one of the newer iron-reinforced masonry embrasures. This particular embrasure is in good condition, unlike the one at bottom right. Most of the masonry embrasures are in bad condition, the masonry has eroded causing the heavy iron bands to fall into the lake. Bottom left: exterior flank howitzer embrasures on bastion C. All lower tier embrasures are of brick. Photos by the author.

Exterior view of the best preserved masonry embrasure at Fort Montgomery. An interior view of this embrasure can be seen on the previous page. This embrasure faces north on what is left of bastion D. Photo by the author.

While the masonry embrasures have not fared as well against the ravages of time, when one stands behind one of the narrow masonry openings it is easy to see why a gun crew would feel much safer in these casemates than behind one of the wide, brick embrasures.

In the autumn of 1854 Montgomery C. Meigs was replaced by Lieut. C.E. Blunt. Charles Evans Blunt would oversee construction at Fort Montgomery in one capacity or another until the end of the Civil War.

Work continued on the fort at a very slow pace. Funds would run out, Congress was asked for additional appropriations. Much depended on the influence of Chief Engineer Totten and local representatives in Congress. The massive network of coastal forts deemed the "Permanent or Third-System" was seen by some in Congress (and even within the Engineers themselves) as a costly mistake. Fortifications along the northern frontier were considered even less important by some. With the advent of railways and better roads, an invasion via inland waterways was considered less of a threat. Within the Engineers Corps one officer loudly advocated for floating batteries over costly fortifications.[20] Yet, Totten firmly believed in this network of forts; he was a force to be reckoned with. Construction always resumed again, long-time fort masons John Sweeney and Joe Hamelin along with newly hired John Kearny; men who had fanned out into the countryside hoping to ply their trade building homes and churches, were always called back to Island Point.[21]

Fort construction provided a significant boost to the local economy. Local people were called on to work at the site (under the direct supervision of a Corps of Engineers officer) and local businesses were more than happy to provide the materials necessary for such a huge undertaking. Quarries, brickyards and sawmills were never busier. Men moved into the area, oftentimes bringing their families with them. Fort construction periods were prosperous times.

By spring of 1857 work had progressed to bastion D and the north end of the gorge officer's quarters. Lt. Blunt's report to headquarters detailed the work to date: "...all the lower tier of embrasures and loopholes are finished..." (bastion D and north end of gorge). The parade wall on this end of gorge "is carried up (stone) to the level of the top of foundation only (about 8.33')"...Within the gorge officer's quarters "none of these partition walls have been commenced..." Blunt also writes "The scarp of the south front is of variable height- the lowest point is about (18'), the highest about (20')." He then pointed out what appears to have been a rather serious error on someone's part; referring to the *three* openings in the bastion D magazine- the proper entrance at the southeast, one on the west side and yet another on the east side *directly opposite a flank howitzer embrasure!* He wrote "The two openings A & B [east and west] have been constructed as <u>doors</u> [underline in original]; I believe they are to be closed entirely." These openings were supposed to be much smaller ventilation shafts, not doors. An examination of the bastion today shows these large openings were closed, as was the flank howitzer embrasure on the east side, evidently the only embrasure to be bricked up. As bad as it was to have lost this gun on a crucial face of a north facing bastion, keeping it open would have made an already vulnerable location much worse.[22]

Work continued through the end of the decade, albeit slowly. On November 14, 1860 an alarmed Engineers Dept. decried the neglect of northern frontier fortifications and complained that Fort Montgomery was only about half finished.[23]

In January, 1861 all work on the fort was suspended.[24] On January 18, the Engineer Dept. report to Secretary of War Holt listed the fort as "About half built, capable of some defense."[25] A look at the state of the works after 16 years is telling. Rev. Taylor tells us that the while the "foundation" of the fort was complete, the "super-structure" (ramparts) only of fronts IV and V were complete to their full height. The scarp wall of the rest of the fort was only raised "perhaps 18 feet above the foundation". Minimal work had been done on the cover face. Taylor opined that "the fort was thus unprepared to receive any part of its proposed armament."[26] Totten's report to Secretary of War Simon Cameron of November 30, 1861 included the following remarks about the state of the work at Fort Montgomery:

Above left: The outline of the door is clearly seen. Above right: View within Bastion D east toward the wall where the door was mistakenly constructed. Photos by the author.

"The small amount of appropriation has prevented any considerable progress being made with this work. The expenditure has been applied principally upon the scarps and connected masonry of Curtain II, in which part of the work 731 cubic yards of masonry have been laid. With the appropriation asked it is expected to prepare the fort for most of its armament. Appropriation asked, $100,000."[27]

The January interruption was short. Within a few months Rouses Point and Island Point would witness a frenzy of activity. On April 12 another of Totten's forts was bombarded. The bloodiest conflict in American history opened with the shelling of Fort Sumter. The Civil War had begun.

C.E. Blunt (now a Brevet Colonel) was ordered from Lake Champlain to Washington to assist with the defenses of that city at Arlington Heights. While there he retained nominal control of the works on the northern frontier. In July some work resumed at Rouses Point when Totten ordered the capable Capt. David White to assume full local charge of construction as Engineer Superintendent. Some $3,000 in unexpended funds was supplemented by an

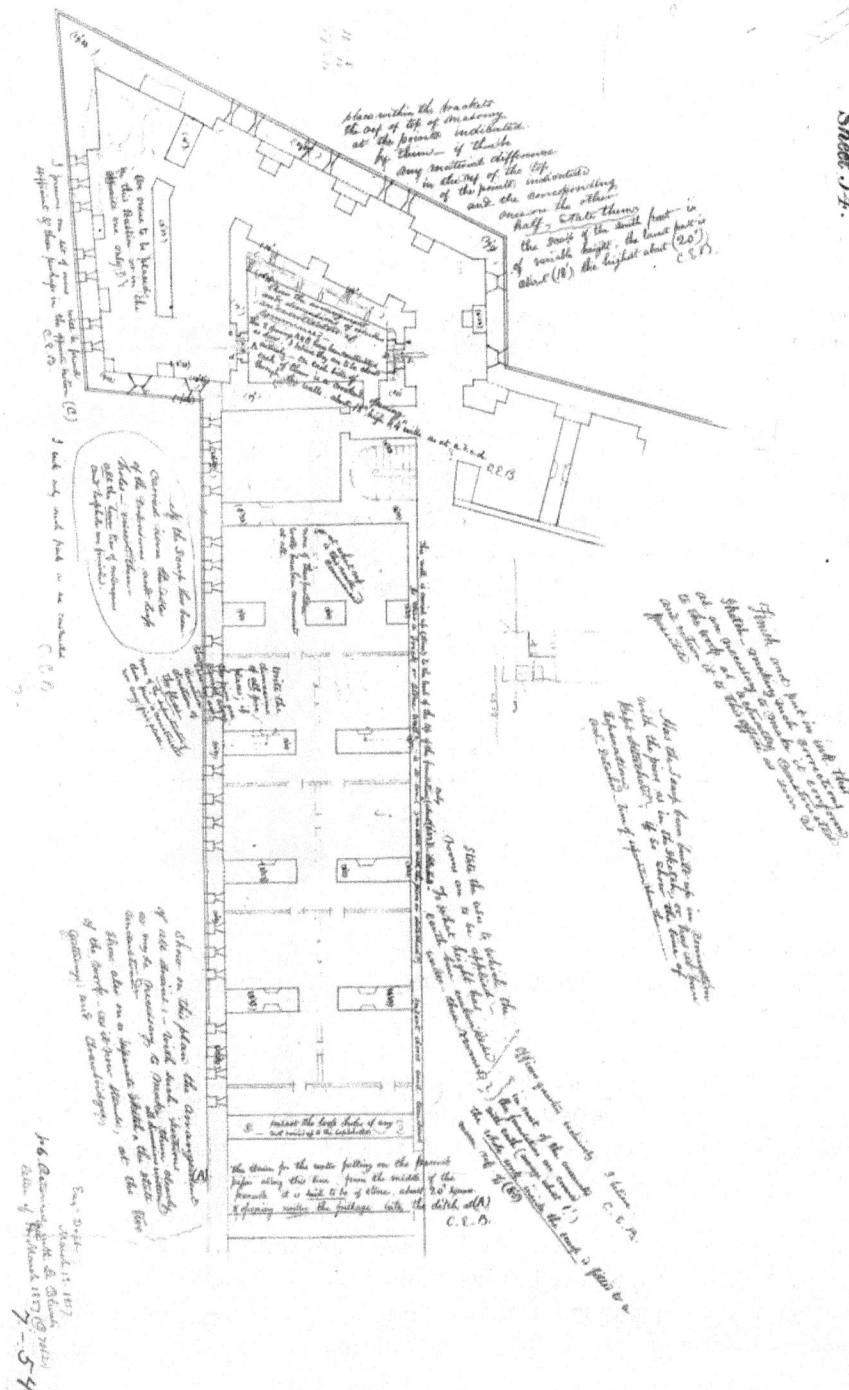

Notes written by Col. C.E. Blunt within the magazine reveal the error made when contractors constructed a door immediately opposite a flank howitzer embrasure. NARA: Records of the Chief of Engineers, Fortification File. Drawer 7, sheet 54, 1857

additional $10,000 that Totten had reportedly secured by appealing directly to President Lincoln. Evidently this money was "borrowed" from another fortification project — work at Island Point was to be pushed "as rapidly as possible."[28]

Once again in November the ominous specter of war with England loomed. As if the problems in the south were not enough, the Trent Affair brought Anglo-American relations to a new low. The nation was potentially the closest it had come to war with England since the signing of the Treaty of Ghent. In addition, France declared its willingness to support Great Britain in a conflict with the United States.[29] Defenses along the frontier with British Canada gained new importance.

That autumn Totten visited the works at Rouses Point; on December 30, 1861 he was able to report significant progress at Fort Montgomery. His report to Governor Morgan of New York stated:

> "The new fort there placed [Fort Montgomery] is well advanced, and measures are in train for the most rapid progress in the spring. It may even now resist escalade, and by the opening of the lake will be prepared to mount a number of heavy guns. All this winter will be devoted to inside finish of magazines and gun casemates, and the preparation of materials for outside walls. It is easy to see that a war in the North may make this well adapted. This fort will overlook a large surface of ground as well as the channel of the lake. Its armament will be seventy-six 10-inch guns, ten 32-pounders, forty 24-pounder howitzers, ten mortars — 136 pieces. Provided this fort fulfill its object, there will be no need for fortifications higher up the lake, and all the advantages of lake communication will be preserved to us during the war. Strategical considerations indicate certain positions farther back from the boundary line as points of assemblage for troops, but these would not need fortifications so long as Fort Montgomery shall be held."[30]

On February 20, 1862 Congress appropriated an additional $900,000 for defenses along the Canadian border. Work at Fort Montgomery and three other northern frontier forts were carried out aggressively.[31]

Taylor described the situation at Rouses Point in a remarkable sentence as descriptive as it is long:

> "...the work to be carried on so large as scale rendered it necessary to provide an entire new plant or outfit of implements for doing the work— such as new, powerful steam and hand derricks, steam engines, stone trucks, etc., all of which were gotten ready and the work of construction commenced in an incredibly short time, and then the wonderful flow of material to the fort, stone, brick, sand, lime, iron, timber, lumber, etc., transported by boats, cars and teams; and, then, the little army of employees, at times, we believe, numbering nearly 400 men, of various trades and occupations, going to and from the fort to the village morning and evening, the busy scenes inside and outside, the work so thoroughly organized, every man seeming to

know his duty and doing it without clash or jar, and all this labor conspiring to the daily phenomenal growth of that immense structure..."[32]

Taylor also tells us that within a few months one third of the fort's armament was mounted.[33]

In a significant development, 15 soldiers of the 14th Infantry are briefly garrisoned at the fort. They remain for about three months.[34] This is apparently the only time Federal troops are stationed at Fort Montgomery. One account tells us that "the fort was used as a prison camp, and a detachment of Federal troops was there as a guard company."[35] I have found documentation to show the troops were there, but nothing to verify the claim about the prisoners. It would seem unlikely that rebel prisoners would be held so close to the border.

Totten again visited the fort in the autumns of 1862 and 1863.[36] All through 1863 work continued under Capt. David White, with Frank H. Dupont as civilian overseer.[37]

The threat of England entering the war on the side of the Confederacy continued. On March 2, 1864 the House passed a resolution requesting "that the Committee on Roads and Canals...inquire as to the importance and expediency of enlarging the Champlain canal, in the State of New York, for the passage of armed and naval vessels from the tide waters of the Hudson River to Lake Champlain..."[38]

Gen. Joseph Gilbert Totten. Library of Congress, Prints & Photographs Division

On April 22, 1864, Brigadier General Joseph Gilbert Totten, Chief of Engineers, designer of the earthen batteries at the Battle of Plattsburgh in 1814, builder of Fort "Blunder" and driving force behind the "Permanent" or Third System of Fortifications and Fort Montgomery, died at Washington, D.C. of pneumonia. He had served almost sixty years in the army. The great Civil War still raged. The effectiveness of his vast network of masonry fortifications was as yet still unproven.

In September 1864 General Henry W. Halleck ordered a company of laborers to be organized into a military-type unit to serve as a first line of defense of the works. Uniforms and small arms were requisitioned and distributed. The unit drilled every day in infantry and heavy artillery tactics. The good citizens of Rouses Point got a good taste of what it was like to hear the fort's 32-pounders and flank howitzers fired as gunnery practice took place.[39]

On October 19, 1864 the northernmost land engagement of the Civil War took place at St. Albans, Vermont. Twenty Confederate raiders led by Lt. Bennett Young entered the city and staged simultaneous robberies on three banks. Their plans to burn the city failed but they were quite successful in causing uproar in the North Country. Word reached Fort Montgomery the same day when Vermont Central Railroad employee George L. Stone received word by telegraph. Stone rushed the word to Captain White at his home. White hurried to the fort and arrived just as the workday was ending, around 5:00 pm. The fort went on full alert with half of the workmen taking up assigned posts there. Another large group quickly marched to the village where they took up guard positions along the roads into town. The raiders fled into Canada but the fort remained on high alert for several days.

On November 20, 1864 another account of rebel activity, probably spurious, was reported in the Rouses Point area. Supposedly a gang of rebel raiders on horseback appeared in the village that Sunday evening. When challenged by pickets they reportedly fired on the guards. The fire was returned, resulting in one of the raiders falling from his saddle. The raiders fled with their wounded man.[40] Again that month jittery residents sounded the alarm, probably false also. Taylor wrote that an O&LC engineer reported a large group of men assembled just outside of town preparing to attack Rouses Point and Champlain village. He insisted he saw signal rockets fired. While the fort went on high alert again, no raid ensued.[41]

Despite the various alarms and concerns caused by the St. Albans Raid, the war years were good times for Rouses Point and Champlain. After years of languishing, construction on the fort proceeded rapidly. In 1864 alone some 400 men toiled at the site each day. With this great construction project came prosperity. With all of these laborers, masons, carpenters, teamsters, etc. came a need for housing, food and other goods. Local quarries, brickyards and blacksmiths flourished as did lumberyards, stores and other businesses. Trains brought more men and materials to the fort each week. The dock adjacent to bastion B often was seen with ships unloading various cargos. Among that cargo were guns and munitions, Fort Montgomery's reason for existing.

On January 31, 1865 Major Blunt filed his yearly Armament Report. It is particularly useful in that it shows the guns mounted during the period of conflict. It is also an important document in that it shows the fort was acting as a deterrent to any attack south up the lake while still unfinished. It listed:

- Seven 32-pounder smooth bore guns mounted *en casemate*
- Thirty six 24-pounder flank howitzers mounted *en casemate*
- Carriages on hand for the remaining four flank howitzers

The report also stated that by June 30, 1865 seven center-pintle and three fore-pintle mounts would be ready for guns *en barbette* [this was overly optimistic, the center-pintle mounts were never completed]. Blunt annotated the report with his hopeful notation that the seven 32-pounders smoothbores "are, I believe, only temporary."[42]

So, as 1865 dawned, the nearly completed fort mounted roughly a third of its full complement of guns. These guns were not the serious ordnance Blunt expected. His "only tem-

Daily Report of Service Rendered at Fort Montgomery, November 14, 1865. Courtesy: Clinton County Historical Association

porary" remark is of interest since all of the guns mounted by late winter were the old-style and nearly obsolete 32-pounders and 24-pounder flank howitzers, a much smaller anti-personnel weapon mounted only in the flanks of the bastions. The larger guns would arrive shortly with the cessation of fighting in the south.

On April 9, 1865 the American Civil War came to an end with the surrender of Lee at Appomattox. Although the great conflagration finally came to a halt, work on Fort Montgomery continued.

On October 30, 1865, Companies C and I of the 4th Infantry took up posts at Plattsburg Barracks. They were commanded by 1st Lieutenant Thomas F. Quinn under Post Commander Henry M. Judah.[43]

Judah and the 4th were intended to garrison Fort Montgomery. The Plattsburg Sentinel reported that Judah was "temporarily stationed at Plattsburgh, waiting until Fort Montgomery could be prepared for the reception of his troops." That transfer never occurred and Judah died at Plattsburg on January 14, 1866.[44] The 4th remained at Plattsburgh until March of 1867 when they were sent to Omaha, Nebraska.[45]

In November, 1865 Major Charles Evans, "C.E." Blunt was replaced by Gen. Chauncey "C.B." Reese.[46] Blunt, in charge of several fortifications, including those on the Niagara frontier- Fort, Wayne, Fort Porter, Fort Niagara and Fort Ontario, is one of the key figures in the construction of Fort Montgomery. C. E. Blunt graduated from West Point in 1846. He served honorably and accomplished much during his 41 years in the Engineers. He retired in 1887 and died in 1892. He and his wife, Penelope Bethune Blunt, are buried together in Arlington National Cemetery.

A "Daily Report of Services Rendered at Fort Montgomery" from November 14, 1865 gives us a fascinating look at the state of the fort at the end of that year. Seventy-six workers toiled at Fort Montgomery that day. Although there are still derricks in place, tended by five laborers, it is obvious that the fort is largely finished. Masons are plastering in Curtain III (the gorge officer's quarters). One carpenter is making "earth boxes." Nine double teams are hauling earth, wood, water and stone. Eighteen laborers are digging, loading these teams, and hauling earth on the Commons and cover face, while another ten men are digging and hauling earth in the moat. One overseer was on site. Also present were one clerk, two sub-overseers, three masons, and six stone-cutters. Two smiths were "sharpening tools", four laborers were "running and tending engines", one was "tending the B. Smith", and another two were sawing wood.

The 1866 Report of the Chief of Engineers report of work done during the period reads "Stone and earthen parapet and breast-high wall of the land front [gorge, curtain III] completed, setting parade wall coping [the top-most layer of stone] and turning floor arches; embanking terreplein and cover-face; constructing masonry barbette platforms (20), and excavating the moat."[47]

In the spring of 1866 the northern frontier again erupted. The first of the Fenian Raids was attempted at Compobello Island, New Brunswick, just north of the Maine border. This raiding party was dispersed by the US government before hostilities could take place but it did set the stage for five years of mischief by the Fenian Brotherhood. In early June 1866, Company C of the 4th Infantry was sent from Plattsburgh Barracks to Buffalo and then to Malone to "prevent the crossing of the "Fenians" into Canada."[48]

It was during this time, early 1866 that Major Charles J. Allen was assigned to Fort Montgomery. He was to remain only a few months.

On June 7, 1866 the Second Fenian Invasion of Canada took place, this time just across the lake. Some two thousand Fenian raiders crossed the border at Franklin, Vermont (near Highgate). After a brief skirmish at Pigeon Hill, these raiders abandoned their attack and fled back across the border. Despite the best efforts of the US government to prevent such incursions, these attacks worsened Anglo-American relations. This worsening situation made the ongoing efforts at finishing Fort Montgomery seem even more prudent.

Colonel Chauncey B. Reese filed his armament report on June 30, 1866. In addition to the seven 32-pounders, four more 24-pounder flank howitzers had been mounted, the fort's full complement of this anti-personnel weapon. In addition, ten 10-inch Rodman's were mounted *en casemate* and another eight 8-inch Rodman's *en barbette*. Though not completely finished, with the arrival of the Rodman's the fort was now mounting significant ordnance. The big

Rodman guns were all mounted on iron carriages. As of this date sixty-five guns had been mounted. Two of the huge 15-inch Rodman's planned for the barbette tier were on site but not mounted. Reese's report also states that fore-pintle mounts are ready for en *casemate* for an additional fifteen 8 or 10-inch Rodman's and thirty-four fore-pintle mounts and seven center-pintle mounts are ready for Rodman's *en barbette*. Seventeen of these, however, need traverse irons and pintles to be complete.[49]

Much had been accomplished since Congress dramatically increased funding in 1862. The Engineer's Report for the fiscal year July 1, 1866 to June 30, 1867 tells us much about this progress:

> "At this work the principal operations have been the following: Completion of seventeen barbette gun platforms; laying coping of parapet wall on curtains one, two and four, and bastions A and B, (thus completing the scarp wall of the fort); raising staircase of bastion C from foundation to level of gun casemates (23.58'), laying of flagging in lower story of bastion C, and concrete foundation for lower floor of bastion E; turning communication arches in lower story of bastion C; advancing interior finish of officer's quarters; embanking and laying stone facing on coverface; driving piles on south end of wet ditch with a view toward a modification of the counterscarp. During the present year it is proposed to complete the staircase to bastion C, the parade wall of curtain three, and the barbette magazines on the land front, and to continue the interior finish of the officer's quarters, &c. The fort is now ready for a considerable portion of its armament. Appropriation asked for the next fiscal year, $60,000."[50]

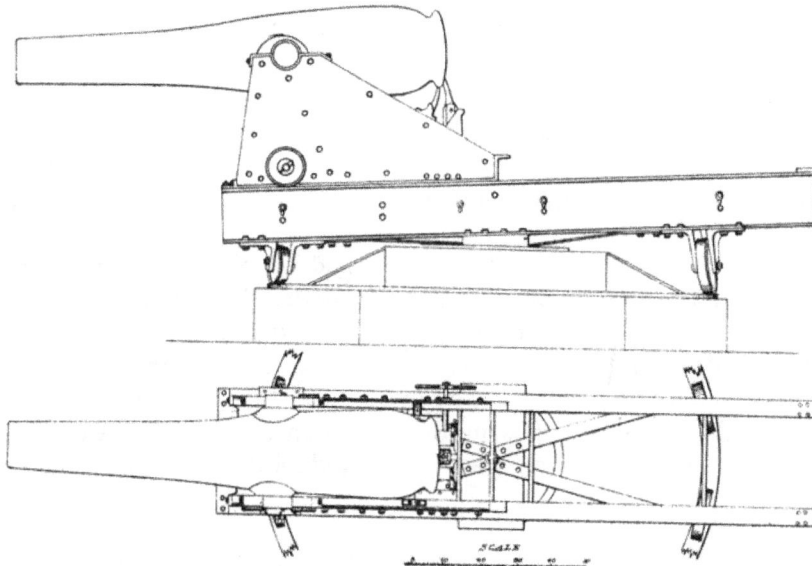

Center-pintle barbette mounted Rodman gun of the type planned for Fort Montgomery but never mounted. Two of these enormous 15-inch guns were on the parade for years.

Drawer 246
Sheet 32 - 3

Fort Montgomery

Col. Blunt's Armament Report of June 30, 1867. NARA, Records of the Chief of Engineers, Fortification file, Drawer 246, Sheet 32-3 1867

The June 30, 1867 Armament Report of C.E. Blunt also reflected this progress. Over the past year another ten 10-inch Rodman's were mounted *en barbette,* bringing the totals to 35 "seacoast" guns and forty flank howitzers— 57 *en casemate* and 18 *en barbette.* Blunt also reported an additional twelve platforms ready for guns in the casemates and 23 platforms available on the barbette tier. It appears that all center-pintle mounts were changed to fore-pintle since there is no entry for center-pintle mounts at all. The two massive 15-inch Rodman's would remain on the parade.

Fronts I and V [bastions A and E and curtains I and V] were constructed with wooden floors rather than with the stone and masonry that supported the rest of the fort's casemated guns. These floors would only support the obsolete 32-pounders and would have to be replaced if these critical eastern facing fronts were to receive modern ordnance. Four 32-pounders were mounted in curtain V and another one was placed in curtain I. On September 21, 1867 plans were drawn up for replacing these wooden casemate floors on the first and second tiers of Fronts I and V.[51] Funding was not received for the modifications and the work was never begun.

Casemate tier, Curtain I or V showing wooden floors and traverse irons for gun carriages. This rare photo also shows the iron reinforcing rods in place to inhibit further separation of the scarp wall. Courtesy: Powertex.

Col. Blunt's report to the Chief of Engineers for FY 1867-1868 read much like the previous year's report:

"The principal operations at this work have been the completion of the flagging of the first and second stories of bastions C and D; raising the south end of the parade wall of curtain III, and the staircase in bastion C, to reference (30.80′); turning the lower passage arches in bastion C, and the second story arches of curtain III; advancing the interior finish of the officer's quarters, and constructing the revetment wall of coverface. During the present year it is proposed to complete the staircase in bastion C, the parade wall of curtain III, and the revetment wall of coverface. Appropriation asked for the next fiscal year, $25, 000."

Also of interest in Blunt's report is the notation that Capt. J. W. Barlow was now assigned to Fort Montgomery. Captain James W. Barlow would continue to visit Fort Montgomery until 1900 and would later hold the distinction of being Chief of Engineers for one day before retiring in 1901. In 1869 Barlow was "Commandant" of the Fort. The Champlain Journal of August 4, 1869 tells us that Barlow "resides in Burlington, VT with frequent attendance at the Fort. Mr. David White is still in charge."[52]

Civil Engineer David White spent much of his career at Fort Montgomery. First assigned to the work in 1856, White superintended construction during the height of activity in the Civil War years. A long-time Rouses Point resident whose ancestors were among the region's first settlers, the well-respected White lived in the village until his death in 1900.

The Chief of Engineer's report for fiscal year July 1, 1868- June 30, 1869 detailed the years work:

"During the year staircase bastion C has been raised to the height of 39'.78; the adjoining pier[?] completed; the south end of parade wall of curtain III raised to 39'.58, and that of the west end of curtain II to 38'.33. The last main arch and drain of curtain III and the remaining two of bastion C have been turned. The second floor arches of one suite of rooms in the quarters, and the roofing of curtain III and bastion C have been completed. The terreplein of the former and a part of the latter have been filled with earth. The stone facing of the west salient of cover-face has been raised to its full height, and the cover-face embanked with earth. It is proposed to replace the wooden floors of curtains I and V, and bastions A and E with masonry; rebuild counterscarp, and make some other necessary repairs. Appropriation asked for next fiscal year, $65,000."[53]

In September 1, 1870 proposals were advertised for construction of a "one story and attic Frame Building" to be built at Fort Montgomery. Bidding was to end at midnight on October 1 and construction was to be completed within sixty days of acceptance of the bid. This building was undoubtedly the Fort Keeper's cottage on the Commons.[54]

The turbulent decade of the 1860's closed out with this report from the Chief of Engineers highlighting work for the previous fiscal year:

"Completion of staircase bastion C, parade walls, asphaltic covering, and terrepleins of curtains 2 and 3; turning four arches of second-story floors of curtain 3, and completing earthen parapet of right flank bastion B." Also recommended was "...substitution of brick arches for the decaying wooden floors in some of the gun casemates, and also that it be kept in suitable condition as a depot for stores and ammunition for troops either moving to invade Canada, or for the defense of this frontier line." They also recommended "additional thickness to be given to the exposed magazine walls. The modification of the barbette battery was intended to be delayed until some demonstrations were made by the Canadian authorities to deepen the Chambly Canal."

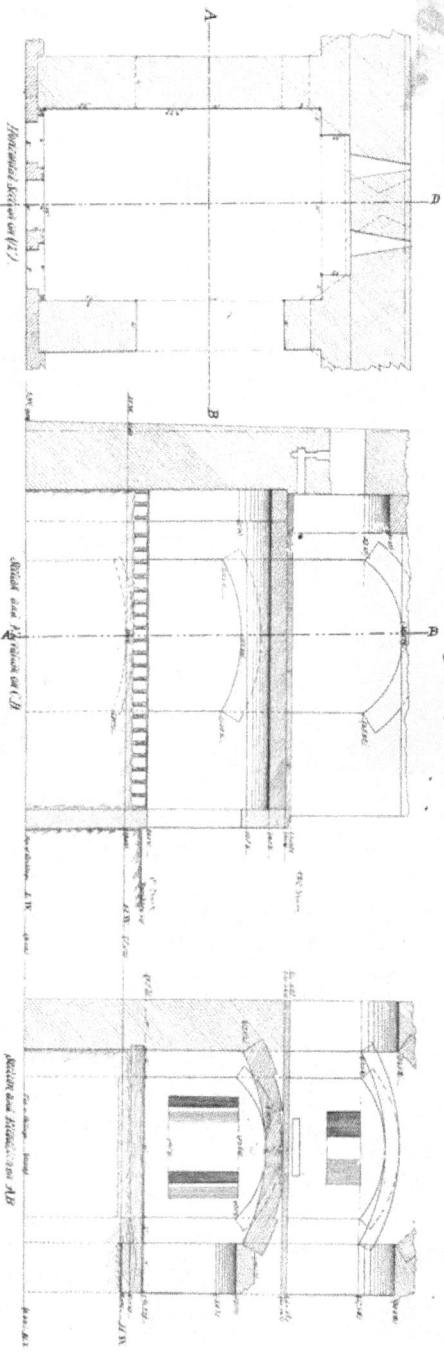

Sketch showing arrangement & dimensions of the existing masonry floors in Curtain IV & proposed modifications in 1st & 2nd floors of Fronts I & V. This is the plan designed for replacement of the wooden floors to enable the placement of Rodman guns and the removal of the obsolete 32-pounders. NARA, Records of the Chief of Engineers, Fortification File, Drawer 7, Sheet 66. 1867

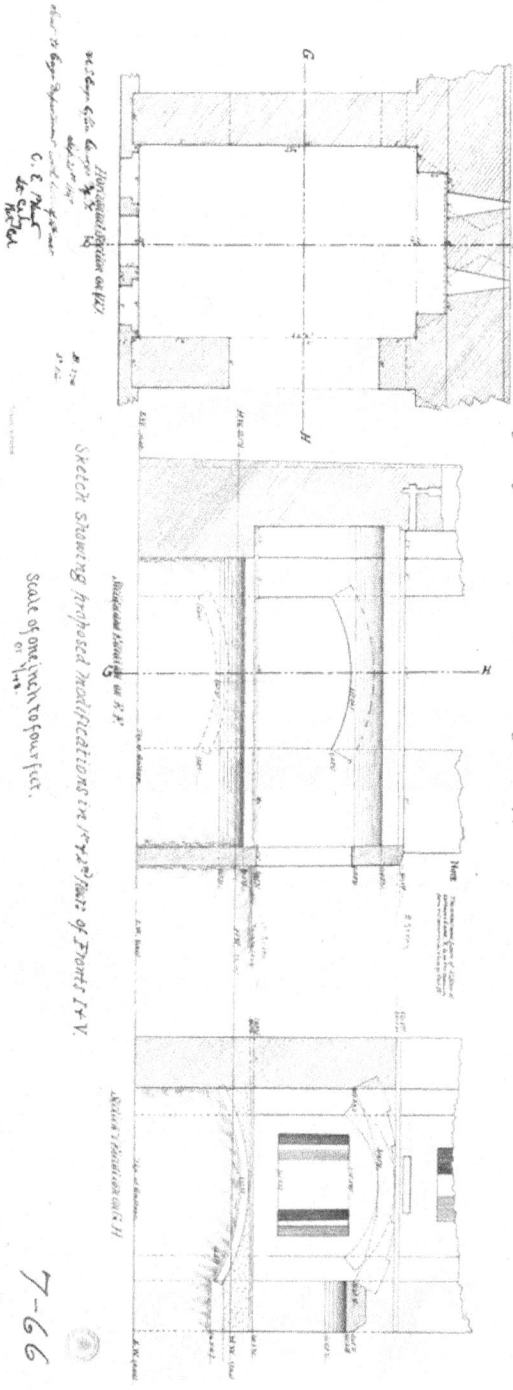

Fort Montgomery, largely completed and bristling with more than half its full complement of heavy ordnance.
Courtesy: Clinton County Historical Association.

The report went on to state that the fort was "essentially complete for the old styles of armament."[55] With the new decade came approval by the Board of Engineers of the "Project for modification for modern guns."[56] This modernization would not be forthcoming.

On May 8, 1871 the Treaty of Washington was signed in Washington. It was ratified in London on June 17th. This treaty settled claims between the United States and Great Britain, particularly the Alabama Claims. It would contribute greatly toward furthering peaceful relations between the two nations. It had a significant impact upon Britain's perceived need for troops in Canada. It also effectively ended the need for a major fortification along the northern frontier at Lake Champlain in the view of many military and political figures. Some twenty-seven years after it was begun, Fort Montgomery was now largely complete. It was also viewed by many as largely unneeded.

View northeast from the parade. Seen in this photo are a part of Curtain IV, Bastion E, Curtain V, Bastion A, and even some of Curtain I. Courtesy Ray Seguin

US Reservation: Rouses Point, NY. Records of the Adjutant General, Record Group 153.5 Lands Division, Sheet 1. This document states that [Fort Montgomery] "was garrisoned for about three months in 1862 by a detachment of fifteen men from the 14th Infty."

CHAPTER VI

The Treaty of Washington, 1871
to Private Sale, 1926

The Treaty of Washington was a significant factor in easing Anglo-American tensions. To say that relations between Washington and London were good, however, would be inaccurate. Problems remained, and one of the most significant was the oft-heard call for annexation of Canada. As early as 1850, William Seward, American Secretary of State during the Civil War, had been pushing the idea that British Canada should become part of the United States.[1]

The idea that the United States would even consider annexing Canada might seem rather incredible to some today. Yet it was considered inevitable in some quarters, witness this quote from the Plattsburgh Republican of February 4, 1871:

> "...*annexation is only a question of time* and doubtless the time will be long ere the cannon of this formidable fort shall be pointed toward a hostile fleet from Canada. *Hence, the immense fortress is a useless thing,* and so far as being necessary for military purposes is concerned, Heaven grant it remain so."[2]

On July 2, 1866, Massachusetts Congressman Nathaniel Prentiss Banks had introduced H.R. 754, "A Bill for the admission of the States of Nova Scotia, New Brunswick, Canada East, and Canada West, and for the organization of the Territories of Selkirk, Saskatchewan, and Columbia."[3] The bill was introduced largely as a gesture of support for the Fenians and never made it to the Senate. It certainly did nothing, however, to improve relations between the United States and Great Britain. Talk of annexation would continue well into the Twentieth Century. So also would discussion about the importance and future of Fort Montgomery.

After the Treaty of Washington was ratified work on Third-System and Northern Frontier fortifications slowed significantly. The Engineers Report of 1872 listed "Slight repairs made to magazines, retaining walls; general care of work" as the extent of efforts directed at Fort Montgomery.[4]

By 1872 Fort Montgomery had received all of the guns it was going to mount. The Armament Report of that year listed:

En casemate

- Seven 32- pounders on wooden carriages
- Ten 10-inch Rodman's on iron carriages
- Forty 24-pounder flank howitzers on wooden carriages

En barbette

- Eight 8-inch Rodman's on iron carriages and fore-pintle mounts
- Nine 10-inch Rodman's on iron carriages and fore-pintle mounts

Seven of the eight center-pintle mounts on the barbette tier had yet to receive their traverse circles and the eighth (on bastion C) had yet to be commenced.[5] Two 15-inch Rodman guns planned for the barbette tier remained un-mounted on the parade.

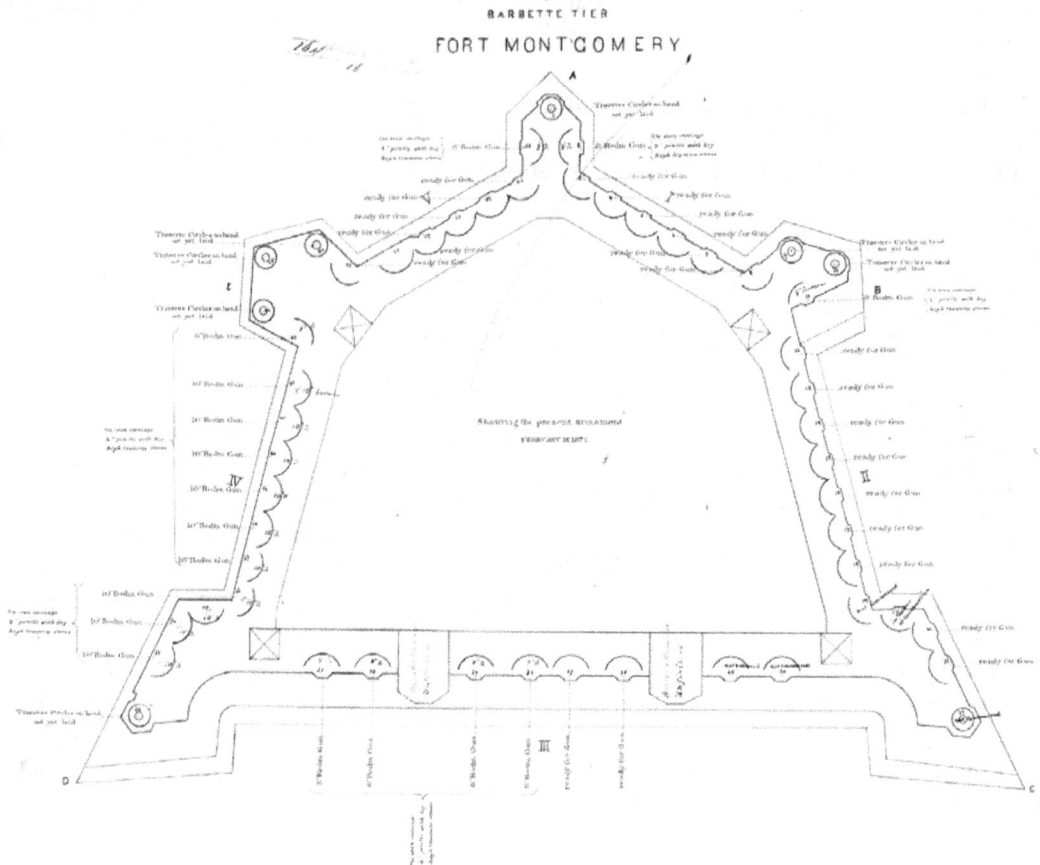

Armament of the barbette tier, February 1872. NARA, Drawer 259, Sheet 95

The following fiscal year brought only "minor work" to the fort and in the fiscal year July 1, 1873 to June 30, 1874, "No operations were carried on..." although "Projects for the modification of this work to suit its armament to heavy guns have been prepared by the Board of Engineers for fortifications, and *should be carried out.*"[Italics added]. No appropriation had been made for the fiscal year and none was asked for the next. Lieutenant Col. John Newton was in charge of the works at Rouses Point.[6]

In December of 1873 an effort was made to remove the un-mounted 15-inch Rodman's by water from the fort. They were to be placed at another fort. The effort was postponed indefinitely by bad weather.[7] These enormous 15-inch guns would remain on the parade until at least 1900.[8]

Some work was performed in 1874-75, "6 shot and shell beds built on parade, and repairs made to earthen parapet, footbridge over marsh, and cavities in causeway and revetment."[9] The following year brought some activity also, "... the parade was graded as far as practicable, new bridge constructed and placed in the main postern, and the repair of the causeway, together with the sodding of parapet of Curtain 3 has been commenced. Six hundred yards of earth and gravel were employed in grading parade."[10]

In 1876 the announcement came that the fort was "complete."[11] That year also brought an ominous new discovery, one that would have implications for the fort to this day. The scarp wall, purposely designed to be separate from the casemates to allow for heavy damage to it without taking down the casemates themselves[12], was separating in places from the rest of the ramparts. Included in that year's work was the first attempt at repairing a serious structural flaw that would plague not only Fort Montgomery but other fortifications as well.

This photo of a section of the gorge shows how the scarp was purposely built separate from the rest of the rampart. In theory, it was a great idea. Unfortunately, too often the scarp would settle away from the rest of the structure resulting in the need for major repairs. Author photo.

"Portions of earthen parapet have been resodded, repairs made to the asphalt covering of curtain III, and *tie rods for strengthening the right or north face of bastion D have been put in.* No appropriation was made for the fiscal year ending June 30, 1878. No appropriation asked for next fiscal year."[13]

This pulling away of the scarp wall was a serious issue. The very next year's report stated "The right or north face of bastion D has been strengthened by large tie-rods, *which appear also to be required on Curtain III* [the gorge officer's quarters]..."[14] This problem continued to worsen and would lead to some dramatic conclusions about the fort's structural integrity and its continued viability in the years ahead.

During this period there were two men assigned to Fort Montgomery, both retired veterans. McComb of the Engineers was in charge of the maintenance of the fort infrastructure and Martin Canavan, retired from the Ordnance service, was on site to care for the ordnance and munitions.[15]

Gen. William T. Sherman ordered that Plattsburgh Barracks be closed and the garrison moved to Fort Montgomery. National Archives photo.

With the New Year came minimal work, "Care and preservation."[16] The New Year also brought a visit from General of the Army William Tecumseh Sherman.

In the summer of 1879 Sherman came to Fort Montgomery. Like Totten before him, Sherman was impressed with the fort and its strategic location at the entrance to Lake Champlain. Sherman decided it made more sense to garrison Fort Montgomery than Plattsburgh Barracks:

"This most valuable fort and property has never been garrisoned but should be, for it is the true key-point of all that frontier."

He advised the removal of the Plattsburgh buildings to Rouse's Point, and the further improvement of the post at an expense of $20,000. Speaking of the Government's use of the fort when the Fenians endangered our international relations with Canada, he said:

"In my judgment, this is the time to prepare for any complications which can possibly arise in that quarter. Plattsburg Barracks have lost their value as a strategic point, and the garrison should be transferred to Rouse's Point... It is proposed to expend $51,253.26 at Rouse's Point..."[17]

Sherman made his recommendation on July 12, 1879.

During the 1879-1880 fiscal year work resumed on the bridge, causeway and parade. Some repairs were also carried out on the wharf to curtain I near bastion B.[18] Finally, in 1880 an appropriation of $33,000 was requested for Fort Montgomery.[19] During fiscal year 1880-1881 work continued:

"Asphalt coverings of curtains 1, 2, 4, and 5, and of bastions B, C, D, and E around staircase, and wooden stair roofings repaired; casemate doors painted and terreplein graded."

Appropriate and necessary repairs were being made. The fort had its detractors; indeed, the entire system of masonry forts was being criticized as being hopelessly outdated and obsolete. Still, in December, 1881 the Secretary of War, in his report to Congress on the Condition of the Fortifications, stated:

"..."There can be no doubt that Fort Montgomery, at Rouses Point... should be retained... [referring to the Report of Dec. 1870] ...it should be kept in suitable condition as a depot for stores and ammunition for troops either moving to invade Canada, or for defense of this frontier line...In its present condition, if armed with suitable guns, the fort would doubtless be efficient in preventing the passage up the lake of hostile gunboats. This, however, is not the sole function this fort may be called upon to perform. For an invasion of Canada on this line of operations it would at once be a fortified base and storehouse for the invading army. For the reasons above given this fort should be retained and be kept in a state of efficiency."[20]

By 1882 the full extent of the scarp wall separation problem was becoming evident. The Report of the Chief of Engineers for that year had an unusually long entry about Fort Montgomery. The Secretary of War may have wanted to keep the fort "in a state of efficiency" but it would not be possible without major repairs:

"...The casemates of this work were reported as having been always damp and unfit for quarters. Operations, therefore, during the past fiscal year were mainly conducted with a view of repairing these defects as far as they could be discovered and as the available means allotted from the general appropriation for the preservation and repair of fortifications would permit.

In excavating to the arches it was found that the asphalt covering was much more injured than anticipated, and that this was partly due to a separation of the scarp wall from the arches, it is believed from the effects of frost, leaving, often, spaces of an inch or more in width for the water to pass to the casemates below. Many of these cracks were directly under the gun-platforms and difficult to get at; and the ground being still frozen hard during the latter part of April, the excavating of the earth cover could only be proceeded with slowly. Even as late as the end of May the vertical conductors were one mass of ice, as reported, and so were also the blind drains in the valleys of the arches; and, of course, the water, instead of being readily carried off by the means provided, would remain stationary over the arches, and eventually find its way through defects in the asphalt covering to the masonry underneath; and evil which will be difficult to remedy in that severe climate, as the common asphalt covering now in use has failed to make the casemates waterproof. Besides these repairs— principally made on bastions A, D, And E, and on curtains I, II, III, and V— depressions in the terre-plein have been filled to prevent the settling of water in such spots; but the water flowing over the coping of the parade wall, a gutter there, as at Fort Hamilton, might aid in keeping this part of the masonry dry.

The brick arches of the embrasures of the second tier and the breast-height wall have been repaired and repointed, as have also the undersides of the arches of bastion D. On curtain III the slopes of the breast-height wall have been resodded, and the wooden covers of the barbette magazine and the thresholds of the casemate doors renewed.

To complete the modifications or repairs of this work as at present planned and approved, the following sums are required, viz:

> For strengthening casemate arches, curtains I and V...$12,000.00
>
> For thickening magazine walls..18,000.00
>
> Total..30,000.00

No appropriation having been made, no work was done at this fortification during the last fiscal year beyond its protection, preservation, and repair, as far as was possible with the general appropriation made for this purpose, and no other work is contemplated during the current fiscal year for the same reason.

> Appropriation asked for next fiscal year..30,000.00"[21]

In April, 1882, the citizens of Plattsburgh, anticipating the imminent closing of the base there and the withdrawal of the garrison to Fort Montgomery, attempted to have a bill introduced in Congress asking that the reservation be donated to the village for the purpose of forming a public park:

"...it is a foregone conclusion by the War Department that the reservation is absolutely to be abandoned, and the bill introduced will not hasten the event. Gen. Sherman, as early as July 12, 1879, in a very decided letter gave his reasons for the abandonment of the post and for the occupation of Fort Montgomery and the reservation at Rouses Point...Gen. W. S. Hancock...fully concurred in this..."[22]

From May through June, 1882 workmen labored at the fort reinforcing the scarp walls. [23] On October 16, General Sherman reiterated his earlier statements about Fort Montgomery in a report to the Secretary of War:

"... [Regarding] The northern or Canadian frontier. The posts which should be maintained in permanency are: Fort Montgomery, outlet of Champlain; [listing of other forts]... All these places are now occupied, but need changes involving cost. Fort Montgomery is a costly fort, nearly if not complete, mounting sixty sea-coast guns, but without barracks. I advise that an appropriation be asked for of $60,000 to erect thereon (the reservation is ample, 600 acres) permanent barracks for four companies of artillery. Plattsburgh Barracks could then be sold, or donated to that city for a park. It should have been abandoned after the war of 1812."[24]

In March 1883, the Plattsburgh Sentinel reported that Major Walter McFarland, Engineers, had been ordered to proceed from Oswego to Rouses Point and to return upon "completion of business." McFarland was probably going to the fort to check on the condition of the scarp walls. The Sentinel thought otherwise, as shown in a statement that reflects the concern in Plattsburgh— "The object is undoubtedly to prepare plans for the changes at Fort Montgomery, to enable the troops at Plattsburgh to be transferred there."[25]

From November, 1882 to May, 1883 twenty-five men under the supervision of Lieutenant William V. Judson labored at the fort "bracing up some of the arches which had settled and cracked and making other repairs."[26] The fort was deteriorating badly enough it was important to work through the winter. The Chief of Engineers Report for that year spelled out the problem in alarming detail:

"Work accomplished Fiscal Year July 1, 1883- June 30, 1884: ...rebuilding in its present form was accomplished in 1876, and completes the work, except the interior fittings of a part of the casemates intended for quarters, and also parts of Bastions A and E, temporary wooden floors have been built for the second tier of casemates. During the past fiscal year forty-four sets, or eighty-eight, tie-rods were placed in Curtains I, III, IV, and V [note that curtain II did not receive rods], these rods were for the purpose of restraining the tendency to separation of the scarp-walls from the casemates. To remedy the evil resulting from the flow of water over the coping and masonry of the parade-wall, gutters were placed along the drip of the coping and connected with down-spouts. To provide for the drainage of the parade, three lines of surface drains were laid, connecting with the sewer discharging into the lake. Minor repairs were made to the drawbridge and dock. By the formation of ice during the severe winters, the methods of drainage, as now provided, become inoperative, and consequently the work is severely subjected to the destructive action of frost and water. The vertical conductors connecting with the drains in the valleys of the arches become choked through the formation of ice, and the water, instead of being carried off by the means provided, finds its way eventually through defects in the asphalt covering to the arches beneath. The casemate arches require repointing, but so long as the radical difficulty lies in the proper drainage of the arches above, such work of repointing would be almost useless. This defect in the drainage of the upper surfaces of the arches is an evil which requires remedy, for if it is permitted to continue it must result in serious injury to the work. During the year no change has been made in the armament of this work or in its condition to receive armament.[27]

In February, 1884 the "Macdonough Park Bill" was introduced in the House of Representatives. The bill, first promoted in April 1882, sought to have Plattsburgh Barracks donated to the Village of Plattsburgh for use as a park upon the transfer of troops to Fort Montgomery.[28] Again, one last time, in November of that year, General W.S. Hancock urged establishment of a garrison at Fort Montgomery.[29] Yet, Plattsburgh Barracks was not closed, nor was a garrison transferred to Rouses Point. As influential and famous as they were, neither Sherman nor Hancock had the political influence of some of Plattsburgh's more prominent citizens. Instead of closing Plattsburgh Barracks was dramatically enlarged, and Fort Montgomery continued its long slide into obscurity.[30]

The Chief's Report for fiscal year 1884-1885 showed other work still being done at the fort. "Wooden shutters fitted to embrasures and loophole openings, waterfront sally-port gateway repaired, and interior gates placed at the land-front sally-port entrance."[31] Another report addressed other issues. It mentioned that Fronts I and V still had wooden casemate floors and that the replacement of these had commenced but been suspended "for want of funds." The modifications needed on the barbette tier were not finished for the same reason. —"arranged for 8 centre pintle and 45 front pintle platforms, and for 2 service magazines; the magazines are barely commenced..." The report listed the state of other platforms by number on the barbette tier and placed the "present armament (mounted)" at 74 guns. The report concluded with this ominous warning— The scarp wall has "settled in places, and has separated from the casemate arches, to prevent further separation, iron tie rods have been introduced...Very significant leaks exist in the casemate arches...with these exceptions the present condition of the work appears to be fair."[32]

A significant development regarding America's network of fortifications was just beyond the horizon. Stung by criticism of the deteriorating state of the nation's defenses, newly elected President Grover Cleveland directed Secretary of War William Endicott to study the state of fortifications along the seacoasts, major ports and along the "lake ports." Endicott formed a board that would come to bear his name and recommend sweeping changes to the nation's coast and northern frontier fortifications.[33] In 1885 General Nelson B. Miles visited Fort Montgomery in order to make his recommendation to the Endicott Board.

Above: This view of the scarp wall of Bastion C show the large bolts between the embrasures of tiers I and II securing the iron supporting rods installed in the 1880's.
Below: the interior of the same wall showing the cut rods.

While Rouses Point and the rest of the nation awaited the recommendations of the Endicott Board work continued at the fort. In May, 1885 Major Milton B. Adams advertised for "proposals for repairing the gun platforms at Fort Montgomery."[34] This work was noted in the "Report" of 1886 — "operations at this work have been confined to the repairs of five center pintle and six front pintle platforms, and the renewal of the wood-work of the bridge over the moat."[35] Work was finally proceeding on the center pintle gun mounts on the barbette tier. These mounts were important in that they allowed a gun to be rotated a full 360⁰. Unfortunately, the guns they were to mount were obsolete. Every gun at Fort Montgomery was a muzzle loading smooth-bore.

The 8 and 10 inch Rodman's, 24-pounder flank howitzers, and especially the ancient 32-pounders were seriously inferior to modern ordnance of the type needed to protect against modern iron-plated gunboats.

On January 16, 1886 the Endicott Fortifications Board made its recommendations. Fort Montgomery was to receive 4 8-inch 13-ton guns and eight 10-inch rifled mortars. The Board also stated "In its present condition, if armed with suitable guns, the fort would, doubtless, be efficient in preventing the passage up the lake of hostile gunboats. This, however, is not the sole function the fort may be called upon to perform. For an invasion of Canada on this line of operations it would at once be a fortified base and storehouse for the invading army."[36] Over the next decade, optimistic local press accounts would point to the Endicott recommendations and stress that it was only a matter of time before the modernization would occur. Fort Montgomery would never receive this new ordnance.

Only minor repairs were made in the years following the installation of the iron retaining rods and drainage down-spouts. The 1884 Report had made clear how untenable the situation was with regard to water seepage into the casemates. It also made it quite clear that the major repairs required were not going to be undertaken. No appropriation was made nor was any asked for. Still the harsh winters and melting snow and ice of spring continued to take their toll.

The "Report" for fiscal year 1885-86 read:

"...rebuilding in its present form was accomplished in 1876, and completes the work, except the interior fittings of a part of the casemates intended for quarters, and also parts of Bastions A and E, where temporary wooden floors have been built for the second tier of casemates. During the fiscal year ending June 1886, operations at this work have been confined to the repairs of five center pintle and six front pintle platforms, and the renewal of the wood-work of the bridge over the moat. No appropriation was made for the fiscal year ending June 30, 1887. No appropriation asked for next fiscal year."[37]

This would be the last Report of Chief of Engineers detailing work at Fort Montgomery until 1897.

By 1891 no effort had been made to modify Fort Montgomery for the heavy ordnance recommended by the Endicott Board. Still hopeful references were made to the report and there was belief in some quarters that the Fort would receive the new guns. On February 26, 1891 the Fort Covington Sun reported—"The committee or board of fortifications have recommended the armament of Fort Montgomery at Rouses Point, with 8 inch rifled cannon. Secretary Proctor says in his report in relation to the better condition of defense along our border: "'These are not measures of provocation, but rather of prevention, and for the continued preservation of peace'"[38] Still, nothing happened at Rouses Point, while Plattsburgh Barracks was soon to undergo a dramatic enlargement of its facilities.[39]

It appears that the Fort Keeper position was occupied by a James Fawdry in 1895, witness this statement from the Plattsburgh Sentinel— "Ordnance Sergt. James Fawdry has been ordered from Fort Montgomery to this post for medical treatment."[40]

Again, in 1896, a full ten years after the Endicott Report was released, locals were referring to the recommendations hopefully. Under the heading "Fort Montgomery— The War Department convinced of the strategic value of the old fort" the Sentinel reported:

"One point on the great lakes has been selected by the war department for fortification under the provisions made at the last session of congress, namely Fort Montgomery, at Rouses Point, commanding the northern entrance to Lake Champlain. This was one of the places on the Canadian border mentioned by the Endicott fortifications board , more than ten years ago, as needing to be furnished with modern guns...It was recently visited by General Miles, who formed a high opinion, we believe, of its military importance. The Fortifications Board of 1885 recommended for it four 8-inch and eight 10-inch mortars as a suitable armament, but a recent statement represents that it is to be far more heavily fortified, receiving many more mortars, and also a great many more heavy guns, some of them of calibers much exceeding the 8-inch. If this is so, reflection on the situation and possibilities of the fort must apparently have increased the sense of its importance. At all events an allotment has been made for repairing and improving the fort, which is now without a garrison, and has lacked one for many years. This work will be vigorously pushed. We may add that Fort Montgomery is not the only point in the Lake Champlain region which has lately received attention from the military authorities. In recent years the post at Plattsburgh has been enlarged, and a new post, Fort Ethan Allen, has been built and garrisoned on the Vermont side of the lake near the Canadian border. The military purpose plainly is not only to secure the lake region from an inroad, but to furnish fortified rallying points from which forces could be hurried to wreck the British canals and to prevent the enemy from using his waterways in case of war."[41]

With fiscal year 1896-97 came another attempt to fix the severe water leakage problems— "103 f. of parade wall covered with patent granite roofing laid in hot mastic to prevent the percolation of water."[42] Unfortunately, the efforts at stopping the leakage were futile, as is shown in the following year's "Report":

"To prevent the percolation of water from the terreplein down the joint between the facing and backing of the parade wall into the masonry of the casemate arches, a length of 103 feet was covered with patent granite roofing during the previous fiscal year, as an experiment. It was intended to continue this work during the present fiscal year, but as the experimental work previously done had not proved satisfactory it was recommended that the repairs be deferred until the alterations of the fort were begun in accordance with the amended plan, as an inspection of the fort developed the fact that much more extensive work would be required than was previously contemplated. In view of the representations made, the Department directed that no further steps be taken for the present to stop the leakage referred to.

The amount expended during the year was $908.57
It was applied as follows:
To services of a fort keeper.......................$540.00
To mileage, traveling expenses, and services of laborers in refilling
trenches previously excavated..$368.57 [43]

Work at Fort Montgomery over the next three years was limited to "Care and preservation."[44]

Ordnance Sergeant Robert Moore was in charge of the fort at this time. The Plattsburgh Sentinel referred to him as "the commanding officer and enlisted force at Fort Montgomery."[45]

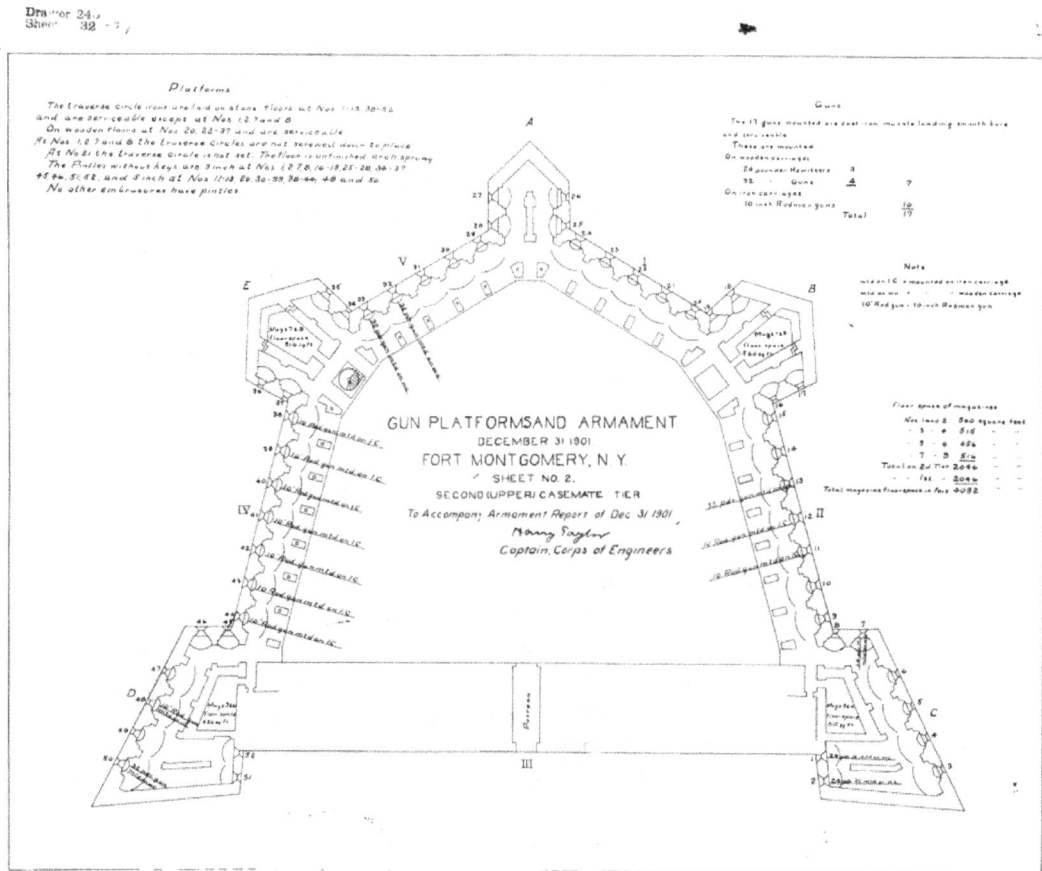

Armament sheet No. 2, Second (upper) casemate tier for Armament Report of December 31, 1901. At this point many guns were being removed although there was still a good number of each type of ordnance on site. NARA, Drawer 246, Sheet 32-37, Capt. Harry Taylor.

By 1900 some of the obsolete ordnance was being removed from the fort. Colonel J.M. [John] Barlow's Armament Report of that year reported the following:

Second (upper) Casemate Tier
- Four 32-pounder Smooth bores (three have been removed)
- Three 24-pounder flank howitzers (seventeen have been removed. Some wooden carriages for those guns remain on the second tier)
- Ten 10-inch Rodman's

Barbette Tier
- Ten 10-inch Rodman's
- Eight 8-inch Rodman's

First (lower) Casemate Tier
- Twenty 24-pounder flank howitzers

The un-mounted 15-inch Rodman's originally intended for the barbette tier are still reported as being on site.[46] Within a few years of the dawning of the new century Fort Montgomery would be a fortification without guns. The Fort Keeper would mend fences on the Commons, record the water level at Bastion B and watch as the big guns were removed one by one.[47] Capt. Harry Taylor's Armament Report of December 31, 1902 told the tale:

En Barbette
- Ten 10-inch Rodman's
- One 8-inch Rodman

En Casemate
- Eight 10-inch Rodman's

All of the 32-pounders have been removed, as have all forty 24-pounder flank howitzers. [48] It is believed that all forty of the flank howitzers were donated to municipalities around the country. [49]

On May 8, 1908 the Plattsburgh Sentinel reported on 'The End of "Fort Blunder."' The article is interesting for a lot of reasons. It is remarkable in its inaccuracy but is quite prescient in that inaccuracy. It refers to the removing of the fort's guns as the "dismantling" and "demolition" of the "old stone structure." Also fascinating is the contractor hired to do the work. It not only details the removal of the rest of Fort Montgomery's ordnance but it may very well be one the earliest examples of the merging of the two forts into one in print. We have established in the earliest chapters of this book that the first work, Fort "Blunder", and Fort Montgomery were two different and unique fortifications. Fort "Blunder" was not Fort Montgomery and Fort Montgomery was not Fort "Blunder." This incorrect "merging" of the two forts into one continues to this day in the media and in a number of latter day works referring to the forts at Rouses Point. The Sentinel article reads:

"One of the old landmarks of Lake Champlain, Fort Montgomery, near Rouses Point, will soon be a thing of the past, the work of dismantling it now being underway. The War Department some time ago determined to abandon the fort entirely and a contract was let to a Philadelphia firm to demolish the old stone structure, the contract later sub-let to Weston Brothers of Rouses Point, who have for some time past been dismantling the cannon, which for years have guarded the entrance to the lake from the casemates of the fort. These obsolete guns are now to be broken up and used as scrap iron by the Philadelphia Roll & Machine Co. of Philadelphia.

Late Tuesday afternoon a schooner [ironically named the "Montgomery"] under full sail landed at the wharf in this city, having as her cargo the first shipment of these guns. There were twelve cannon in the cargo and of these eleven weighed seven and one-half tons, while the other weighed twenty-five tons. The large crane used by the D&H for cleaning away wrecks was brought into play and the work of unloading the vessel commenced. This work was no easy task, especially when the largest gun was moved. The work was not accomplished until early in the evening when the eleven smaller guns were placed in two cars and the big gun given a car by itself, on Wednesday forenoon they were started on their way southward. Another shipment of the old cannon will be made on Saturday of this week. There were two of the twenty-five ton guns at the fort, but neither of them had been mounted for service.

Fort Montgomery was commenced by this government shortly after the war of 1812, and work continued until 1818, when it was discovered by surveys that it was on British territory. Work was then suspended and for years the unfinished walls were known as "Fort Blunder." In 1842, a treaty was signed ceding to the United States the land upon which the fort stands. The structure was then completed, but it has never been regularly garrisoned, only an ordnance sergeant being stationed there as care taker."[50]

Again, on May 15, 1908:

"Another Boat-load of Cannon" — Taken from Fort Montgomery and to be shipped from here to Philadelphia by Rail— Another boat load of the cannon which for years guarded the entrance to the lake at Fort Montgomery arrived in this city Tuesday and was on Wednesday shipped by rail to Philadelphia where they will be broken into scrap iron.

The cannon were brought here on the schooner Montgomery, the cargo consisting of two fifteen-inch guns, each weighing twenty-five tons and seven-inch [sic] guns, each weighing seven tons. With the cannon, were the carriages upon which they had for so many years rested at "Fort Blunder." The old fort is now practically bare of guns and it will be but a short time until it is a thing of the past."[51]

On June 29, 1908, Fort Montgomery's last Fort Keeper, Thomas Bourke, retired from the Army at Fort Mason, California. Six or seven years later Bourke moved to Rouses Point to take on Fort Keeper position. Bourke came to a fort without guns and in poor condition; the casemates having suffered from the effects of excessive water leakage for years. The February 21, 1916 Report of the Chief of Engineers made clear the situation at the fort:

- No repairs of any kind have been made since 1897 except to repair places of entry that have been breached by "depredation."
- Interior plaster of the quarters is cracked; some of the ceiling has fallen.

- Fixtures and fittings, such as gutters, drains, sally port doors, interior plastering, etc. are in poor condition
- Casemate floors are usually covered with snow and ice throughout the winter due to drifts and leakage
- Scarp walls are leaning away from interior walls in many places, allowing drainage from the parapet to enter the casemates and magazines.
- Watchman is paid salary of $540 per year.
- Pasturage rent amounts to $340 per year."[52]

Despite one rather bizarre account from the Sentinel of April 11, 1916 that the War Department's plans for "added national defense include the rehabilitation of old Fort Montgomery"[53] it was obvious that Fort Montgomery would soon be declared surplus military property. During the 1920's the huge fort stood hulking in its repose at Island Point, a playground for the Bourke children its only apparent use. Oral tradition has it that the fort was used by smugglers during Prohibition although this writer has found nothing to support that legend.

The beginning of the end of Federal ownership finally came in July 1926 when the Quartermaster General of the Army wrote Clinton County asking if the county would be interested in acquiring the Fort Montgomery Military Reservation. The County Board of Supervisors met in special session on July 29 to consider the option and other matters. The county waived its option to buy the fort but decided that they would encourage New York State to purchase the property for a State Park.[54]

Clinton County didn't want the fort but it certainly did want the State of New York to purchase it. "Tourists motoring into Canada" would bring tourist dollars into the county. An appraisal of the fort's value showed it wasn't worth much— "...the reservation... appraised at $14,470, while the old fort itself is valued at only $500, with the causeway and right of way to the mainland thrown in."[55]

The United States government auctioned off the Fort Montgomery Military Reservation, including the fort and "Commons" on September 16, 1926. The property, comprising a total of 563 acres, was sold in five separate parcels:

- Delaware and Hudson Railroad, one parcel for right of way— $1,655.
- Champlain and St. Lawrence Railroad (Grand Trunk) one parcel for right of way— $827.
- G.I. Fox, Fort Montgomery Development Company, Inc. (said to represent Fox Film Corp.), three parcels including Island Point— $43,000.

Evidently there was interest in the property from Universal Pictures also. The Sentinel reported a "Mr. Simpson, said to represent the Universal Film Corporation, was a heavy bidder but stopped within $300 of the price paid by the Fox organization."[56] The description of the fort from Abstract No. 7 (United States of America to The Fort Montgomery Development Company) merits quoting here:

> "The Fort proper is a massive stone casement fort on the Canadian border at the head of Lake Champlain, commanding the outlet of the Richelieu River. On three sides, the walls of the fort rise sheer from the waters of the Lake. On the land side there is a wide moat filled with water, and beyond that a great glacis partially faced with stone covers the approach to one entrance. The whole constitutes what is practically an island and is reached from the mainland by a causeway. There are emplacements and embrasures for 128 guns in two tiers; magazines, storerooms, shops, kitchens, quarters for officers and men, in all about 64 rooms; water is obtained from a well. Construction was started in 1843 and was discontinued in 1868. The quality and material in the fort are of the best and it remains in a reasonably good state of preservation. Some of the metal fittings are of heavy bronze such as the hinges on the doors of the Sally Port, etc., The property - the Old Fort Site especially - might appeal to a person in search of a novel site, for a summer resort and particularly as a location for the taking of Moving Pictures."

The entire property, not including the eastern parts of lots 60, 61 and 62 which were sold in 1936 by the government to The Lake Champlain Bridge Commission netted the government a grand total of $45,482.

On November 7, 1926 The New York Times ran a notoriously inaccurate story. Under the headline "Fort Blunder, Near Border, Becomes Camp for Tourists," the paper published a fantastic account that again merged both forts into one and described plans for a fancy resort with camping sites, tennis courts and a golf course.[57] Magnificent old Fort Montgomery was entering a period in its colorful history that at times bordered on the surreal.

CHAPTER VII

Fort Keepers: Sergeant William McComb to Sergeant Thomas Bourke

"Fort Keepers" were quite common on Permanent or "Third System" fortifications. Early on, even as these great fortifications were just being started it was determined that the majority of these great stone fort would not be garrisoned in peacetime. Fort Montgomery, like so many other forts along the east and gulf coasts would only be garrisoned in time of war.

There was a need for maintenance, repair and supervision of these great structures, however. Particularly if the fort had received its guns was there a need to see to the care of the ordnance and associated structures, such as magazines. Fort Montgomery, being located on the northern frontier, was especially susceptible to the harsh effects of winter and the effects of melting snow and ice during the spring.

During the early years of the "Third System" it was not unusual for each fort to have two men assigned to it.; one a retired veteran of Engineers and the other with ordnance experience. In later years it this policy was modified so that only one man was assigned to each fort. It appears that this person was usually a retired Ordnance Sergeant.

The Fort Keeper's duties varied with the location and fort. Some tasks were common to all, however. Foremost among them was protecting the government's investment from damage due to the elements, depredation and theft. The 1857 Regulations for the Army of the United States[1] detailed how these fortifications were to be cared for by the garrison [bold face text added]:

ARTICLE IX
CARE OF FORTIFICATIONS
"38.….No person shall be permitted to walk upon any of the slopes of a fortification, excepting the ramps and glacis. If, in any case, it be necessary to provide for crossing them, it should be done by placing wooden steps or stairs against the slopes. The *occasional* walking of persons on a parapet wall will do no harm, provided it be not allowed to cut the surface into paths.

39.…...No cattle, horses, sheep, goat, or other animal, shall ever be permitted to go upon the slopes, the ramparts, or the parapets, nor upon the glacis, except within fenced limits, which should not approach the crest nearer than 30 feet.

40.….**All grassed surfaces, excepting the glacis, will be frequently and carefully mowed** (except in dry weather), and the oftener the better, while growing rapidly — **the grass never being allowed to be more than a few inches high.** In order to cut the grass even and close, upon small slopes a light one-handed scythe should be used; and in mowing the steep slopes, the mower should stand on a light ladder resting against the slope, and not upon the grass. **Crops of hay may be cut upon the glacis; or, if fenced, it may be used as pasture**; otherwise it should be treated as other slopes of the fortification. On all the slopes **spots of dead grass will be cut out and replaced with fresh sods. All weeds will be eradicated**. A very little labor, applied steadily and judiciously, will maintain the grassed surfaces, even of the largest of our forts, in good condition.

41.....**The burning of grass upon any portion of a fortification is strictly forbidden.**

42.....Particular attention is required to prevent the formation of gullies in the parade, terreplein, and ramps, and especially in slopes where grass is not well established. If neglected, they will soon involve heavy expense.

43.....Earth, sand, or ashes must not be placed against woodwork; a free ventilation must be preserved around it; and **all wooden floors, platforms, bridges, &c.; will be kept swept clean.**

44.....**The machinery of draw-bridges, gates, and posterns must be kept in good working order by proper cleaning and** oiling **of the parts; the bridges will be raised, and the gates and posterns opened as often as once a week.**

45.....The terrepleins of forts, the floors of casemates, caponniers, store-rooms, barracks, galleries, posterns, magazines, &c., and the sidewalks in front of quarters and barracks, as well as other walks, are sometimes paved with bricks or stones, or formed of concrete. These surfaces must be preserved from injury with great care. In transporting guns and carriages, and in mounting them, strong way-planks will be used, and neither the wheels nor any other part of the carriages, nor any machinery, such as shears, gins, &c., nor any handspike or other implement, will be allowed to touch those surfaces. Unless protected in a similar manner, no wheel-barrow or other vehicle, no barrels, hogsheads, &c., will be rolled upon these surfaces. No violent work will be suffered to be done upon them, such as cutting wood, breaking coal, &c., and no heavy weight be thrown or permitted to fall upon thereon. In using machines, as gins, &c., in casemates, care must be taken not to in-jure the arch or ceiling, as well as the floor. Neglect of these precautions may cause injuries slight in appearance but serious in effect from the leaking of water into ma-sonry and casemates, and expensive to repair.

46.....**The doors and windows of all store-rooms and unoccupied case-mates, quarters, barracks, &c., will be opened several** times **a week for thorough ventilation.**

47.....The masonry shot-furnaces will be heated only on approach of an en-emy. For ordinary practice with hot shot, iron furnaces are provided.

48.....The foregoing matters involve but little expense; the labor is within the means of every garrison, and no technical knowledge is called for beyond what will be found among soldiers. Other repairs requiring small disbursements, such as repairing exposed wood or iron work, can also be executed by the garrison; but reports, estimates, and requisitions may be necessary to obtain the materials.

49.....No alteration will be made in any fortification, or in its casemates, quarters, barracks, magazines, store-houses, or any other building belonging to it; nor will any building of any kind, or work of earth, masonry, or timber be erected within the fortification, or on its exterior within half a mile, except under the superintendence of the Engineer Department, and by the authority of the Secretary of War."

We do know that the grass cutting and ventilation responsibilities were actually assigned to Fort Keepers.[2] It is obvious that properly maintaining a masonry fort required a considerable amount of work. Fort Montgomery's cover face alone was some three acres in size. The fort proper, including the parade, terrepleins, etc. was another 2.5 acres. The gorge officer's quarters included forty-one rooms; within the rest of the casemates were another twenty-three rooms with windows. This was a lot of windows to open "several times a week for thorough ventilation!"

The care of ordnance was also carefully detailed:

ARTICLE X
CARE OF ARMAMENT OF FORTIFICATIONS

50.....At each permanent post with a fixed battery, and garrisoned by not more than one company, there will be kept mounted, for purposes of instruction and target practice, *three* heavy guns, and at posts garrisoned by more than one company, at the rate of *two* for each of the companies composing its garrison. The other guns dismounted will be properly placed (see page 21, Ordnance Manual for 1850) within their own traverse circles, and **the carriages preserved from the weather.**

51.....**All guns should be sponged clean and their vents examined so that they are clear. The chassis should be traversed and left in a different position, the top carriage moved backward and forward and left alternately over the front and rear transoms of the chassis; the elevating screws or machines wiped clean, worked and oiled if required, and the nuts of all bolts screwed up tight. This should all be done regularly once in every week.**

52..... **When tarpaulins, or pent houses, are placed over the guns, they should be removed once a week when the weather is fair, the carriages and guns brushed off, and if damp, allowed to dry.**

53.....An old sponge-staff and head should be used for drill. The new sponges should never be used unless the gun is fired. The implements should be kept in store, under cover, and be examined wiped clean or brushed at least once a month. In the case of leather equipments, the directions for the preservation of harness in the Ordnance Manual should be followed.

54.....**The magazine should be frequently examined to see that the powder is well preserved. It should be opened every other day when the air is dry and clear. Barrels of powder should be turned and rolled occasionally.** Under ordinary circumstances, only a few cartridges should be filled. If the paper body of the cartridge becomes soft or loses its sizing, it is certain that the magazine is very damp, and some means should be found to improve the ventilation. Cartridge bags may be kept in the magazine ready for filling; also port-fires, fuzes, tubes, and primers. Stands of grape, canisters, and wads for barbette guns, should be kept in store with the implements. Fort casemate guns, wads may be hung in bundles, and grape and canisters placed near the guns. Shot, well lacquered and clean, may be placed in piles near the guns.[3]

We know Fort Montgomery had at least 75 guns mounted, many on the exposed barbette tier. We also know there was shot on site and powder in the magazines. Civil War era muskets have been found at the fort.[4] There was plenty of work to keep the Ordnance Sergeant busy.

During the course of its active service (1844-1926) Fort Montgomery often had both a Fort Keeper and an Ordnance Sergeant assigned to it. At other times it appears the "garrison" consisted of only one man, usually he was a retired Ordnance Sergeant. We do know there were two men assigned to the fort as late as 1900.[5]

The first and longest-serving Fort Keeper was William McComb. Sergeant McComb, of the Engineers, was First Sergeant of the "Fort Company" in 1864. He served simultaneously with Ordnance Sergeant Martin Canavan from at least 1871 until Canavan's death in 1883.[6]

In 1875 Fort Keeper William McComb received additional duties. From this year on a daily chore of the caretaker would be to record the water level at the fort:

"...Through the courtesy of Capt. Harry Taylor, the gage readings taken by William McComb, the fort keeper, at 9 a.m. each day, are reported weekly to the United States Geological Survey. The depth of the water is taken on a reference mark on the base of the scarp wall, at the north face of bastion B, about three feet from the angle with the east curtain [I] of Fort Montgomery...In winter the depth as the water rises in a hole in the ice is commonly taken. On windy days the depth is taken in a well within the fort inclosure by measuring the depth on a flagstone in the bottom of the well."[7]

In 1885 the Plattsburgh Sentinel reported McComb had been "reappointed" Fort Keeper,[8] and several sources state he is still on the job in 1893.[9] We do know he served in the role for a very long time:

"Of all the old employees at Fort Montgomery but one remains connected with the work at present [1892], who is Sergt. Wm. McComb, of this place, the present Fort keeper. McComb, on obtaining honorable discharge in 1863 from service in the U.S. Infantry, was employed at Fort Montgomery. In 1864, at the organization of the Fort Company, he was appointed 1st sergeant of the company, and made himself useful at the time in drilling the men in infantry tactics. The Sergt. has served since in the capacity of watchman and fortkeeper. That his faithfulness to duty and merits have been appreciated may be judged by his long retention in office."[10]

Ordnance Sergeant Martin Canavan was at Fort Montgomery from 1871 until his death in July, 1883. Canavan had been at the fort for almost 12 years, but was only 49 years old when he died on July 5, 1883. Canavan left a wife, four sons and a daughter. He is said to have died of wounds received during his service under McClellan on the Delmarva Peninsula.[11]

Canavan was replaced by a "Sergeant Qualey." Qualey, however, was quite ill with pneumonia when he arrived at Rouses Point. He died within a month and was replaced by a "Sergeant Burns, of San Francisco, California."[12] Burns was evidently only on the job for about a year when he was replaced by a Sergeant Gallagher.[13] Gallagher served from 1883-1886.

Local press accounts reported a number of changes in the Fort Keeper position in 1886-87. Rather than clear up an already confusing picture of the Fort Montgomery Fort Keeper position, these accounts tend to make who was custodian at what time even more uncertain. The knowledge that *two* men were assigned to the fort, one each from the Engineers and Ordnance services, helps to clear up the picture some.[14]

The Plattsburgh Sentinel of September 3, 1886 reported that Ordnance Sergeant Anthony McGuire, one of the "oldest soldiers in point of service in the U.S. Army, he having enlisted nearly fifty years ago." was ordered to report to Fort Montgomery to take charge of that work. He did not report- "death has called him higher."[15] The same paper reported on October 8th — "Sergt. Gallagher, who has had charged [sic] of Fort Montgomery for the past three years, has been placed on the retired list and has purchased a home in New Hampshire. He will not leave the Fort until his successor arrives."[16] On November 5th — "Sergeant Gallagher, who has been in charge of Fort Montgomery at Rouses Point, but who has been retired, is succeeded by Sergeant [William J.] Russell, who recently came from a fort in southern Texas..."[17] And finally, on August 19th — "Ordnance Sergeant H. Young, of Co. G, 24th Infantry, U.S.A., now at Fort Sill, Indian Territory, has been ordered to proceed to Fort Montgomery at Rouses Point and relieve Ordnance Sergeant Wm. J. Russell..."[18]

It appears that Russell served as Fort Keeper from November 1886 to August 1887 when he was replaced by Ordnance Sergeant H. Young. Young serves a long time—from the summer of 1887 to around 1895.

In 1889 Sergeant Young hosted a tour of the Fort by Plattsburgh High School "cadet corps" students in June of that year. The Plattsburgh Sentinel reported the students traveled from Plattsburgh to Rouses Point on the steamer "Reindeer" and "The sergeant in charge of the fort has granted permission for a thorough inspection of the fort, with its great magazines, its large arsenal of 77 guns, and other points of interest, both in and about the fort. Tickets 50 cts."[19]

Could this be Ordnance Sergt. Martin Canavan or other Canavan family members? This undated, unidentified tintype was acquired by the author from a person in the area. The 10-inch barbette mounted Rodman gun is of the type mounted at Fort Montgomery. It is possible that this is also the only known closeup photo of Fort Montgomery ordnance in place. Author collection.

Around 1895, James Fawdry, also a retired Ordnance Sergeant, came to Rouses Point where he served as custodian for about two years. After Fawdry retired, Ordnance Sergeant Robert Moore arrived. Moore came to be well-liked and "known not only by everyone in Rouses Point but by many from places throughout Northern New York and in many other states." Moore served at Fort Montgomery from around 1897 to 1906.[20]

Finally, in either 1914 or 1915 Ordnance Sergeant Thomas Bourke arrived at Rouses Point. Bourke was to serve as Fort Montgomery's last Fort Keeper. Thanks to the previously unpublished memoirs of his son, Harold, we know much about Sergeant Bourke and his time at the fort. What follows is an excerpt from Harold Bourke's reminiscences about his father, used here with permission.

Sgt. Thomas Bourke by Harold Bourke

Photo: Sgt. Thomas Bourke during his service in the 7th Cavalry. Courtesy of the Bourke family.

"Thomas Bourke was born in Ballon, County Carlow, Ireland on 5 June 1858. Dad arrived in the US at Philadelphia and worked in a bar in some capacity or other. When he enlisted in the 7th Cavalry, on 26 July 1882, the Recruiting Sergeant told him to list his occupation as a teamster, since there was no need for bartenders in the Army. Dad's military career consisted of fifteen years in the Cavalry and eleven in the Engineers. His first unit was Troop H, 7th Cavalry, which was at Fort Meade in the Dakota Territory. This was near the area of the Wounded Knee Massacre, which occurred on 29 December 1890, but Dad was long gone from the area at that time. During his first five year enlistment, he advanced to Sergeant.

Dad was in the Oklahoma Territory patrolling the starting line, when two million acres of Indian Territory were opened to white settlement. The Sooners were attempting to sneak through the line to pick the better sites before the official opening occurred. At noon on April 22, 1889, more than 40,000 settlers raced from the borders of the Unassigned Lands to claim 160 acre tracts or town lots. He was also in the Arizona Territory chasing Geronimo, the Apache renegade chief, through the mountains. Dad mentioned the fatter troopers having to give up the chase, whereas the more slender ones, like himself, were able to continue on. His various records show that Fort Apache, Fort Huachuca and Fort Lowell were his posts at that time with the 4th Cavalry.

He didn't talk much about his experiences in the Spanish-American War, but his records indicate that he was "Engaged in submarine running in Mobile Bay", whatever that meant. Shortly after that, he went to the Philippine Islands with the Engineers. That was during the Philippine Insurrection and they were building roads and bridges. Dad got involved with photography at that time.

He was eligible to retire and did so on 29 June 1908, at Fort Mason in California. At that time, military personnel on active duty were not allowed to vote, so he saw no reason to apply for citizenship during his time in service. He returned to Ireland to see his family. Probably when he was visiting his brother John in Dublin, he met and married our mother Mary Masterson of 17 Emmett Street, North Circle Road, Dublin. A daughter, Lilyan was born on 27 April 1912. Because of his military experience, Dad was offered a Majority in the infamous IRA, but he refused to get involved.

When World War I broke out, Dad decided that he had better get back to where his pension checks were coming from. So he came alone to find employment and locate a home. Upon landing in New York, he applied to become a citizen. The judge involved, after learning of Dad's military service, held a special session of court and immediately gave him his citizenship. He then had to find employment and had a choice being a policeman in Washington, DC or a caretaker of Fort Montgomery in Rouses Point, N. Y. Dad chose the caretaker job and sent for his family. The previous caretaker was a Sergeant Moore, whose daughter was Mrs. J. M. Gettys.[21]

Mother and Lilyan arrived on the liner Lancaster in 1915. His military experience caused Dad to be recalled into the Army and he trained troops at Fort Slocum in New York for some time. He was fifty-eight years old and because of back problems, a doctor told him that he had seen enough soldiering and sent him home.

The Fort Montgomery complex included some six hundred acres west of the fort along the Canadian border. Dad called this the "Reservation" while the town's people referred to it as the "Commons". The area was divided by the extension of Lake Street, which was Route 14 to Montreal through the Canadian village of Cantic. This road sliced off a triangular section of the reservation, which came to a point at the north end, where the Canadian National R. R. crossed Route 14 at the border. Both areas were fenced in and the smaller section was called the "small commons". The access road to the fort was an extension of Montgomery

The Caretaker's Cottage on the Commons. Referred to as the "summer house" by Harold Bourke. Harold was born in this house. Courtesy: Elizabeth Clark (Bourke family).

Street that skirted the lake shore. It ran due north to a point opposite the fort and then turned east around a long curve. The road continued through a swamp of alders to the lake and then made a slight left turn on a causeway to the fort. The roadway was always under water in the spring floods and there were the remains of pilings that supported a bridge in earlier times. The annual ice floes probably destroyed the bridge.[22] A hawthorn tree and several apple trees, including a crab apple, were in the swamp along the road. Their isolation seemed to keep them free of worms and insects, so we had many good snacks from them.

Our house on the reservation was on the west side of the access road, just before it turned toward the lake. It was a two story unit with a porch on the southeast corner.[23] The two large cottonwood trees shaded the house on the south side and were just far enough apart to swing a hammock between them. The house was just used as a summer place and we moved to an apartment on State Street for the school months. My brother, Thomas, was born on 9 August 1917 and I was born on 16 August 1919 in the summer house. That was when doctors, such as Dr. Remilard, made house calls. The only memories that I have of the place when we lived there, was Dad lighting a kerosene lamp and placing it in a steel wash tub on the floor, as we were about to depart for the State Street place. The light was to fool any vagrant into believing some one was at home. At another time, I remember that he had to remove some loose bricks off the summer kitchen roof, where they had fallen to when a wind storm had damaged the chimney. Saint Patrick School would hold their annual picnic at the fort, but changed it to our summer place, when the bridge across the moat became dangerous.[24] It was sponsored by the Catholic Daughters, and the meal consisted of hot dogs, baked beans and ice cream. The picnic site was still used long after we had moved away and I attended a couple of them when I started school. The average boy would eat his hot dog, launch the paper plate with the beans into space and then hang around for the ice cream.

In addition to being caretaker of the fort, Dad had to collect fees from the locals, who kept their livestock on the reservation. For the first few days of the pasture season, which probably began in late April or early May, he would set up office at the gate on Montgomery Street to register the owners and the number and type of animals being boarded. The charges were five dollars for a horse, three for a cow and one and a half for a calf for the full season. The little used horses, the non-milking cows and the calves seemed to have been pastured in the larger area, where they were less accessible because of the wooded section called the "cedars" and the swamps along the lake. The town's people who had milking cows or horses that were used quite often, would keep them in the "small commons", where they were easier to catch. Some of the owners would bring their pails and milk the cows in a corral type enclosure near the gate on Lake Street. Most of the cows were herded through the town every afternoon and each cow would know its home and stop there. After the evening milking, they were bedded down in their barn stalls and spent the night there. The following morning, after being milked again, they were released to join the other cows enroute to their pasture in the "commons". There was less work to be done after the initial registration of the livestock. Keeping the miles of fence in repair was the major job in connection with the pastureland. One individual cut the fence to get his cow out of the large "commons", rather than take it to the Montgomery Street gate. Dad soon found out who did the cutting, located him at home and marched him back with tools and supplies to repair the fence. A pedestrian stile was located at the Montgomery Street gate, so it wouldn't be necessary to open the gate to enter.[25] Dad's job of caretaker of the fort and reservation was quite time consuming, especially in the spring and summer. His other job of water gage reader, consisted of checking the water height of Lake Champlain at ten o'clock each morning and sending a monthly report to the Army Engineers in Albany. There were gages at the fort and the railroad bridge on Montgomery Street. It was an easy task in the warmer months, but became increasingly more difficult when the lake water froze. Dad would use a hatchet to cut the ice at the gage, but would change to a long handled ice chisel, when the ice got thicker. One extremely cold winter, the water froze to the ground. A second hole had to be cut at the next piling of the bridge, where the water was deeper and a trench chipped in the ice to flow the water to the gage. A temporary gage was then made at the second piling and used until the spring thaw. I was glad to see the end of winter that year, as I seemed to be doing a lot of the ice cutting. A Technical Sergeant, which was Dad's rank when he retired, received ninety-six dollars ($96) a month pension. Each of the Fort Caretaker and Gauge Reader jobs paid thirty dollars ($30) each month.

Every morning at ten o'clock, Dad would walk to the railroad bridge, take a water height reading and then continue on to Pardy's store to get his New York newspaper. He would then walk north on Lake Street and then east on Rose Avenue to our home. Rose Avenue paralleled the reservation and the Canadian border beyond. About half the homes on the street were either involved in smuggling booze and/or the selling of it. On the one

The Montgomery Street gate, entrance to the Commons of Fort Montgomery. Author photo.

morning that I remember accompanying him on his circuit, he said he had to stop and see a Mr. Gebo. Anyway, he ended up having a glass of some liquid that he said was tea. I must have mentioned it when I got home, because I don't remember being invited to go again.

When I was about four, Dad got us two large rabbits. We couldn't seem to keep them in their pen and they always ended up in Jim Callopy's garden. He would catch them in a box trap and return them to us. Dad said they had to go and took them to the fort, where they could be confined. Since he made daily inspection tours to the fort, he could check on the rabbits and bring them any table scraps that rabbits would eat. It was on one of those trips that he met a bull that had broken through the north fence from a Canadian farm. The bull started after Dad and he managed to hit it on the nose with a large monkey wrench that he was carrying for some reason or other. The bull decided he had enough and left the scene. From then on, Dad carried his revolver with him on his trips to the fort. He was burning grass on the fort top one day and the fire got out of control. It burned his coat that he had taken off and the revolver in the pocket. He had to stop fighting the fire and seek shelter when the bullets started exploding from the flames. In the mean time two wooden buildings burned on the west wall.[26] He made weekly trips to the library, bringing home two books each time and he probably read every worthwhile book in the library. Between his books and the daily New York newspaper, his spare time was occupied. Occasionally, I was taken to the fort with him. Once it was to show Andy Weston and his party around the place. We had our picture taken with them. About fifteen years later, Andy tore down a lot of the fort to build the motor vehicle bridge piers. At another time, Dad and I met a convoy of military trucks at the gate. I was able to ride in the back of the high truck to the fort. The owner of a carnival show and his crowd asked to let them see the fort.

The Commons at Fort Montgomery Military Reservation. In the distance is the Montgomery Street gate. Author photo.

Upon leaving, he told Dad to bring us two boys to the carnival for free rides. We got on the Ferris Wheel and went around and around. People got on and got off, but we kept going. Finally Tom got sick and they let us off.

Fort Montgomery and the Reservation was sold to private interests in 1928 [sic][27], so we lost the thirty dollar per month pay that was connected with it. Shortly after the stock market crash in 1929, all military pensions were reduced by 12.5%, so Dad's monthly pay from the military was now eighty-four dollars.

He died on 18 December 1939, at the age of eighty-one."[28]

Sergeant Thomas Bourke, much like his very first predecessor, William McComb, was well liked and highly respected in the community. He carried out his duties at Fort Montgomery conscientiously and on schedule each day. He was responsible for "keeping" the great stone fort in as good a condition as was possible within the limited means provided him. The Fort Keeper was, indeed, the garrison. A capable garrison indeed.

This house at the corner of Rose Avenue and Montgomery Street was a home to the Bourke family in the winter when they were not staying in the "summer house" on the Commons. Photo by the author.

CHAPTER VIII

Fort Montgomery in private hands, 1926-2009

Despite the sensational story in the New York Times about Fort "Blunder" becoming a "Camp for Tourists" complete with a golf course, tennis courts and camping sites[1] very little happened at Fort Montgomery in the first decade of private ownership. The "gaunt barrack rooms" were never "tricked out by the arts of interior decorators" nor were "its dim interiors" made to "re-echo to the jests of holiday-makers and the strains of jazz tunes."

The most excitement the property was able to generate was in the meeting house where the town fathers gathered to complain about not being able to collect taxes on a huge property that had now passed into private ownership. One of the provisions of the sales contract between the government and the Fort Montgomery Development Company was that the title of the property would remain with the government until the full purchase price had been paid. As of August 2, 1932, that title remained in the hands of the United States of America, and was exempt from state, county and municipal taxes.[2] The tax matter was only the first in a long line of controversies that would result from Fort Montgomery being in private hands.

The Fox Film Company, under the auspices of the Fort Montgomery Development Company never made any films at Rouses Point. They did not do any "development" either. It is clear that a group of New York City area business people held an option on the property but there is some question as to whether the group actually owned the property.[3]

We do know that the fort was used as an enterprise of sorts in the 1920's. Vermont Senator, entrepreneur and Lake Champlain ferry operator Elisha Goodsell leased the fort for a time and attempted to make the massive parade into a very unique campground. Unfortunately, the endeavor was not successful.[4]

Harold Bourke, in his memoirs, reminisced about when he and the other children of Fort Keeper Thomas Bourke worked for Goodsell at the time. What follows are excerpts of Harold Bourke's memoirs, again, used with permission.

The Memoirs of Harold Bourke (excerpts)

"My first job, or rather my first chance to earn money, was when Mr. Goodsell, who owned auto ferrys on the lake, leased Fort Montgomery and got it ready to exhibit to tourists. He repaired the drawbridge to enter the fort and graded the road leading to the area. Soon the cars were arriving and my sister Lilyan, Tom and I were guides to show the visitors through the fort. Elisha, the youngest Goodsell boy would collect the entrance fee. Our additional duties were to unlock the doors in the early morning, raise the flag on the new pole and keep the grass cut. The latter job was quite involved, as we had to clear a large area for the cars to park and there were no power mowers available to us.

When a car load of tourists arrived, they would select one of us for a guide. We would start out on our tour by heading south from the entrance. The officer's quarters was the first stop, with the large fireplaces and beautiful plaster work on the ceilings. Next, it was into one of the wings of fort where the bakery was with the large ovens and a bellows that were of great interest. Then they were directed up the first circular stairs to the second floor to view the portholes and tracks for the large cannons that were not there, having been removed in 1910. The powder magazines were also of great interest, with their double stone wall protection and their interior wood construction to keep the ammunition dry. We would light up the magazines with our flashlights, since there were no windows. After walking them through a quarter of the heavy gun area on the second floor, we took them up to the top floor, which was open. The sundial was at the top of these second stairs. There were also gun emplacements to see on top and we would continue on and go down to the second floor at the next stairway. Through the gun ports, a good view of the Richelieu River to the north could be seen. Then it was down to the ground floor at the last stairway, where we went by the remaining officer's quarters to the parking lot. We received no pay and depended on our tips for compensation. A tip of five or ten cents was considered proper for our efforts. A group of well dressed business men gave Lilyan a tip of five dollars. Mom sure asked her a lot of questions about that tour.

When things were quiet and we had no customers, we would set up the croquet set and have a game or two. Elisha was called back to the Custom House by his father to advertise their Rouses Point to Alburg car ferry and also the fort. My brother, Tom, took over the collection of fees at the fort and was given a salary. One day a number of trucks arrived with men in uniforms, probably CMTC's (Citizen's Military Training Camp) from the Plattsburgh Barracks. They ignored the sign that listed the entrance fee and went in like they owned the place. They found our croquet set in the officers quarters, took all the mallets to beat on things as they went. Tom complained to the colonel in charge of the group and he gave Tom ten dollars, probably to pay for the croquet set, Tom turned it in as an entrance fee to the Goodsells. The tourist business at the fort proved to be unprofitable, so the project was given up."[5]

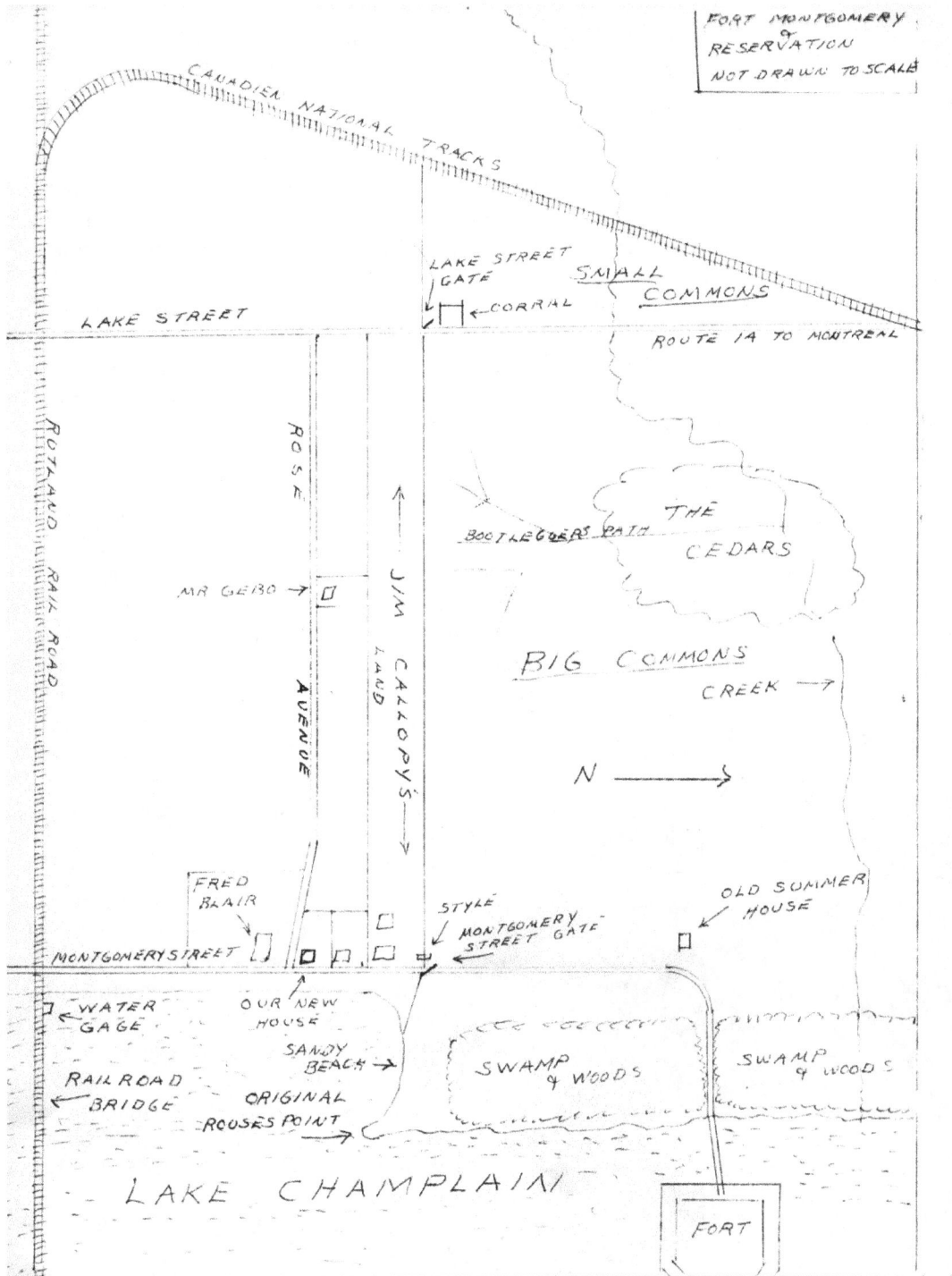

FORT MONTGOMERY
or
RESERVATION
NOT DRAWN TO SCALE

CANADIEN NATIONAL TRACKS

LAKE STREET GATE

SMALL COMMONS

CORRAL

ROUTE 14 TO MONTREAL

LAKE STREET

ROTLAND RAIL ROAD

ROSE AVENUE

JIM CALLOPY'S LAND

MR GEBO

BOOTLEGGERS PATH

THE CEDARS

BIG COMMONS

CREEK →

N →

OLD SUMMER HOUSE

FRED BLAIR

STYLE
MONTGOMERY STREET GATE

MONTGOMERY STREET

WATER GAGE

OUR NEW HOUSE

SANDY BEACH →

RAILROAD BRIDGE

ORIGINAL ROUSES POINT →

SWAMP & WOODS

SWAMP & WOODS

LAKE CHAMPLAIN

FORT

Harold Bourke's hand-drawn map of the area surrounding Fort Montgomery. Courtesy of the Bourke family.

With the '30's came the Depression and plans for building a new bridge across the lake at Rouses Point. That another bridge was needed there was no doubt. There was only one bridge crossing the lake, far up the waterway, at Crown Point. Despite the best efforts of men such as Goodsell, crossing the lake by ferry was costly and time-consuming. Plus, a project such as a bridge would bring jobs. Any talk of jobs during these difficult times was welcome.

On February 19, 1936, the Lake Champlain Bridge Commission purchased the eastern parts of lots 60, 61, and 62 from the United States of America for $3,000.[6] This included the actual "point" of old Rouses Point, the southeastern part of the Commons, and a significant chunk of wetland along the shore.

A more ominous development took place on April 21 when George Bierman, President of the Fort Montgomery Development Company sold Island Point to the Mott Creek Corporation of Long Island. This corporation, owned by the Weston family of Long Island and Rouses Point, was buying the fort for the expressed intention of "demolition and removal of said masonry fort." The sales agreement provided for the Fort Montgomery Development to finally pay off the United States government the remaining $1373.22 balance owed from the original purchase some ten years earlier. In exchange for the $5500 purchase price, the Weston interests would receive Island Point (Fort Montgomery proper, but *not* including the cover face, "all rock and stone now located on the westerly side of the moat near the masonry fort, and… the right to remove the same within six months…, the right to remove sufficient fill from an embankment [the cover face] located to the west of the masonry fort, to fill in the moat between said embankment and the masonry fort." Also included in the agreement was the "right and privilege to repair" the roadway between the Commons and the embankment and fort. The purchaser would have the right "to use as much fill as necessary, from the embankment…in order to repair said roadway" and was granted the right to allow "all equipment necessary for the demolition and removal of the said masonry fort" along the seller's property and rights of way. All personal property within the fort proper was included in the sale. Of the $5500 dollar purchase price, $3500 was the "agreed value of the masonry fort" and the "value of the stone and building materials." The granted right of way, removal of stone and fill from the embankment [cover face] and demolition of the fort was to occur within two years.[7]

Demolition of Fort Montgomery. Windows and doors have been removed from the Gorge Officer's Quarters and stone is being pulled from the postern. Courtesy; Charles Barney

A gathering at Greystone, home of the Andrew Weston family in Rouses Point. This building is believed to have been built with stone from the first fort, Fort "Blunder." Reportedly Montgomery C. Meigs lived here with his family during his tenure at the fort. It is now the residence of one of the current owners of Fort Montgomery. Courtesy: Clinton County Historical Association.

Local entrepreneur Andrew Weston had purchased the Fort so that he might tear it down and use the stone as fill for the new Rouses Point-Alburgh Bridge across the lake. Various agreements were made between Insurance companies, the Guardian Bond and Mortgage Company, and Clinton County to allow this to happen.[8]

Shortly after the sale of the Fort proper all glass, doors, wooden fixtures, hardware, etc. with value was removed. An auction was held and these items disappeared into the hands of local contractors, homeowners and history buffs.[9]

Much of the furnishings of value had disappeared in the years previous to the auction; doors and fireplaces were stripped of brass and copper, oak trim had been removed and interior walls were vandalized. [10]

Actual construction of the bridge had begun in March of that year. Thomas Cunningham of Ticonderoga was awarded the contract for construction of the west embankment and started work on March 16, 1936. This initial contract for $35, 750 included only grading and rip rapping of the west embankment.[11]

Andrew Weston was awarded his contract for construction of the east embankment and 15 piers of the bridge on May 4, 1936. His agreement with the Lake Champlain Bridge Commission included his use of large scows to bring the stone from the demolished fort to the Vermont side where it would be used as concrete aggregate and rip rap for 3500 feet of

The demolition of Fort Montgomery. Bastion B is at the right. Courtesy: Clinton County Historical Association

bridge embankment.[12] Demolition of the massive structure began that summer.

Weston brought his heavy demolition equipment in along the newly reinforced road and causeway. The bridge across the moat was torn down and the moat was filled in. An enormous crusher was erected on the parade close by Curtain I. The lake bed alongside Curtain I was dredged to allow for the barges or scows to come alongside the stone walls.[13] Since the stone was to be removed by barges brought alongside Curtain I, demolition began there at the junction of Bastion B. There is no small amount of irony in this as it was here, where Curtain I ran between Bastions A and B that the stone for the fort was brought in from the quarries during construction. Weston erected his massive crusher near the same location where the big derricks had been placed for offloading the newly quarried limestone.

Workmen first drilled holes into the massive walls. They then placed dynamite into the drill holes which, when ignited, took down the parade and scarp walls and arches. Once the walls came down, laborers, glad to have the work during these dark days of the Depression, tackled the largest limestone blocks with sledgehammers, breaking them into pieces small enough to fit into the crusher. Methodically, work continued due north from the south eastern face of Bastion B. First, Curtain I was removed down to the level of the first story floors. The massive pillow blocks for the axle of the "water gate" were left in place; it may not have seemed worth the effort to remove them. They remain in place today, firmly bolted into the limestone below.

Here at Curtain I, demolition began when the ramparts were removed to the level of the drawbridge. Author photo.

The demolition of Fort Montgomery. Top: Limestone from the crusher is loaded onto Weston Company barges at the site of newly demolished Curtain A. Bottom: View northwest across the parade. The postern in the gorge (Curtain III) is at far left and at right is Curtain IV. Courtesy: Clinton County Historical Association.

The demolition of Fort Montgomery. Two views from the barbette tier of Bastion B north toward Bastion E and Curtain IV. Most of Curtain V has been demolished. Courtesty: Clinton County Historical Association.

The demolition of Fort Montgomery. Top: This photo, taken from the Barbette tier of Bastion C, shows the view northeast toward what is left of Bastion A and Curtain V. Curtain I has been completely removed. Bottom: View a little further to the west showing Bastion E, Curtain V and Bastion A at far right. Courtesy of Ben Arno.

The demolition of Fort Montgomery. Top: view northwest toward Bastion C. Workmen are removing the limestone from the parade wall of Curtain III. Bottom: Scene near the crusher. Courtesy of Ben Arno.

The demolition of Fort Montgomery. Counterclockwise from top: View northwest from the cover face. The scarp wall has been removed from the gorge. Some of the men employed by Andrew Weston to demolish the fort. View south from the vicinity of Bastion D shortly after the demolition crews left. Three photos courtesy of Ben Arno.

The demolition of Fort Montgomery. Weston Company workmen break stone just inside the parade wall of Curtain III (the Gorge). Courtesy: Clinton County Historical Association.

Next in line was Bastion A, then Curtain V, Bastion E, and finally Curtain IV, facing due north, the only curtain at the fort that had ever received its full complement of guns. Almost all traces of Curtain IV were scraped from the earth. Once removed, the site of Bastion E was used as fill for unwanted material.

For some reason, demolition did not proceed past Curtain IV on the north before attention was focused back onto south-facing Bastions B and Curtain II. The parade wall and staircase of Bastion B were removed and the entire top tier of long Curtain II was pulled down, leaving only the scarp wall to support itself. The parade wall of Curtain II was pulled down and the entire second tier was removed. The interior of Curtain II's lower tier was gutted but the massive interior supporting arches at ground level were left in place. Attention was then focused on the Gorge Officer's Quarters of Curtain III. Almost all of the land front's scarp wall was pulled into the moat. On the inside, the entire parade wall was removed. The quarters themselves had been gutted and indications are that Weston may have actually experimented with using fire to burn the interior prior to attacking the walls with dynamite. Except for some lathe and plaster left clinging to the huge vaulted ceilings of the second story, all traces of the finely finished rooms vanished. Although it is not know what its final

Aftermath. Curtain III (the Gorge Officer's Quarters) viewed from the cover face across the filled in wet ditch.
Courtesy: Charles Barney

Aftermath.Views across the parade after the Weston Company crews had finished their work, 1937. Courtesy: Charles Barney

Aftermath. View northwest across the parade toward the Gorge and Bastion D. The Weston crews are largely finished with their work at this time. They have yet to remove the floors from the second story of the Officer's Quarters. Courtesy: Charles Barney

disposition was, an enormous amount of brick was removed from the casemates.

For some reason, Weston did not demolish either Bastion C or D. He did tear down their magnificent stone staircases, probably because the finely finished limestone steps were such easy marks. With the notable exception of gutting the large powder magazines within each bastion and tearing out the wall in front of the garrison ovens deep within Bastion C, the interiors of both bastions were left pretty much as they had always been. A couple of courses of stone were pulled from the scarp of the remaining bastions and Curtain II. Despite these missing blocks, the southern front of Fort Montgomery looks fairly intact to the casual viewer. It is this largely intact section of fort that has so fascinated travelers crossing the Rouses Point, New York-Alburgh, Vermont Bridge for generations.

On July 16, 1937 the new bridge opened to much fanfare. Andy Weston, regarded by many as a local hero who brought jobs to Rouses Point, took part in the dedication ceremonies. The bridge was impressive by North Country standards. The total length of the bridge and approaches was approximately 1.5 miles. It consisted of one draw span and twelve fixed spans. The draw was a swing span for two channels, each 125 feet wide to allow for navigation. The cost of construction was paid for by collecting a toll of one dollar for a one-way trip or $1.50 for a round-trip. The cost of demolishing Fort Montgomery has never been paid for.

Photo courtesy of Ben Arno.

By the fall of 1937 Weston had pulled all of his demolition equipment from the fort. The massive crusher was dismantled and local legend has it that he sunk the barges in the lake. The Depression lifted, the great new bridge contributed much to commerce and ease of travel between New York and Vermont. Another casualty of the bridge was Goodsell's ferry; everyone wanted to cross on the grand new bridge. The stark ruins of Fort Montgomery were left to nature, the explorations of the curious and the illicit drinking parties of young people. Gradually, nature started to reclaim the bare earth of the parade. Sumacs, alders and burdock took seed among the scarred ruins of Fort Montgomery.

On December 18, 1939, the last in a long line of Fort Keepers, Thomas Bourke, passed away at 81 years of age. Bourke had lived to see the magnificent structure that had played such a large role in his life demolished.

There was little news of Fort Montgomery in the years to come. The nation and the world would become enveloped in a great World War. Rouses Point sent its young men off to fight. Incredibly, Fort Montgomery would also play a role in this conflict as well.

In January, 1940 the Guardian Bond and Mortgage Company ran an ad in the Plattsburgh Daily Press advertising 450 acres of the military reservation for sale at the "tremendous sacrifice" price of $4,000. The ad stated the property must be sold by February 1 of that year.[14] There is no record of the property being sold by February 1 or at any other time that year. Weston would have to content himself with income from the time honored practice of renting the property for pasture.[15] It is possible he received some additional income from further scavenging of the ruins of the fort during the war years. Or, perhaps his next assault on the fort would come from a patriotic impulse during one of the many scrap drives held during that period. We probably will never know. Sometime during the war years it is believed that the remaining iron retaining rods that were introduced during the 1870's and 1880's were cut and pulled from within the casemates. It is not likely these rods were removed during the 1936 demolition. Photos of the walls being demolished show the long rods intact and clinging to broken sections of scarp. When these rods were cut Fort Montgomery contributed to the war effort by effectively sealing the fate of its remaining stone walls.[16]

Andrew Weston died on May 3, 1947 in Palm Beach, Florida.[17] Less than a year later his widow, Vivian C. Weston, sold the fort and Commons property to William and Belle Castine for a paltry four thousand, five hundred dollars.[18] The Castine's held on to the property until November 21, 1957 when they received an excellent return on their investment.

The Castine's had sold the former Fort Montgomery Military Reservation property to Quebec Lithium for a reported $115,000.[19] On November 22, the Plattsburgh Press-Republican trumpeted the big news— "Quebec Lithium Selects Rouses Point for $3 Million Plant. 300-400 Workers, 2 Million Yearly Payroll Set for Plant."[20] On December 2, the Press Republican reported that construction for the giant plant's employee housing would "start immediately." Quebec Lithium's President Pierre Beauchemin said at the time that the fate of the fort was not definite but that it was likely the site would be used as a dock "since the water is deep at that point and would easily accommodate ships." Beauchemin also said he did not know if the fort's walls would remain intact.[21]

Unfortunately for Rouses Point and Champlain, the excitement over Quebec Lithium would prove to be much ado over nothing. Almost four years would pass before the Rouses Point Village Board decided to approach Quebec Lithium to determine what their intentions were with regard to the property and development. Nothing had happened with the property, not even the housing that was to "start immediately" in 1957 was begun.

In September, 1961 the Rouses Point Chamber of Commerce began a push for development of a public beach and campsite on 50 acres of lakeshore north of the Village. This property was owned by Quebec Lithium. Included in the campsite plan were the ruins of Fort Montgomery, although there were no plans to restore the fort itself.[22] On September 29, Rouses Point Mayor Leo Letourneau announced that Quebec Lithium "was not presently planning to build in the village." This encouraged the Chamber of Commerce to continue pushing their plan for a beach/campsite at the site of the fort. The Chamber president announced that they would approach Quebec Lithium to see if they would sell the fifty acres desired. The hope was to preserve the fort with an eye towards possible development in the future.[23]

Quebec Lithium's response to the Chamber's offer was not encouraging. They were willing to sell the entire 400 acres but were not interested in selling part of it. Furthermore, the company made it clear that they were no longer considering the property for industrial use.[24]

The Chamber's plan to build a beach and campsite did not meet with universal approval in Rouses Point. Village residents were quite divided on the plan. Two camps emerged— The "North Countryman" newspaper under owner Kenneth Crouse came out against the plan and stated his belief that most village residents agreed with him while Al Ryan's "Banner"[25] said his paper was backing the plan.[26]

By mid-summer, 1962 hopes were still alive for the proposed beach and campground. The Chamber was reportedly still trying to get Quebec Lithium to drop their asking price and was looking into obtaining federal aid for the purchase.[27] On August 3, 1962 local officials toured the Fort site with New York State officials to "give the state an idea of just what was available."[28] Village residents were still clearly divided into "pro-industry" and "pro-campsite" groups, however. By August 13, divisions among Village residents were very pronounced. On one side was the Chamber of Commerce pushing for the plan. Leading the opposition was Kenneth Crouse of the "North Countryman." The Chamber made it clear that they knew of no business interest that was considering acquiring or developing the Fort Montgomery site. They explained that it was not a matter of development or recreation being a choice; currently there were no interested parties.[29]

On August 16 Rouses Point Chamber of Commerce president Percey Bosley wrote a letter to the editor of the Plattsburgh Press-Republican encouraging public support of the campsite plan. He said he knew of no community that had allowed a State Park and come to regret it. He strongly believed Rouses Point could have no better neighbor than the State and issued a rallying cry to village residents to urge State purchase of the fort.[30]

Village residents did not "rally together" in support of State purchase. The State, in turn, did not buy the fort property. In February, 1963 another option came up, this time from the private sector. Rouses Point developer William Kirk obtained an option on the 400 acre Commons and Fort Montgomery tract. Kirk, the developer of a recreational center in St. Luc, Quebec and the newly constructed beach and campsite at King's Bay, had quite a vision. He wanted to set aside the northernmost section of the Commons for industrial development, with access to the Lake for "shipping purposes." His plans also included an 18-hole golf course surrounded by low-cost housing, summer cottages along the lakeshore near the fort, and a shopping center with other commercial development along Route 9-B.[31]

Kirk's plans for development did not come to fruition either. This writer has not been able to determine if Kirk gave up his proposed development because he could not secure financing or because of opposition to the development. There can be no doubt that there was strong pro and anti development sentiment in the Village. Some wanted heavy industry and others thought the best use was recreation with its part-time warm weather employment being sufficient. Pro-park petitions were circulated in the village.[32]

Three years passed. There was no development at the Commons and no effort was made to shore up the deteriorating walls of Fort Montgomery. Exactly 30 years had passed since Andrew Weston tore down much of Rouses Point's most famous historic site. Finally, in mid July, 1966 the Rouses Point Kiwanis Club under the direction of President Michael Polino spoke up about the state of things. Polino said the club was discouraged by lack of interest in the fort by Rouses Point officials and said that there should be an effort to pursue federal financing for possible preservation. The group felt that Rouses Point officials may have been reluctant to act on behalf of the fort since it was outside of the Village's incorporate limits, technically within the Town of Champlain. Polino stressed that a restored fort would benefit Town and Village by bringing tourists to the area.[33]

This was not the first time that *restoration* of the fort was brought up as the preferred option. It is likely that talk of actually restoring the fort, rather than simply preserving the ruins, contributed to the lack of action at the time. Local historian John Ross recognized the folly of pushing for complete restoration. Ross, while frustrated by the lack of attention to the deteriorating ruins, had a much more realistic view. He believed, as does this writer, that the only practical and realistic option is that the ruins be cleaned up, made safe and preserved, largely as they are. The Fort Montgomery ruins as they are could still attract visitors in droves.[34]

On November 5, 1966 New York State officials notified interested parties in Rouses Point that budget funds for purchasing park property had been exhausted.[35] The bickering between locals on each side brought significant delays that had caused the state to lose interest. Ironically, a few days later Quebec Lithium made it clear it was definitely ready to sell.[36] It was too late. The money was gone.

In December, 1973 the Town of Champlain was presented with a draft of a land use plan prepared by professional planner Hans Klunder. Klunder's presentation to the town highlighted the unique character of the area around the lake and referred to its wetlands status, pointing out there was limited potential for development there because of the wetlands. The planner's ideas for Fort Montgomery included preservation and possible restoration. Klunder believed the fort was a "key landmark" that should be made into a park with lake access.[37]

Despite the recommendation by respected land use planners Hans Klunder Associates, nothing happened with the Commons or Fort Montgomery during the 1970's. Instead, the bridge between the village and the Vermont shore would command attention over the next few years.

By May, 1976 the Rouses Point-Alburgh Bridge was in need of major repair. At least two expansion joints were in danger of failing by summer. In addition, frequent pavement washouts had occurred on the Vermont embankment during periods of high water and the bridge infrastructure was insufficient to handle the increase vibration caused by modern vehicles and traffic.[38] Discussions would soon begin about replacing the bridge. These talks would serve to reignite interest in Fort Montgomery.

On August 22, 1977 Fort Montgomery was added to the National Register of Historic Places.[39] The designation was a good thing for the fort. The owners of properties with National Register designation become eligible for grants from the National Park Service to aid in preservation. The designation does not change ownership of the property in any way and the property is not removed from any taxable status as a result of the designation. There is no real protection given to the property as a result of the designation; the owner is still free to manage the property in any manner that he or she wishes and they may dispose of or sell the property at any time. The only restrictions actually placed upon the Register-designated property are in regard to any future federally-assisted project that might include it. In that case its historical significance must be taken into account."[40]

In January, 1980 the Lake Champlain Bridge Commission determined that federal funds for repairing the Rouses Point Bridge were unlikely. An audit had determined that the only practical course was full replacement of the now obsolete 43 year old span. The bridge was some twenty feet narrower than federal guidelines for two-lane bridges and there was a strong likelihood that several of the concrete piers would need to be replaced soon.[41] The new bridge, like the one before it, would have an impact on the old fort to the northwest.

Catastrophe arrived with the spring thaws of April, 1980. The west-facing scarp wall of Bastion D collapsed into the moat. Slowly pulling away from the rest of the structure, the scarp had held itself up for a good 35 years. Once the rods introduced in the 1870's to prevent this event[42] were removed it was only a matter of time before the collapse. The scarp pan caked into the moat. The wall collapse was bad enough. Unfortunately, the bastion's arches and second floor ceiling, weakened by years of leaking, freezing and thawing, went down with the scarp. Everything west of the magazine collapsed.[43]

In June and July, 1982 archaeological surveys were made at the site of the proposed new bridge. Other than "one button...which may have been worn by a soldier garrisoned at Fort Montgomery," nothing of significance was found. There was nothing of archaeological significance that would prevent the new bridge from being built.[44]

With spring, 1983 came yet another significant event. Fort Montgomery was sold to the Podd family, owners to this day. On April 29, Sullivan Mining Co. (formerly Quebec Lithium) sold 338 acres including Island Point and the fort to Victor and Julia Podd of Montreal for "industrial and commercial development." Podd was not unaccustomed to doing business in the region. He already owned and operated a firm across the lake at Alburgh, Vermont. The business, Powertex, Inc. manufactures plastic liners for shipping containers. Podd also owned Powercast, Inc., an aluminum castings plant based in Montreal. Podd told the Press-Republican that it was safe to assume he would relocate both of his manufacturing plants to the Rouses Point site. The purchase was handled by Kavanaugh Realty of Rouses Point with the assistance of local management consultant Mark L. Barie. Barie would prove instrumental in future negotiations regarding Island Point and Fort Montgomery. New York State Senator Ronald B. Stafford was also a key figure in helping the sale process along.[45]

On May 9 Podd revealed some of his development plans to Champlain and Rouses Point officials. His fairly modest plan was to develop only four acres initially. He would build a 20,000 foot industrial plant to house Powertex, Inc. which would move from Alburgh. Initial operations would employ about a dozen employees. Within a year of that construction, Podd wanted to build a second structure, some 10,000 square feet, to house his other business, Powercast, Inc. Powercast would move from Montreal. The second plant would employ twelve to twenty people initially.[46]

Within a month Podd was in the news again. He had informed local officials that "four or five [additional] companies "were interested in locating at the "Commons." One firm, "Raisin People" had provided Podd with a letter of intent to purchase ten to twenty acres. This raisin processing plant would provide at least 150 jobs initially and was to begin operations by April, 1984. Podd stated at the time that the fort itself would not "suffer at the hands of industrial expansion..." He was looking into renovating the fort and possibly constructing a marina and condominium complex.[47]

On July 9, 1983, in what would prove to be only the first in a long series of articles about the fort, Press Republican staff writer Steve Manor wrote about the first fort and early resident Jacques Rouse. Unfortunately, Manor made a number of statements about the first fort on Island Point that continued a long tradition of misinformation.[48] Had this been one isolated incident it may not have been that big a deal. Each time these misstatements were published, however, a long tradition of false information became more firmly established as truth in the public's mind. We have already determined that the first fort was not named Fort "Montgomery." The second fort received that designation well after construction began, in 1849. The survey was conducted in 1816-17, not 1819. And, most importantly, Fort Montgomery never was "quickly named Fort Blunder."

An ominous development took place in the summer of that year. Podd had surveyed and posted the "Commons" property shortly after purchasing it. Shortly thereafter, incidents of vandalism on the property increased and individuals started removing the signs. Podd was advised by State Police to chain the gate at the Montgomery Street entrance.[49] These problems were apparently the first sign of some ill-will towards the new owners by local residents long accustomed to unfettered access to the fort and adjacent lands. The property wasn't referred to as the "Commons" for nothing.

One of the concerns that often came up whenever Rouses Point officials discussed the fort was the fact that it was located in the Town of Champlain and not in the village proper. On January 1984 proposals were made and hearings set for annexing the Commons and Fort Montgomery into the village.[50] Annexation would only be the first in a long series of complicated legal maneuvers designed to promote commercial development of the Commons and get something done with the fort out on Island Point.

That February Manor again wrote of the developments at Rouses Point. In an in-depth article entitled "Podd's development plans extensive," the Press Republican staff writer detailed Victor Podd's ambitions for the property and provided North Country readers with a biography of the Canadian entrepreneur. When Manor wrote of current developments he did a commendable job of detailing the highlights and nuances of the negotiated agreements. Unfortunately, he again made incorrect statements about the fort's history when he merged the two forts into one in a side article— "Fort may have a better future."[51]

The Rouses Point Village Board ratified the Commons annexation on March 29, 1984. This move effectively increased the size of the village by one third. The board also ratified a fourteen point annexation agreement with Fort Montgomery Estates and Powertex. The annexation agreement, made in response to a $153,000 Urban Development Action Grant the village received, spelled out the "detailed do's and don'ts" of how current and future Commons property owners could use the property for the common good.[52]

Some of the terms of the annexation agreement were:

  o The Village of Rouses Point would have the option to buy the peninsula and Fort Montgomery for $1 after 15 years. The Village's option could be exercised only if Fort Montgomery Estates did not do more than $60,000 development work on the peninsula or fort.

o Fort Montgomery Estates was to deed over five percent of the gross acreage of the Commons that did not lie in wetlands. The State Conservation Department would determine just what parts of the property comprised these wetlands. There was to be one parcel of at least three acres for use by the Village on the Fourth of July. In addition there would be a three-acre beach on Lake Champlain if the village determined it was able to construct a beach and obtain the required permits.

o Fort Montgomery Estates was to deed over a boat launch site near any marina it developed.

o In order to finance the building of recreational facilities on the lands deeded there was to be a $200 surcharge per residential unit on any building permit issued for construction on the Commons.

o After the initial two years, no building permits would be issued until the required road was built up to at least a base course of asphalt.

o The agreement stipulated that there were to be no junkyards, motor vehicle storage yards, explosives storage, kennels, livestock (except horses), poultry raising, blinking or flashing lights, outdoor sound systems or dumps...[53]

In late summer 1984, the Town of Champlain formed a new development agency. The Industrial Development Agency (IDA) was created as the town's promotional agency while the Local Development Corporation (LDC) would be its financial arm. The LDC and its Executive Director Mark Barie would play a key role in the ongoing negotiations regarding potential sale and development of Fort Montgomery and the Commons over the next few years.[54]

The first project for the new IDA/LDC was a $500,000 bond issue to finance the new Powertex plant on the Commons. Now that the Champlain IDA was formed Victor Podd requested that his inducement agreement with the Clinton County IDA be reassigned to the Champlain agency. Podd had big ideas for development. His plans were for over $100 million in industrial, commercial and residential development over five to ten years.[55]

It wasn't just pro-industry advocates who were excited about the potential for big things happening at Rouses Point. For decades individuals and groups interested in the history of the region and its precious historical sites had fretted about the neglected state of the ruins of Fort Montgomery. Finally, there was the real possibility of preservation—someone was talking seriously about doing something with the fort. The Clinton County Historical Association, under the able direction of President Dennis Lewis, was prepared to take the lead in advocating for the fort. In September, 1984, at the invitation of the Rouses Point-Champlain Chamber of Commerce Lewis gave a presentation at the Anchorage Hotel highlighting the story of Fort Montgomery. In the audience that day was Fort Montgomery Estates spokesman Laine Jamison. Jamison made an announcement that Podd's plans definitely included "restoration" of the fort.[56]

That September Podd revealed his ten-year master plan for development of the property. His very ambitious plans called for the building of some 300 homes, another 30 condominiums, a 200,000 square foot commercial complex with a shopping mall and offices, a parking lot for 1,000 car and an incredible 30 "industrial plants!" All of this development would take place on 200 acres of the "Commons" while another 130+ acres would be reserved for wetlands, recreation and use by the Village. [57]

In February, 1985 Victor Podd started running classified ads in local papers asking for fort memorabilia "to help start a museum at Rouses Point..."[58] I have been unable to determine what, if anything was collected or what the final disposition of collected artifacts might have been.

Along with the cold and snows of February came additional publicity for the fort. This interest came about as a result of the new bridge that was to replace the 1937 original. On February 8, 1985 the Press-Republican ran an account by Steve Manor entitled "Re-Fortification may be hidden in old bridge." In it, Manor recounted how Podd hoped to recover stone from the fort that was used during the 1937 construction. It also highlighted Podd's desire to purchase the small strip of land just north of the new bridge. This narrow strip constituted the old western approach to the bridge and was owned by the Bridge Commission. Once Podd purchased it he intended to give most of it to the Village for their use.[59] Podd's offer to purchase stone from the Vermont Agency of Transportation ostensibly to be used "to restore the ruins of Fort Montgomery" is puzzling to this writer. Unfortunately, most of the limestone removed from the fort went into the maw of the giant crusher erected on the parade for that very purpose. Photos of the barges hauling stone to the bridge site on the Vermont side show stone far different from the large blocks quarried and cut during construction.

Construction of the new bridge began on June 3, 1985. The bridge would be impressive in size, towering over the old structure. The bridge would be over 7,000 feet long with two 12-foot travel lanes and a pavement width of 40 feet.[60]

That June LDC Director Mark Barie told the Press-Republican he was going to seek state funding for a feasibility study on the restoration of Fort Montgomery[61] and on July 28, Podd hosted the first of a number of public tours of the fort. This first tour, originally intended for some 25-30 members of the Clinton County Historical Association, was organized by CCHA's James Dawson. Podd, himself a member of the Association, decided instead to open the tour to the general public. He planned on a hundred people showing up. Three hundred came. Podd took it in stride; he even served sandwiches and refreshments. In addition to the publicity and good will, Podd got something else in return— a petition was circulated supporting the feasibility study for the fort's renovation. Most of the tour attendees signed it.[62]

In late July LDC Director Mark Barie revealed more about the feasibility study request. They were asking the North Country Regional Economic Development Council for $133,000. The money would not just be used to study potential restoration or preservation of the fort. Part of the study would be for "a complete recreational complex along the shoreline..." that would include "...public boat mooring facilities, a marina, restaurant, public swimming pool, tennis courts, public beach bathhouse and an information booth."[63]

Barie and Podd had some impressive support for their efforts. Clinton County Historical Association President Dennis Lewis stated his organization's support for both the study and preservation or restoration. The Council on America's Military Past (CAMP) endorsed restoration, as did Vermont's Champlain Maritime Society. The Clinton County Chamber of Commerce, Plattsburgh Chamber and the Rouses Point-Champlain Chamber were on board as were a large number of local politicians, business people and entrepreneurs.[64]

Prospects were looking good for a preserved fort. Rouses Point and Champlain appeared likely to experience a boom in construction along with commercial, industrial and residential development. Popular and influential New York State Senator Ronald Stafford was on board as a key supporter. Podd's efforts were generating enough excitement and promise that Rouses Point Mayor Paul Cloutier called his little village a "boom town." The prospect of development and fort preservation were there. Still, the only building constructed to date was the Powertex plant itself.[65]

"Grassroots campaign at work to save Fort." This was the headline atop the regional section of the August 19 issue of the Press-Republican. In the first of a four-part series on the Fort, Steve Manor wrote of the history of the site and explained current and ongoing efforts at preservation or restoration. He wrote of Victor Podd's unflagging enthusiasm for the fort and the massive development project proposed for the Commons and shoreline. He also sounded an alarm from LDC Director Mark Barie. Barie said he feared the fort's condition "worsens each year" and that if something wasn't done "...Fort Montgomery will cease to exist."[66] The series was optimistic, detailed, informative, and despite a few notable errors, fairly accurate with regard to the history of the fort. It also concluded on a somber note— a potential cost of four to six million dollars to "restore" the fort and a statement from LDC director Barie tying any fort restoration to development of the adjacent property. Barie said that a restored fort wouldn't be able to support itself and that a restored fort would have to be supported by "privately owned recreational facilities" and "waterfront development."[67]

The New Year brought the first signs of trouble ahead. The New York State Department of Environmental Conservation (DEC) had weighed in on the development and the news was not good for Podd or the LDC. It was all about wetlands.

By spring, 1986 the Powertex plant had been built on the Commons. It was constructed on a section of land carved out of the old military reservation designated as an industrial park. Some 25 acres in size, the Rouses Point Industrial Park's title was now held by the Champlain LDC/IDA. In addition to Podd's Powertex firm, plans still called for the second Podd-owned facility (Powertex II) and a new building for the Anachemia Company, a Canadian laboratory supply company and chemical manufacturer to be built. It was an access road for the latter that caused the first problems with DEC. While the locations of the proposed plants were not on state designated wetlands, a good section of the access road was. Not just any wetlands, either. The state claimed the road would cross Class I wetlands, considered most valuable and vulnerable. The LDC believed the area in question constituted poor quality Class III wetlands.[68]

Disagreement between DEC and the Champlain LDC continued through July of that year. The state wanted an archaeological impact survey and a habitat study done. Barie and the LDC felt that the access road was far enough away from any significant wetlands that neither of the costly surveys was necessary.[69] This round was won by the development forces. By July 30, DEC had agreed to issue the necessary permits for the access road. The second part of the Industrial Park could now be accessed and built upon.[70]

Earlier that year contractors for the new bridge believed they had found some original stone from the fort on the Vermont side of the old causeway. This stone was supposedly intact and not crushed or ground up. Podd wanted it. He contacted the contractor, Cianbro Corporation about purchasing the stone for potential use in restoration. Unfortunately, the town of Alburg, Vermont, where the stone was now located, felt they had first dibs. Alburg wanted the stone from the causeway for use in reinforcing another road at Windmill Point. Any intact limestone blocks removed from Fort Montgomery now on the Vermont side would remain there.[71]

Efforts also began that May for the establishment of a "Fort Montgomery Foundation" and "Friends of the Fort" Society. Although Barie named several individuals who had agreed to serve as the foundation's board of directors, it is not clear as to whether this foundation or the "Friends of the Fort" were ever formed. That September there was a dramatic new twist; Podd offered to donate the fort to the State of New York.

Much has been made of Victor Podd's offer to give Fort Montgomery to the state for free. While his offer certainly made state acquisition potentially more likely, it is important to understand that the offer was not made without conditions. Podd told Steve Manor that he was moved to make the offer because of developments regarding Crab Island in Cumberland Bay. Crab Island had received much publicity of late due to the State's determination to take possession of the historic island by eminent domain.[72] Here was one example of privately-owned property on the lake being taken over by the state because New York believed it had an overriding interest in protecting what it viewed as a historic site. In addition, Podd now had come up with new information; cost estimates for restoration of the fort had risen to around ten million dollars. Podd felt the project would simply be too large for the nascent "Fort Montgomery Foundation" to take on by itself.[73]

In mid-September Rouses Point Mayor Portugal threw the Village's support behind Podd's proposal to give the fort to the state. In a letter to the Office of Parks, Recreation and Historic Preservation, Portugal stated that the Village supports the donation "as long as the state preserves and restores the structure and not just lets it sit there…"[74]

Victor Podd was determined to do what he could to advance his ideas with regard to the development of his property and, this writer believes, he did have a sincere desire to see the fort preserved. In October he met with Crab Island's new owner, Roger Jakubowski. Jakubowski, an entrepreneur from New Jersey, was getting much attention of late with his plans to develop Crab Island into a recreation area with camping and ski and snowmobile touring.[75] Podd felt that someone needed to show an interest in the fort, if the state wouldn't step up, he was willing to make an alliance with another prominent businessman.[76]

By October 21, several significant developments had taken place. Podd was contacted by Deputy Parks Commissioner Ivan Vamos to set up an "exploratory" meeting about his proposal. LDC Director Barie, Dennis Lewis, State Senator Ronald Stafford and Assembly-man Chris Ortloff were invited to attend. The Town of Champlain went on record as sup-porting state purchase when it adopted a resolution encouraging the state to accept Podd's offer and the Clinton County Legislature adopted a similar resolution.[77]

On Thursday, October 23, 1986, officials of the New York State Office of Parks, Recrea-tion and Historic Preservation toured Fort Montgomery with Podd. Deputy Commissioner Vamos was quoted in the Press-Republican as stating "...the fort is just spectacular...," and that he would "be getting back to Podd in six weeks." It was decision time. Unfortunately, there was no money available for purchase or restoration of another fort.[78]

On Sunday, October 26, Podd hosted yet another tour of the Fort Montgomery ruins. This tour, again open to the public and including an open house of the Fort Montgomery Es-tates Industrial Park, drew an estimated 400 people.[79] Many of those visitors would be disap-pointed, however, by the state's response when it finally arrived in December.

In early December New York Commissioner Orin Lehman wrote Victor Podd that the state had decided against accepting his offer and assuming responsibility for Fort Montgom-ery. The state cited a backlog of work at other state-owned historic sites and the cost in recon-structing the fort in accord with Podd's wishes as reasons for declining the offer. The state also believed that Podd's estimate of $10 million to stabilize and 'reconstruct" the fort was "conservative."[80] That, it would seem, would be the end Victor Podd's efforts with regard to Fort Montgomery.

In the spring of 1987 Podd was back with another offer. This time, it was a revival of the 1961 beach-on-the-island (coverface) idea. Overtures were made to the Village of Rouses Point. Undeterred by the state's refusal to have anything to do with his fort, Podd now of-fered to donate some 1,000 feet of "beach front property" to the Village of Rouses Point pro-vided the Village applied for a grant to develop it. Tied in with the proposal was an offer to donate the fort ruins to a non-profit as long as the organization applied for a grant to stabilize and preserve the fort.[81] The "beach front property" was located in a rather unlikely place-along the southwestern end of the cover face and east end of the causeway. The project would require substantial development of the property since only 400 feet of the proposed beach was along the cover face island proper. The rest of the beach would be created along the causeway. Podd estimated the value of his donation to the Village at $300,000.

In late May the Rouses Point Village Board authorized the Champlain LDC to submit an application for a grant to the NYS OPRHP to build the municipal beach. The state agency that recently decided against purchasing Fort Montgomery because it was too expensive, was now disbursing some $30 million for recreational and historic preservation projects. The Vil-lage hoped to get some of that money for its new beach and for Fort Montgomery. The grant application was to include plans for a new bathhouse, interpretive center and museum, na-ture trails and a bike path along with sheltered pavilions with picnic tables. The fort would be stabilized under a separate application that was tied to the beach project. Fifty-five acres of wetland would be donated to the New York Department of Environmental Conservation. In what he referred to as a "trade-off situation," Podd laid out his provisions "that I at least be given the enjoyment of one-third of that land." Podd would reserve a portion of the shoreline north of the causeway and the northern part of the coverface for future private development. Those development plans included a marina with several building and parking on the coverface north of the public beach.

By the fall of 1987 Rouses Point and Champlain residents had received a "mixed bag" of news. The impressive new bridge was finished, opening on September 22. However, there would be no further development of the Podd property. Nor would there be any funds distributed for the preservation of Fort Montgomery. Victor Podd gave up his efforts to tie development of his property to a 'free" offer of the fort. A headline on page five of the St. Albans Messenger told the tale- "Fort nobody wanted for free now for sale at $2.5 million."

Despite some initial interest, Victor Podd did not sell the fort he had tried to give away. After a long period in the public spotlight little was heard of Fort Montgomery for a decade. March 1999 was the 15th year since Podd's agreement to spend more than $60,000 on development of the peninsula or fort. The Village could now exercise its option to purchase the fort and peninsula for one dollar. That did not happen either. The ruins Fort Montgomery remained in private hands without attention, care or maintenance.

On December 5, 1999 Victor Podd died, leaving his estate, business and Fort Montgomery to his family.

Stephen and Victor Podd, Jr. took over their father's business with apparent skill, enthusiasm and success. They also resumed efforts to rid themselves of the burden of Fort Montgomery. The nation had become a more litigious society. It became more important than ever to keep trespassers away from the deteriorating ruins. Old posted signs were replaced with fresh new ones. Access to Fort Montgomery, was of necessity, limited to a few individuals who would sign a liability release and, hopefully for the new owners, prospective buyers.

In September 2002 this writer and Roger Harwood received permission for a tour of the ruins. We were guided on that first visit by Powertex employees Ann Thurber, George Bombardier and Calvin Hilliker. It was the beginning of a long and mutually beneficial relationship between the owners and this writer. That fall, in response to many questions I had received over the years about Forts "Blunder" and Montgomery, I published my first story about the fort on the America's Historic Lakes website. Titled "Following Fort Blunder: The Strange and Sad Tale of Fort Montgomery," this account told of our visit to the ruins that September. It was also an attempt to clear up many of the misconceptions about Fort Montgomery and Fort "Blunder." The material is still available on the site and remains some of the most popular on the America's Historic Lakes site.

The story led to a spate of attention being given the fort by local media. Over the next few years most of the local television stations did a feature story about the fort, including a joint Lake Champlain Basin Program/WPTZ sponsored "Champlain 2000" segment that ran over five minutes. A few years later a follow-up feature ran on the NBC affiliate, the segment now entitled "Champlain Connection.' Popular local personalities Gordie Little and Calvin Castine did an interview with the author for Castine's popular Hometown Cable television show.

Due to popular demand, this writer gave over a dozen presentations about the fort at local historical societies, libraries, restaurants and school auditoriums. Presented in communities on both sides of the lake, each was very well attended, often standing room only.

In September, 2005 America's Historic Lakes published the first book ever written about the fort. Primarily a photographic history of the second fortification built at Rouses Point, "Fort Montgomery Through the Years" has been quite successful and is still in print.

In May, 2006 Victor Podd listed the fort for sale on the popular eBay web site. This was a shrewd move by Podd, who had some success selling unusual properties online in the past. Utilizing photos supplied by this writer and Roger Harwood, together with a description of the fort and information about land use regulations, regional demographics and permitted uses, Podd put together a listing that drew media attention from around the world. There was also a link to this writer's recent book on the listing.

The fort and adjacent "Commons" property was originally listed for $9,500,000. There was an initial flurry of activity with one bid coming in at $3,000,000. Unfortunately for the Podds, it was not a serious bid. The listing has been renewed repeatedly since 2006 and, as of this writing is still open. The current asking price is $5,000,000. It had gone as low as $3,000,000 and remained at that price until September, 2008 when another important milestone in the fort's recent history occurred.

On September 26, 2008 the Preservation League of New York State notified this writer that Fort Montgomery had been accepted as a "Seven to Save" Site by the League. The designation highlights New York's most threatened historic resources and gives endangered properties increased visibility and triggers enhanced technical, legal, grant and media services from the League. This writer had written the submission proposal at the urging of Steven Engelhart, Executive Director of Adirondack Architectural Heritage. The group, which uses the acronym AARCH, had sponsored public tours of Fort Montgomery, guided by this writer a few years previous. Included in the submission proposal were letters of support from Adirondack Architectural Heritage, the Clinton County Historical Association, Rouses Point-Champlain Historical Society, Art Cohn of the Lake Champlain Maritime Museum, Lake Champlain Basin Program, and Quebec historian André Charbonneau. Even the New York State Office of Parks, Recreation and Historic Preservation submitted a letter in support of the fort's inclusion as a "Seven to Save" Site.

The owners had notified this writer of their support of the proposal in a phone call from their representative, Ann Thurber, the night before the nomination deadline. Their support was important. It also signaled the beginning of some unprecedented cooperation by the owners in promotion of the fort as a historic resource.

Up until the acceptance of Fort Montgomery as a "Seven to Save" site, the owners had limited their active support of efforts to highlight the fort's historical value to allowing guided tours of the property by this writer, providing me with virtually unlimited access to the property for my research, and support of media requests for fort tours. These efforts were important. They paled in significance, however, to the largest and most important effort to promote the site to date. At this writing, the author is engaged, together with a committee composed of Podd-owned Powertex employees Ann Thurber and Karen Lamberton and

Rouses Point-Champlain Historical Society President Geri Favreau, in an event to be held on September 12-13, 2009. This major event, known as Fort Montgomery Days, will be held at the suggestion of the Preservation League of New York State. The event will be a Hudson River/Champlain Valley Heritage Weekend Event promoted as part of the Champlain Quad-ricentennial. The owners have thrown their support behind the weekend, donating the time of their employees and providing most of the financial backing. Official sponsors of the event are the Rouses Point-Champlain Historical Society, America's Historic Lakes, Powertex, Inc. and Stephen and Victor Podd. It is significant that the Village of Rouses Point and Clinton County legislature have thrown their support behind the event.

As of this writing plans are well under way. Weekly fort cleanups have been organized and are well supported by Powertex employees and dedicated volunteers. Fort vistas have been opened up and tons of brush removed and burned. The parade has been cleared and will be prepared for the arrival of anticipated hundreds of visitors to the free public event. Included in the event will be free public tours, live musical entertainment, photo and artifact displays, children's events and vendors offering refreshments. This writer will be making interpretive signs for the fort as soon as this book is

Volunteers for the first Fort Montgomery Cleanup Day, August 2, 2009. Left to right: Dan Letourneau, Jan Letourneau, Jim Thurber, Ann Thurber, Karen Lamberton, Geri Favreau, Ben Arno, Pat Parker, Richard Seguin, George Bombardier, Calvin Hilliker, Dave Rabideau, Randy Lamberton, Not shown, Roger Harwood and Jim Millard. Author photo.

off to the printer. It is an exciting time. It may also be Fort Montgomery's last chance for the public to see what an important historic resource it is. This writer, along with countless other individuals across the nation, earnestly hopes it signals the beginning of a new day for this important "Bastion on the Border."

PART TWO:
FORT MONTGOMERY IN DETAIL
CHAPTER IX

Bastion A and Curtain I

Plans drawn up for Fort Montgomery identified main sections of the fort (bastions and curtains) by letters and numbers. Each of the five bastions was identified by a letter starting with the easternmost bastion, identified as Bastion A. Each successive bastion received the next letter, in a clockwise rotation. The five curtains were identified in the same manner, beginning with curtain I, just south of bastion A.

Bastion A was the smallest of Fort Montgomery's five bastions, long and narrow compared with the other four. It extended due east from adjacent curtain walls about fifty feet into the lake. It was just under forty-four feet wide. The scarp walls were forty-eight feet high and approximately six feet thick at the embrasures. This bastion was unique in that it did not house a magazine, nor did it have an adjacent stairway. Access to the lower tier of bastion A was from a double door on the parade. Access to the second tier was through arches directly into casemates in adjacent curtains I and V. There was a double door that opened out onto the parade on tier II but it was primarily for ventilation and movement of ordnance, not an entryway. The bastion had wooden casemate floors and, since it was one of the first bastions built, had embrasures constructed wholly of hardened brick. Bastion A, like all of the other bastions, had 24-pounder flank howitzers mounted in its flanks, four on each flank, tiers I and II, for a total of eight. All were mounted.[1] Only the bastions had howitzers mounted on tier I, the lower tiers of all curtains were "pierced for musketry" and had loopholes. The barbette tier of Bastion A was designed to mount three guns, two fore-pintle and one center-pintle gun at the salient. The center-pintle mount was one of the five that was completed but it never received its gun.[2] The fore-pintle mounts each received an 8-inch Rodman.

Bastion A was also unique in that it housed the soldier's latrine. The latrine was located just south of the salient or east-facing point of the bastion in the right face. There was one window, a loophole, "pierced for musketry," the only opening on the scarp walls of the bastion other than the embrasures. Below the latrine two openings to the lake were constructed. Their purpose was to remove the waste from the latrine at high water.

Bastion A was completely demolished in 1936-37. While the outline and form of the bastion are intact, only the bottom few courses of stone remain.

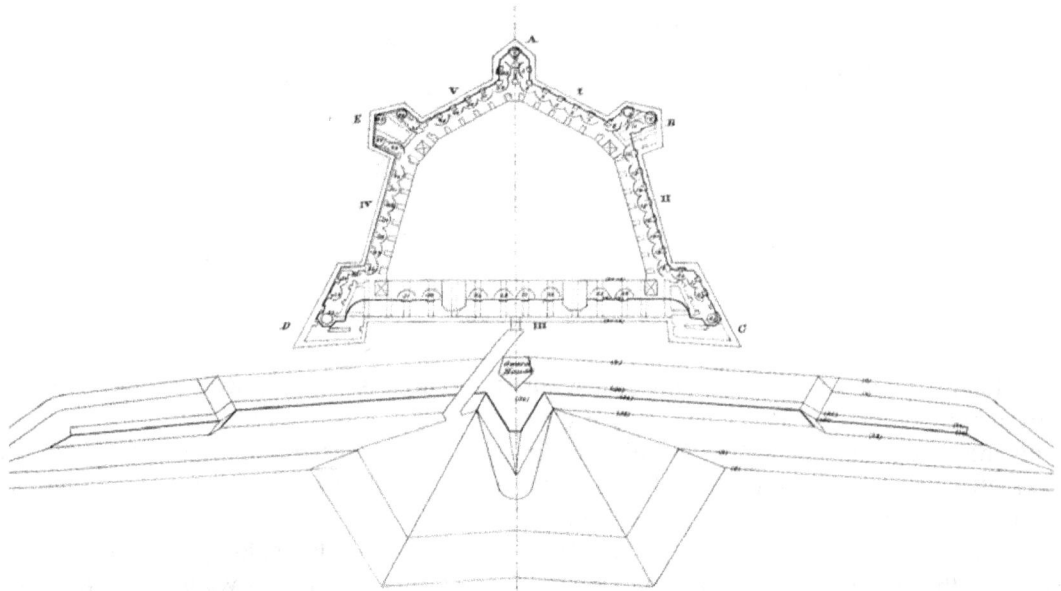

Top: Details of plan from 1886 showing alphabetical and numerical identification of bastions and curtains. NARA, Drawer 7, Sheet A (detail).

Bottom left: Details of plans for Bastion A, casemate tiers I and II. Note that in order to show both tiers on the same plan some features are in opposite locations than actually built, a common practice in these plans. Tier I is on the left and Tier II on the right. Note that the latrine was actually constructed within the south face of the salient. NARA, Drawer 7, Sheet 31 (undated, likely 1850).

Bottom right: Detail of barbette tier for Bastion A. Drawer 7, Sheet 56 (1861).

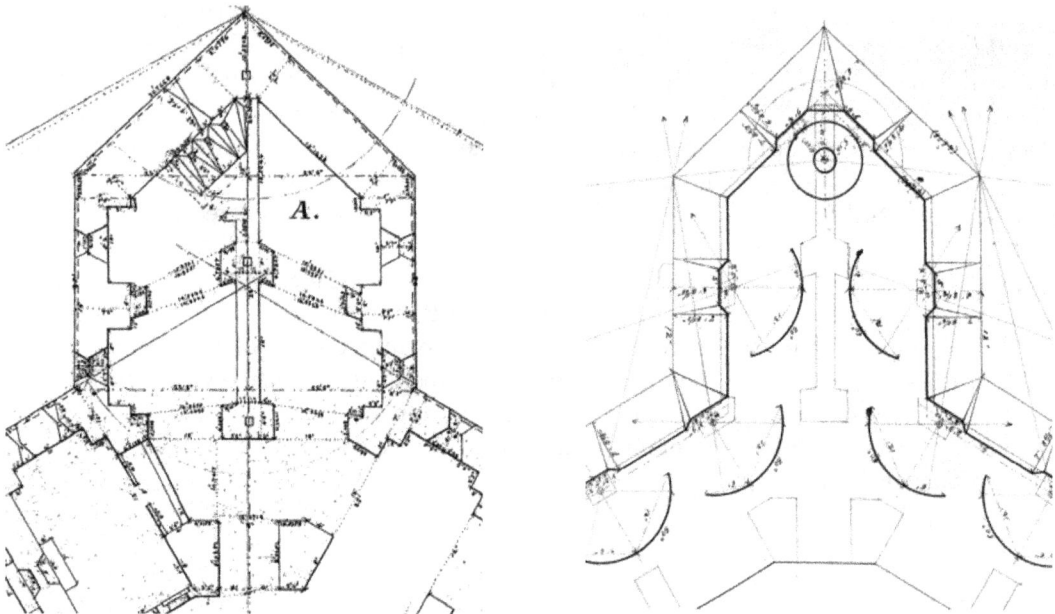

This early photo shows the entrance to Bastion A (center). Note the casemates still have a good portion of their doors and windows intact. Courtesy Powertex.

This photo taken from the barbette tier of Bastion B shows what little is left of Bastion A and Curtains I and V. It also gives a good sense of how small Bastion A was in relation to the rest of the fort. Photo by the author.

These photos of the ruins of Bastion A show the area below the site of the soldier's latrine at low (left) and high water. The photographs at left and below show the drain referred to by some locals as a "secret passage."[1] Top left and below: Author's collection. Courtesy of Raymond Seguin. Top right, photo by author.

Curtain I was located between bastions A and B. Curtains I and V were the smallest curtains at Fort Montgomery, approximately ninety-one feet long from bastion to bastion. The curtain was thirty-one feet wide. The lower tier of Curtain I housed two kitchens, one "Sergeants room," two clothing storerooms, two other storerooms, and the entryway from the lake at the "water gate"[3] adjacent to bastion B. Four fireplaces heated these rooms.

The "water gate" was the "business entrance" to the fort. It was here, at one of only two exterior entrances to the fort, that the massive guns would have been brought in, together with all other ordnance and supplies. This entrance had a "gateway drawbridge" that swung vertically from one end, raised by chains. It was very different in design from the drawbridge at the postern in the gorge. The drawbridge was ten feet

---

[1] I have a rather humorous anecdote to share regarding these openings. During my presentations on the fort, I had occasionally been asked about the "secret passages." Supposedly these passages would allow someone entrance to the fort from the outside simply by swimming underwater under the scarp wall. I was puzzled and could provide no answer until I was sent a photo of the "passage." Sure enough, the "secret passage" was one of the open sewer drains under the latrine. They were "passages" all right, but they certainly were not designed for people.

Plans, Sections & Elevations of Gateway to Drawbridge on Front No. 1, July 27, 1857. These are the detailed drawings of the entrance to the pier at Curtain I, identified as the "Water Gate" on Drawer 7, Sheet 26. NARA, Records of the Chief of Engineers, Fortification File, Drawer 7, Sheet 47

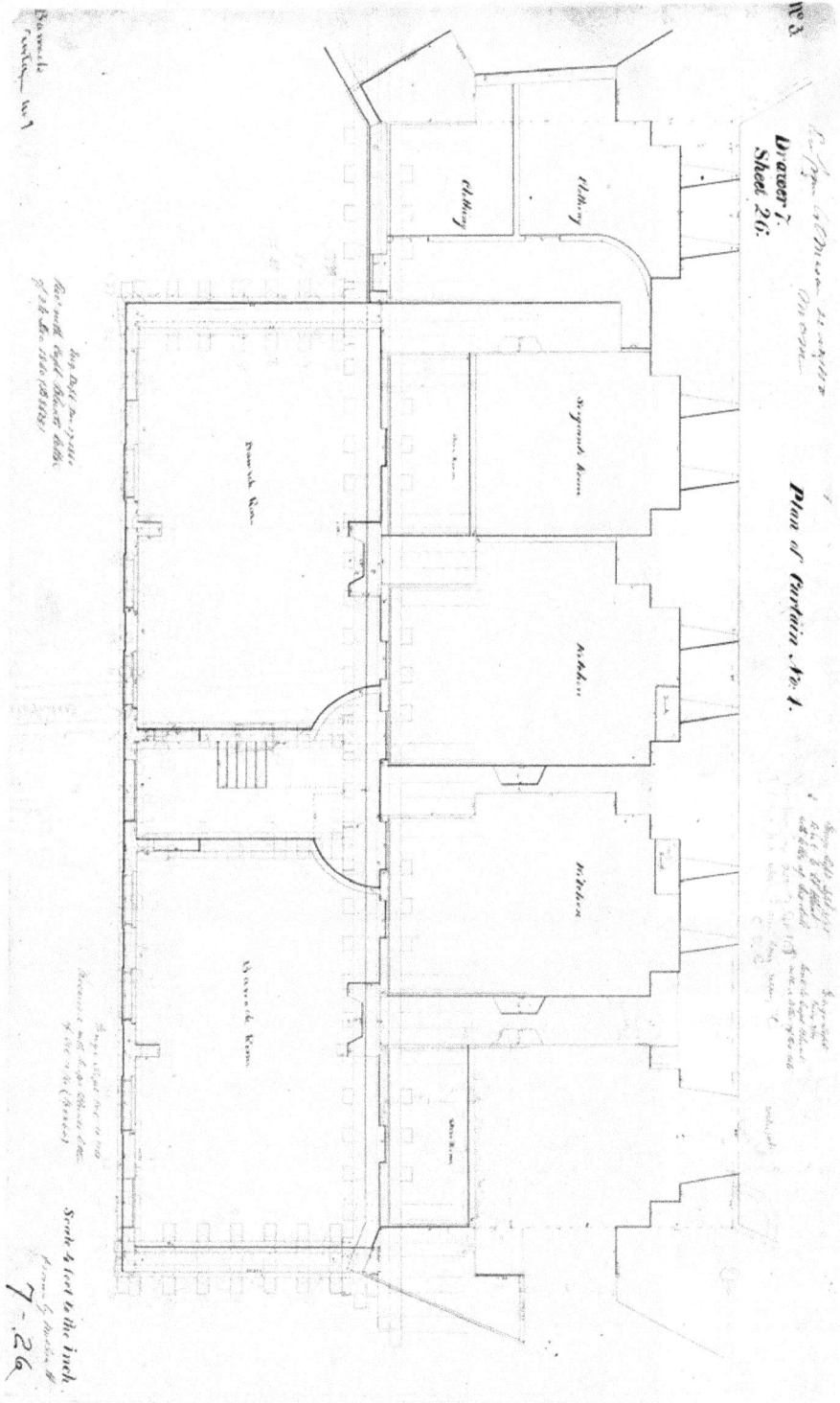

Plan of Curtain I, [Tier I]. This document, originally drawn in 1850 and utilized and annotated for years afterward, shows the planned function of rooms on the lower tier, the "water gate" at far right adjacent to Bastion B, and one of the Soldier's Barracks originally designed but never constructed. NA-RA: Records of the Chief of Engineers. Fortification File. Drawer 7. Sheet 26.

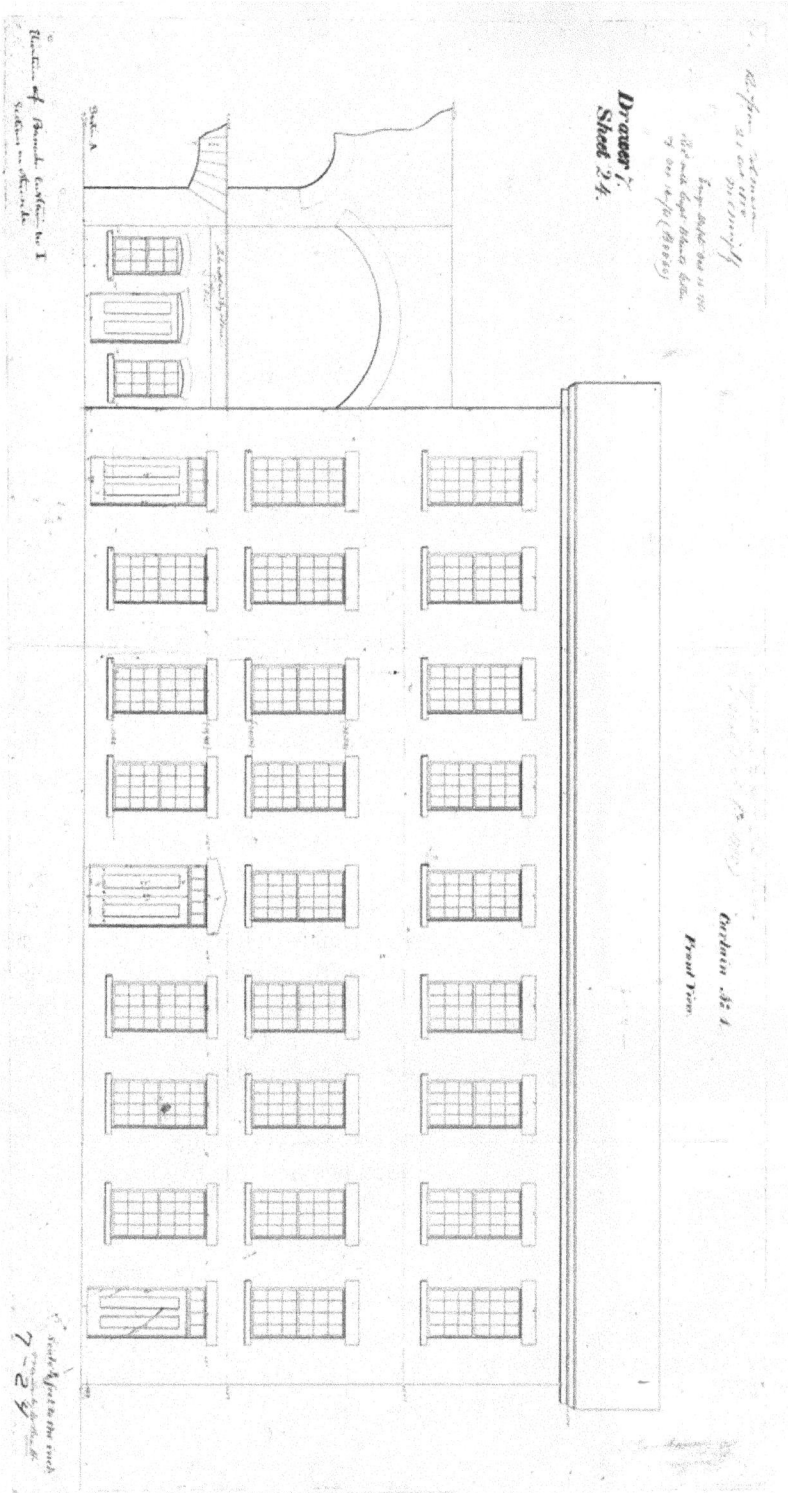

Elevation of Barracks, Curtain I, 1850. This drawing is of the smaller of two Soldier's Barracks originally planned for the fort. See the previous page for a plan of the structure. This building was never built but it does appear that construction was begun and halted. NARA: Records of the Chief of Engineers. Fortification File. Drawer 7. Sheet 24.

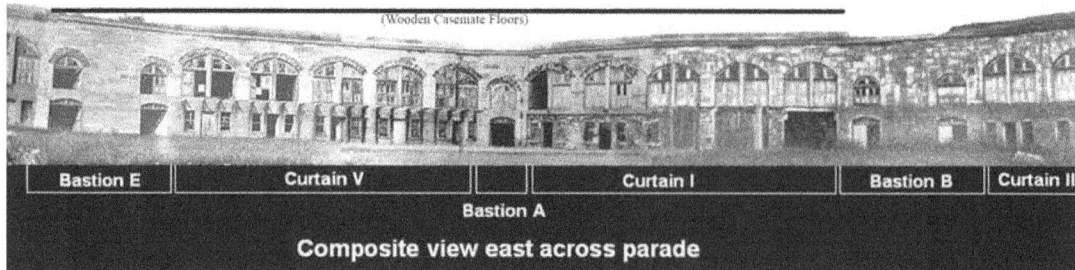

Composite view east across parade

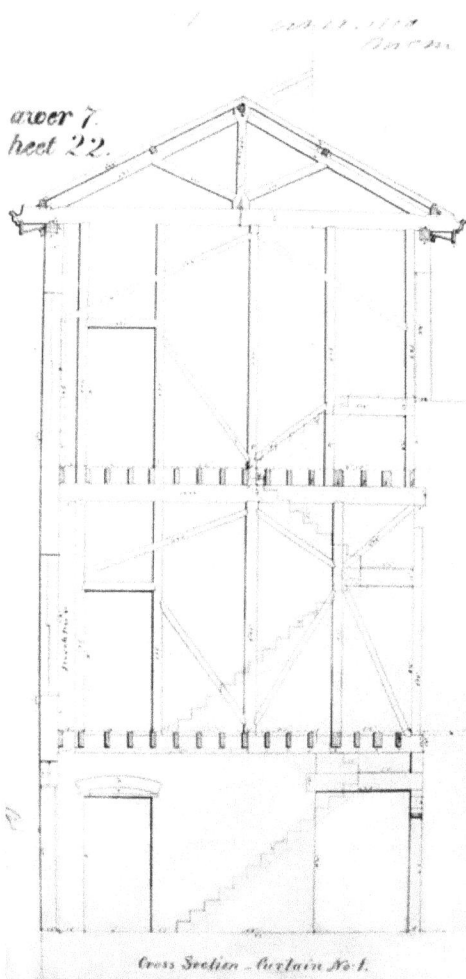

Barracks, Curtain No. I- Sections, 1850. This drawing shows a side view of the Soldier's Barracks featured on the previous pages. NARA, Drawer 7, Sheet 22

long and eight feet, four inches wide. Most of the length of the bridge extended out over the water to a long dock that went out beyond the curtain and wrapped around the left face of bastion B. The drawbridge was nine and a half inches thick, eight inches of pine, topped with another inch and a half of oak plank.[4] This entry point was a vulnerable location. Within the entry way was a second set of thick doors, sheathed in metal. When Curtain I was demolished in 1936, the walls were removed down to the level of the drawbridge. The two huge pillow blocks that seated the drawbridge axle are still in place. The dock was probably taken out by ice in the late 1920's. On sunny days the stumps of the pilings for the dock can still be seen from atop the barbette tier.

It was here, on this dock that William McComb, Thomas Bourke, and all the fort keepers in between would measure the water level of the lake from a "reference mark on the base of the scarp wall, at the north face of bastion B, about three feet from the angle with the east curtain [curtain I]."[5]

Tier II of Curtain I, referred to as the casemate tier, was designed to house five fore-pintle mounted guns. One 32-pounder was mounted here on a wooden carriage.[6] It was never replaced by a much heavier 8 or 10-inch Rodman since the plan to install masonry floors in Fronts I & V [includes Curtain I, Bastion A, and Curtain V] was never implemented.[7] The venerable old 32-pounder was on site for a long time. Mounted in 1862, it was not removed until 1900, long after it had become obsolete. No guns were ever mounted on the barbette tier of Curtain I.

Pillow blocks for the drawbridge axle: Curtain I. These massive blocks pinpoint the exact location of the drawbridge, They supported the large iron rod that was used to swing the drawbridge up and down. They can be seen at center-right in the drawing on page 12. Author photos.

Original plans called for a three-story soldier's barracks building to be constructed on the parade in front of Curtain I.[8] This building, the smaller of two planned for Fort Montgomery, would have been identical to barracks constructed within several other Third-System forts. Excellent examples of the structures, although two-storied rather than three, can be seen at Fort Clinch. It is likely that construction was begun on this building but halted early on. This would explain the lack of limestone facing on the lower tier parade wall, removal of doors, windows, etc. apparent in photographs.

Curtain I had the dubious distinction of being the first section of the fort demolished by the Weston crews in 1936. Just beyond the curtain on the parade the massive crusher was erected. Crushed limestone was fed directly into scows or barges brought directly against the truncated walls here.

Two-story Barracks building at Fort Clinch. The proposed Soldier's Barracks for Fort Montgomery would have been very similar to this with the notable exception of having a third story. Courtesy: Charles Barney.

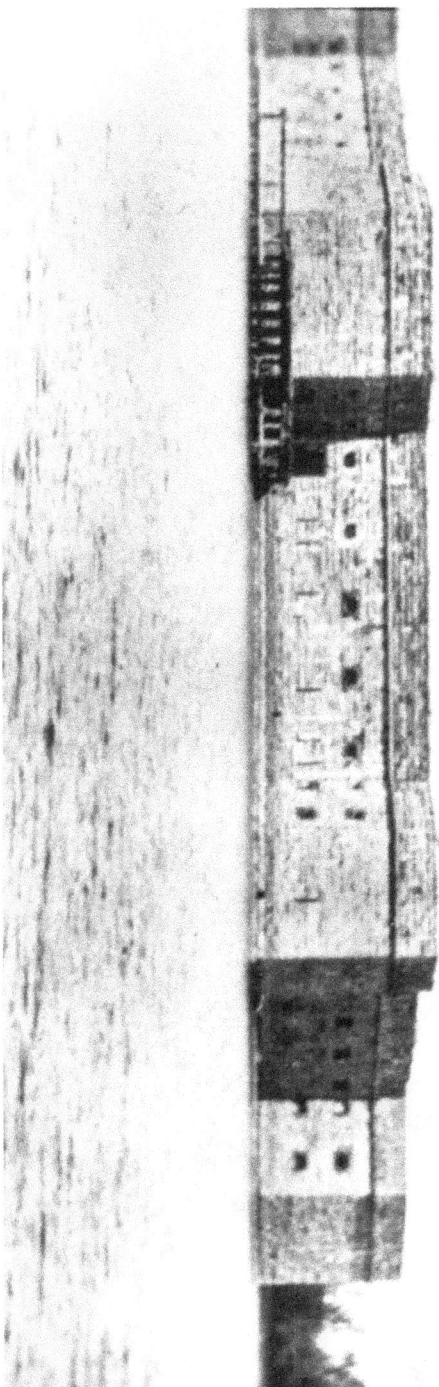

Fort Montgomery, view west from the lake. Courtesy Ray Seguin.

Two views of Fort Montgomery from the water. Top: view north from Lake Champlain, note the intact dock at Curtain I and Bastion B. Bottom: view south from the Richelieu River. This rare photograph clearly shows a row of Rodman guns atop the barbette tiers of Bastion D and Curtain IV. Courtesy: Clinton County Historical Association.

CHAPTER X

Bastion B and Curtain II

Bastion B was considerably larger than Bastion A. While it mounted eight 24-pounder flank howitzers like the smaller bastion to the north, it differed mainly in that it housed two large magazines and a spiral staircase. Bastion B was seventy-eight feet long from parade wall to tip of the south-east pointing salient. It measures about sixty-eight feet wide from shoulder to shoulder.

All eight 24-pounder flank howitzers planned for this bastion were mounted in the casemated flanks. The embrasures for these howitzers were of both types. The earliest ones, on tier I, were built of hardened brick while the second tier embrasures are of masonry reinforced with three iron bands.

The two magazines, one atop the other, tiers I and II, were five hundred, sixty square feet each.[1] Seeing the magazines today, it is hard to visualize what they actually looked like when in service. What appear as damp, massive stone caverns today were actually some of the best cared-for features of the fort. Fully lined with brick (now mostly removed) and then with wood, offset 6-8 inches from the wall, the space was vented by low chimneys to the parapet. Much effort was expended to keep the magazines dry at all times. Wooden pegs were used instead of nails and the doors were heavy wood, probably oak. They were secured from the outside by bronze or brass hinges.

Access to the magazines, casemates and barbette tier was from a round, spiral staircase accessed through two sets of double doors on the parade. The staircase was protected from the elements by a wooden structure with a peaked roof. Measuring some fifteen by fifteen feet square and just over six feet high, the top of these structures actually rose some five inches above the forty-eight foot scarp walls. They were equipped with windows to illuminate the dark stairs and doors to the barbette tier. These wooden structures were removed early on and are featured in the earliest photos of the fort.

The barbette tier of Bastion B was designed to mount four guns. Two of them had fore-pintle mounts while the other two, closest to the outside, were center-pintle mounts. Only the left flank or east side of Bastion B's barbette tier was to mount guns. The right flank, facing southwest toward the cover face consisted of an earthen bank or parapet. One gun was mounted on the barbette tier of Bastion B, an 8-inch fore-pintle mounted Rodman.[2] The gun faced west across the earthen parapet. The two center-pintle mounts were never completely

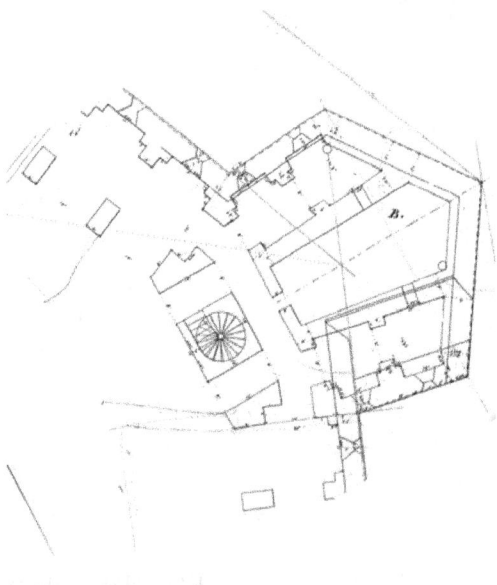

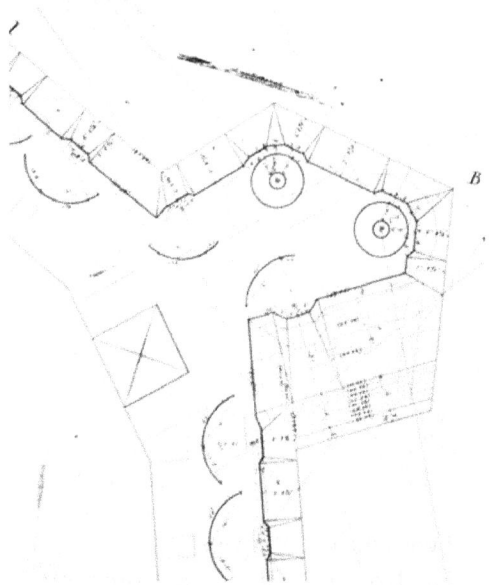

Above left: Bastion B, tier II. This drawing shows the casemates for the flank howitzers, powder magazine and the spiral staircase. Above right: Bastion B, barbette tier. Showing the two center-pintle, two fore-pintle mounts and the earthen embankment on the southwest flank. Details from NARA, Drawer 7, sheets 31 and 56, 1850, 1861.

finished, their high traverse stones were laid but they never received their pintles. The second fore-pintle mount was later used, probably by Elisha Goodsell, as the site for a flagpole. This flagpole, featured in many photos in this book, including the one with Charles Fitch "sitting" atop it, was put up sometime in the 1920's and was not erected by the Army. It was still standing as the fort was being demolished in 1936-37 and the base of it can still be located in the pintle hole for that mount.

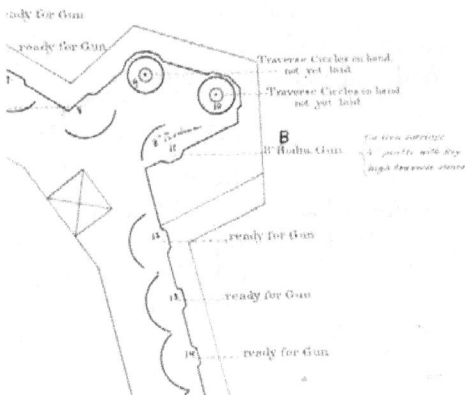

Bastion B has a unique feature on its left face. About half way up, located close to the middle of the face of the bastion the careful observer will notice an upside down "face" carved into a limestone block. Undoubtedly carved into the block by one of the stone cutters it can be called graffiti. Yet, knowing this particular marking was almost certainly cut into the stone by one of the many craftsmen who toiled daily at the fort makes it special and certainly worth looking for if you have the good fortune to be near the fort by boat.

Above: Detail from "Plan of Barbette tier…showing the present armament, February 1st 1872" showing an 8-inch Rodman was mounted here. NARA, Drawer 259, sheet 95.

Above: Charles Fitch "flagpole sitting" atop Bastion B in 1933. This flagpole was probably erected by Elisha Goodsell in the 1920's when he attempted to use the fort as a campground. Courtesy: Charles Barney

Bastion B is about two-thirds intact. Serious demolition started just to the north of it when Curtain I was removed. The parade wall, staircase and part of the left flank of the bastion were demolished.

Curtain II, one hundred twenty-eight feet long and thirty-one feet wide, was designed to mount seven guns *en casemate* and another seven *en barbette*. No guns were mounted on the barbette tier but three were mounted on tier II. Within the casemates of Curtain II's second tier up until 1903 could be found two 10-inch Rodman smoothbores on iron carriages and an ancient 32-pounder on a wooden carriage. Tier I was like the rest of the curtains at Fort Montgomery, there were no guns. Instead the lower tier consisted of three kitchens, three "Sergeant's rooms," three rooms designated for clothing storage and three other storerooms. These rooms were heated by only six fireplaces. The scarp wall was punctuated by 14 south-facing windows with loopholes.

Like Curtain I, Curtain II was originally supposed to have an adjoining soldier's barracks building at the parade. Identical to the one planned for Curtain I but longer, construction on this building was never begun.

Curtain II, visible from the Rouses Point Bridge between Bastions B and C, is the only curtain that still retains its exterior, or scarp wall. Unfortunately, it looks much more intact from the outside than it is. The scarp wall is largely supporting itself, especially at the top since there is very little remaining behind it. The entire second tier was scraped away by the demolition crews. Tier I is but a shell of what it was. The parade wall was pulled away, the interior rooms gutted. Huge quantities of brick and all traces of wood were removed. Most of the brick in the back to back fireplaces was taken out, leaving large openings between casemated rooms that were not there pre-demolition. It is possible to walk from one end of the Curtain to the other inside through these openings, something that would not have been possible when each casemate consisted of individual rooms divided by walls.

Top: Bastion B powder magazine, tier II. Bottom: Same magazine showing tier I. Note the floor joists and the hole in the floor. Some small strips of wood still cling to the walls. This magazine is very difficult to access due to the demolition work in 1936-37. Author photo.

Top: "The Face," Bastion B. Courtesy: Roger Harwood. Bottom: Intact pintle still attached to part of metal frame from flank howitzer carriage, Bastion B. Author photo.

Top: Bastion B as seen from the lake. Bottom: Bastion B from the parade. The parade wall is gone as is the stairway but the magazines remain as do significant portions of the flank howitzer casemates. Author photos

Top: Curtain II, second tier casemates looking west toward Bastion C. Courtesy: Clinton County Historical Association. Bottom: Curtain II as it looks today. The entire row of casemates seen above has been demolished, leaving only the scarp wall standing. Author photo.

Top: View west along scarp wall of Curtain II toward Bastion C. Bottom: The interior of the same scarp wall, view east. When viewed from the south it is not obvious that the casemates of Tier II are gone and the scarp wall is holding itself up with nothing behind it. Author photos.

Above: View of Tier II casemates just prior to demolition. The wooden doors, window frames and glass have all been removed. Courtesy: Clinton County Historical Association.

Left: The same view today. Note how the entire second tier of casemates has been removed as has all the limestone on the parade wall of tier I exposing the massive brick arches. Author photo.

Two views of a casemate, Curtain II, tier I. This room was designated for use as a kitchen or Sergeant's Room. All traces of the interior finish work- wood, plaster, etc.were removed long ago. Author photos

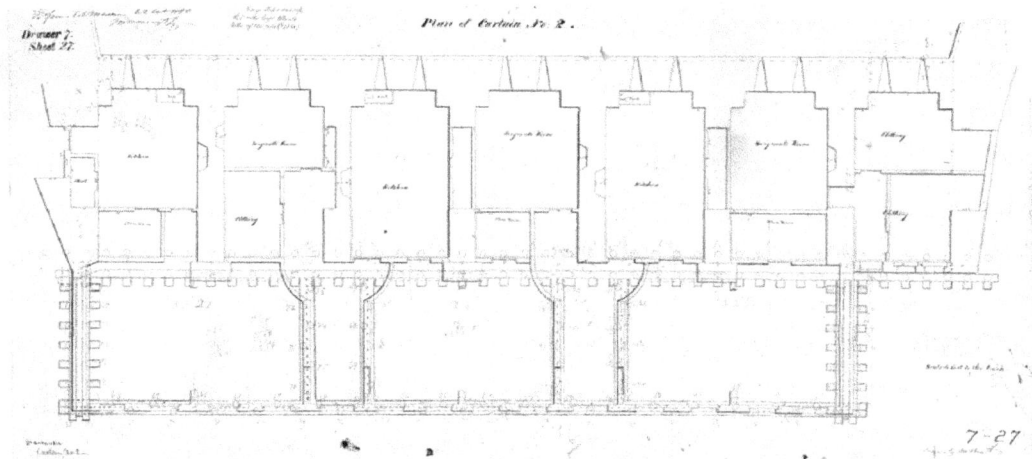

Top: Plan of Barracks Curtain II, Tier I, 1850. This plan clearly shows the large soldier's barracks originally planned. This structure would have been much the same as the one planned for Curtain I but larger. The plan also shows the intended functions of the interior casemated rooms on tier I. NARA: Records of the Chief of Engineers, Fortification file, Drawer 7, Sheet 27.

Bottom: Detail of one of the earliest photos found to date of Curtain II. Had the barracks been built the structure would have taken up most of the open area seen below. The roof of the three-story structure would have actually risen above the level of the barbette tier. From a glass negative, this photo is believed to have been taken by Sergt. Thomas Bourke. Courtesy: Powertex, Inc.

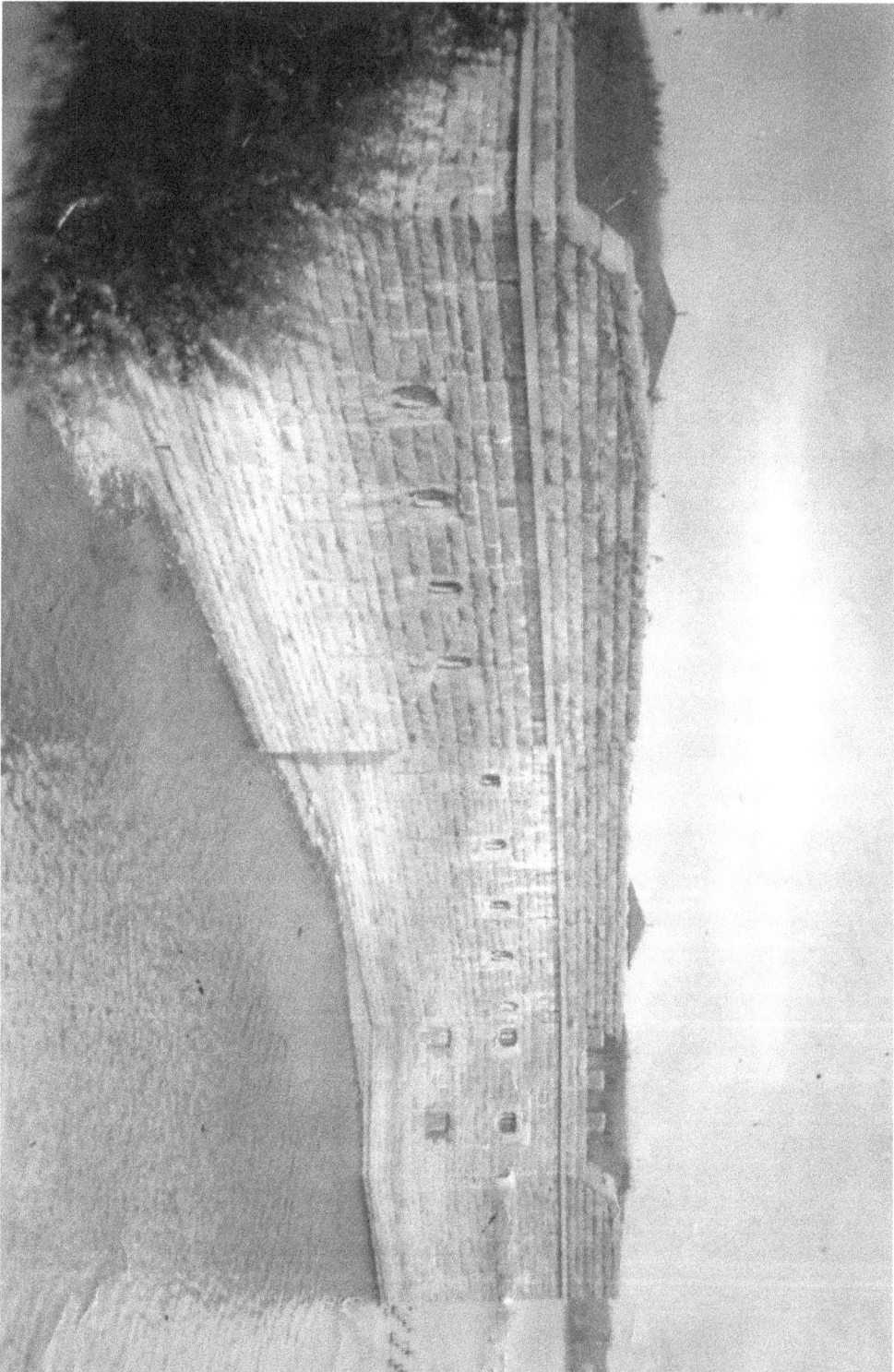

South face from the cover face. Courtesy of Ben Arno.

CHAPTER XI

Bastion C and Curtain III, the Gorge

Bastions C and D are the two largest bastions at Fort Montgomery. Situated at the southwest and northwestern corners of the fort adjacent to the moat and forming part of the Gorge, they are large enough to mount both heavy "seacoast" guns and flank howitzers.

Bastion C comprised the southwestern "corner" of the fort, linking Curtains II and III, the Gorge officer's quarters. It was designed to mount seventeen guns. The lowest level, tier I was to mount four 24-pounder flank howitzers. All were mounted during the Civil War and remained on site until 1902. Tier II, referred to as the casemate tier on fort plans, was designed for another four 24-pounder flank howitzers plus four heavy "seacoast" guns. Tier II of this bastion did not receive any of these big guns but the four flank howitzers were mounted until they were removed in 1900 and 1901. Tier III, the barbette tier, was supposed to mount another five guns, four were to be fore-pintle mounted guns and another was to have a circular, center pintle-mount. Only two of the fore-pintle mounts were ever finished, another was begun but not completed and one fore-pintle mount and the center-pintle mount were "not commenced." There were no guns mounted on the barbette tier of Bastion C.

Like bastions B, D, and E, Bastion C was the site of two large magazines, one atop the other, tiers I and II. Each was five hundred, fifteen square feet in size. The magazines and the rest of tiers I, II and III could be accessed from the parade by another round, spiral staircase very similar to the one previously described for Bastion B. A unique feature of Bastion B was the garrison ovens and bakery located deep within the lower tier. The ovens are still there, although, like most of the easily accessible brick features in the fort, much of the brick has been removed, including the entire front area where the narrow oven doors were located. These massive ovens probably never held a fire.

Bastion C is the best preserved part of Fort Montgomery. The beautiful stone staircase is gone, as are many of the floor stones on tiers I and II. The bakery was wrecked long ago and the second tier magazine, like all of the magazines within the ruins has long since lost its floor, all wood and most of the brick. The two magazines now appear as one enormous, and very dark, cavern. It is not surprising that locals sometimes referred to the magazines as "dungeons."

Despite this damage and the ever present scourge of graffiti, Bastion C still looks much like it did a hundred years ago. A visitor to Bastion C can easily get a sense of what this grand old fort was like in its prime.

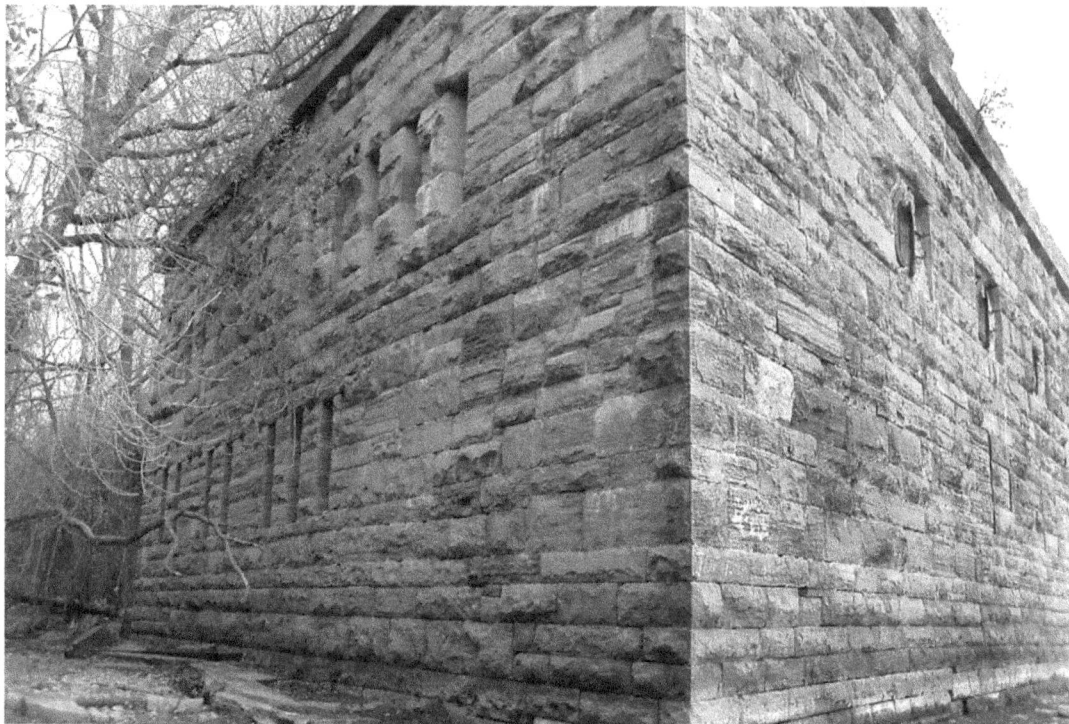

Exterior views of Bastion C. Top: View northeast from within the moat/wet ditch. The area in the foreground has no loopholes since the ovens are located there. Bottom: View southeast from within the moat/wet ditch. Note the locations of the iron reinforcing rods. Author photos.

Two views of Tier II, Bastion C. The top photo looks north and shows a flank howitzer embrasure that protected the drawbridge and postern. The bottom photo was taken in the opposite direction. Both photos clearly show the cut iron reinforcing rods just above the loopholes. Author photos.

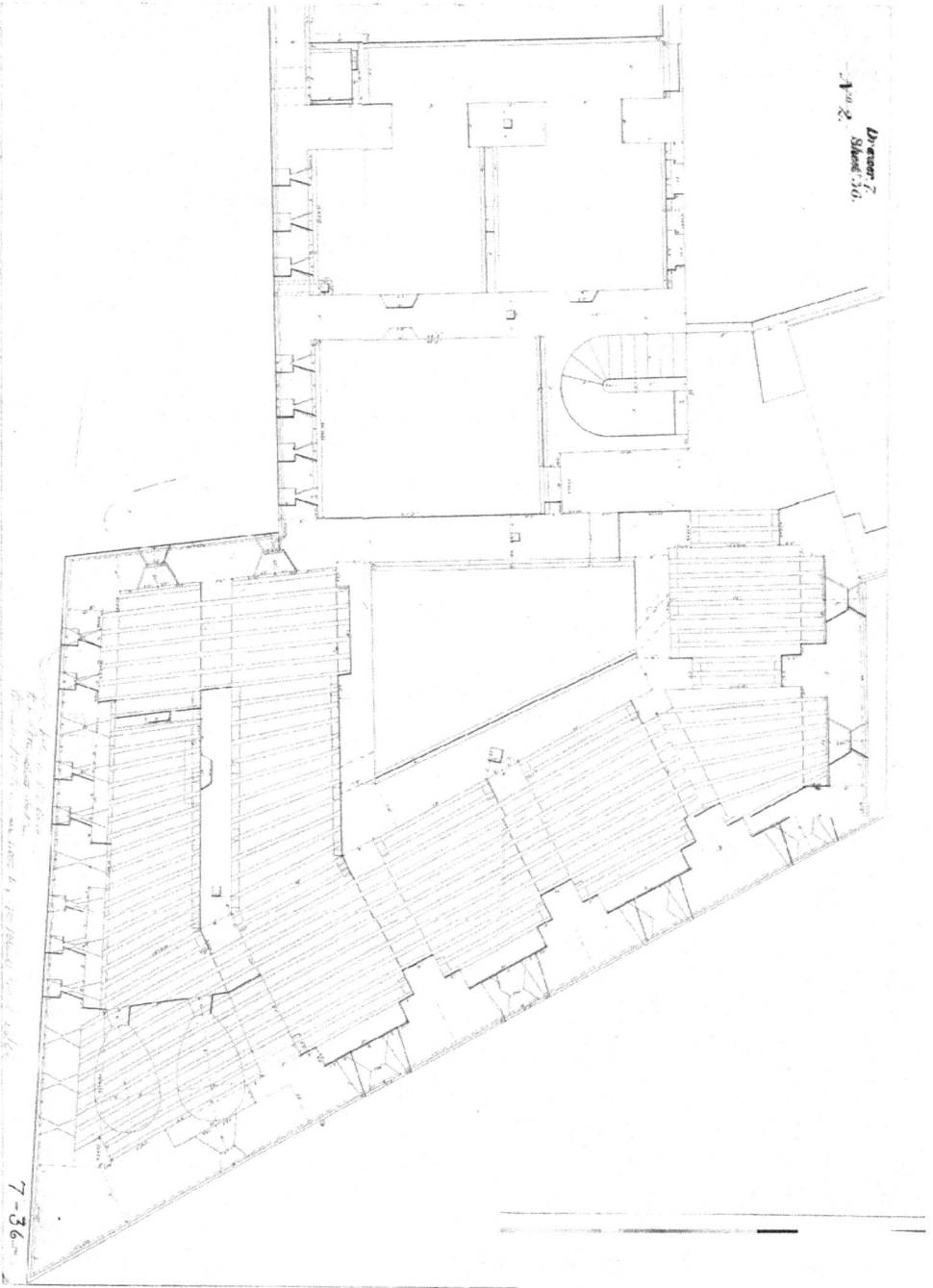

This "Enlarged Plan of Bastion C" is interesting in that both Tiers I and II are shown, superimposed over each other. Three types of embrasures are shown as are the ovens on Tier I. Note also the magazine and the stairway from the parade to levels I, II and the barbette tier. NARA: Records of the Chief of Engineers, Drawer 7, Sheet 36, undated, probably 1850.

Bastion B, tier II, view north. Bastion B is the best preserved part of Fort Montgomery. Author photo.

As the most intact part of the ruins, Bastion C is worthy of particular attention. It is also the part of the fort that this writer is most concerned about. The scarp wall continues to separate from the rest of the structure, something that that has plagued the fort since the 1870's. Visitors to the bastion can easily see what is left of the iron reinforcing rods that were put in place to stop this separation, cut, probably for scrap, during the 1940's. The scarp of Bastion D to the north held itself up until the spring of 1980 when it finally succumbed to the enormous pressures successive North Country freezes and thaws. If this is allowed to happen to Bastion C, what is left intact of Fort Montgomery will be gone forever.

Curtain III, the land front, made up most of what was referred to in Third-system nomenclature as the "Gorge." The longest curtain of the fort, it extended some three hundred twenty-eight feet in length between Bastions C and D. At forty-eight feet wide, it was also considerably wider than the other curtains.

Southeast view of Bastion C, tier II. Tier II was designed to mount heavy "seacoast" guns in addition to flank howitzers. This section of the fort is also among the most difficult to get to today although that is not obvious from the amount of graffiti present. Author photo.

There were many features about Curtain III that made it unique. It was the only part of the fort in which both tiers I and II were made up completely of finished rooms, not gun casemates. Constructed as the Officer's Quarters, there were forty-one individual rooms within the curtain. Most measured eighteen by twenty feet. There were four larger rooms at both ends of the curtain, nineteen by twenty-six feet each. Adjacent to the spiral staircases and magazines, these rooms may have been the armories, used for small arms storage. The rooms were heated by fireplaces and coal stoves. These fireplaces and coal stove enclosures were built within the enormous arches that were well concealed within the curtain. Access to the individual quarters was through a door and hallway to the parade. At the scarp end of the hallway a wooden stairway provided access to the second tier of rooms. There was a second story pass-through above the postern but otherwise access to individual rooms was from the parade only. The builders utilized the open space between the arches as closet space for adjoining quarters. Each of the Officer's quarters was equipped with a privy that drained into the moat. It was located at the west side of the room.

The scarp wall, on both tiers I and II, facing the moat and cover face, was broken by a large number of windows with loopholes to fire from in the event of an attack. Since the Gorge faced the moat or wet ditch and massive earthen cover face, only the barbette tier of

Top left: Bastion C, Tier I, view west toward ovens. Beyond is the wet ditch and cover face. Top right: Approximately the same location within Bastion C but on Tier II. Author photos.

Garrison ovens at Fort Clinch. This photo gives an idea of what the ovens deep within Tier I of Bastion C would have looked like before they were largely demolished. Beyond the narrow oven doors and the brick wall are the huge balloon-shaped ovens similar to those from Fort Montgomery on the following page. Courtesy: Charles Barney

Above: Two views of the ovens within Bastion C, Tier I. At left is the view west and at right is the view east. Author photos.

Left: View of opening to small oven seen at lower left in photo above. Courtesy: Roger Harwood. Below right: The ovens, view southwest. Author photo.

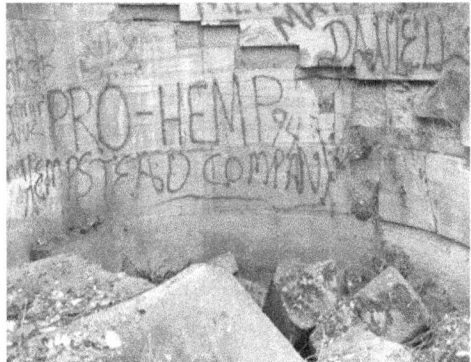

Clockwise from top left: A group of local women sitting atop the Bastion C staircase. The protective wooden structures that topped the stairways were long gone by the time this photo was taken in the 1930's. Courtesy: Charles Barney. The location of the staircase at Bastion C and Curtain III. Remains of the staircase. Author photos.

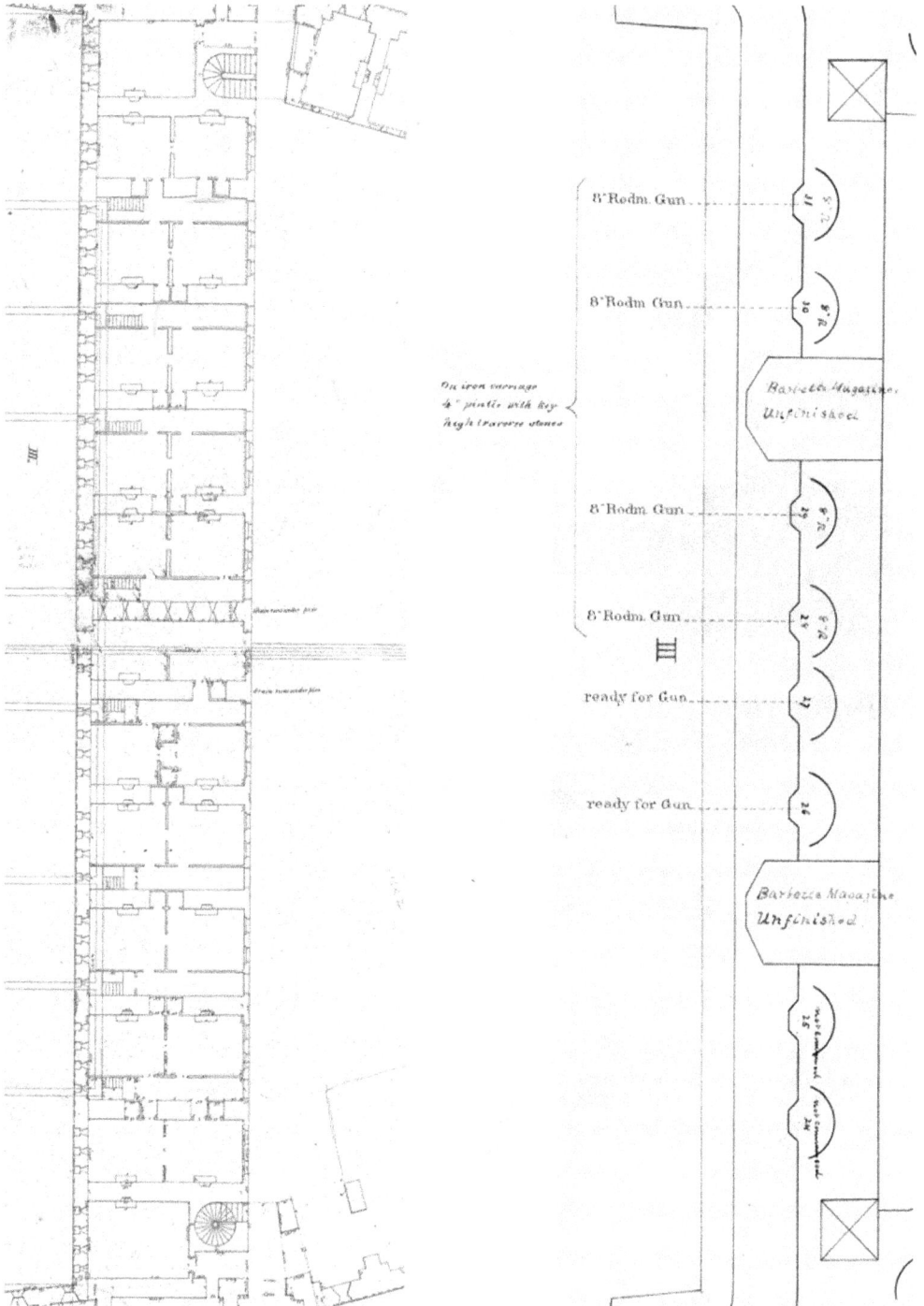

8" Rodm. Gun

8" Rodm. Gun

Barbette Magazine.
Unfinished

8" Rodm. Gun

8" Rodm. Gun

On iron carriage
4" pintle with key
high traverse stones

ready for Gun

ready for Gun

Barbette Magazine
Unfinished

Plans of Curtain III, the Gorge Officer's Quarters. Top: The barbette tier, showing guns mounted and the unfinished service magazines. NARA: Drawer 259, Sheet 95, 1872. Bottom: Plan of the interior showing both levels I and II. In this drawing tier I is at left and tier II at the right. NARA, Drawer 7, Sheet 31, undated, probably 1850.

51.

Curtain III was designed to mount heavy guns. Early plans called for ten fore-pintle mounted guns on the barbette tier[1] but this was modified by 1862 when two service magazines were designed necessitating the removal of two gun platforms. These service magazines were never completely finished.

As the land front, Curtain III also was the site of the main entryway to the fort. The postern was located here, accessed by a stationary bridge across the moat from the cover face through a drawbridge.

The postern was sixteen feet wide and, since it was the passage through

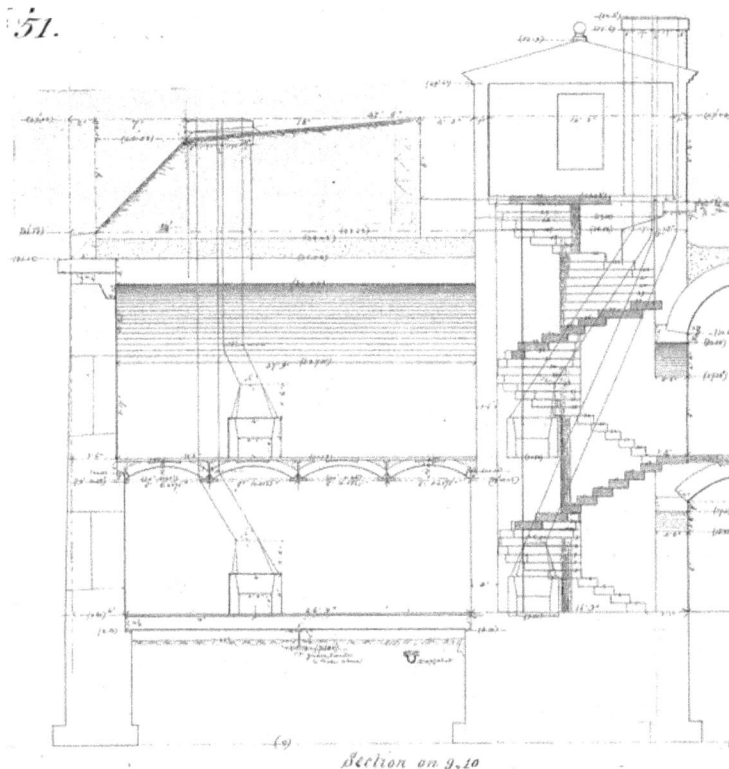

Detail of NARA, Drawer 7, Sheet 51- Sections & Details of Casemates in the Gorge, 1857.

the Curtain, ran the full forty-eight feet from scarp to parade. It narrowed in three places; at the scarp (to nine feet), at the first inner door where the twenty foot long drawbridge was drawn up by chains, to nine feet, and, at the parade, where a second set of doors are supposed to have opened outward (this is uncertain, photographic evidence seems to show these doors opened to the parade). The postern here narrowed to ten feet. The floor of the postern descended from the drawbridge at a five degree angle to the parade. The two "great doors" were made of heavy oak. Each side of the passageway was lined with loopholes or rifle slits. Any invader who gained entrance to the postern would face a withering fire at point-blank range from both sides of the passage. An interesting fact about these loopholes on each side of the postern is that they were placed directly opposite each other, seemingly not the optimal position for firing should they actually have to be used!

The drawbridge itself was quite different from the "water gate" located in Curtain I. Twenty feet, eight inches long and nine feet wide, the massive pine and oak drawbridge was a huge door that swung vertically on an axle. When raised (its default position), it was posi-

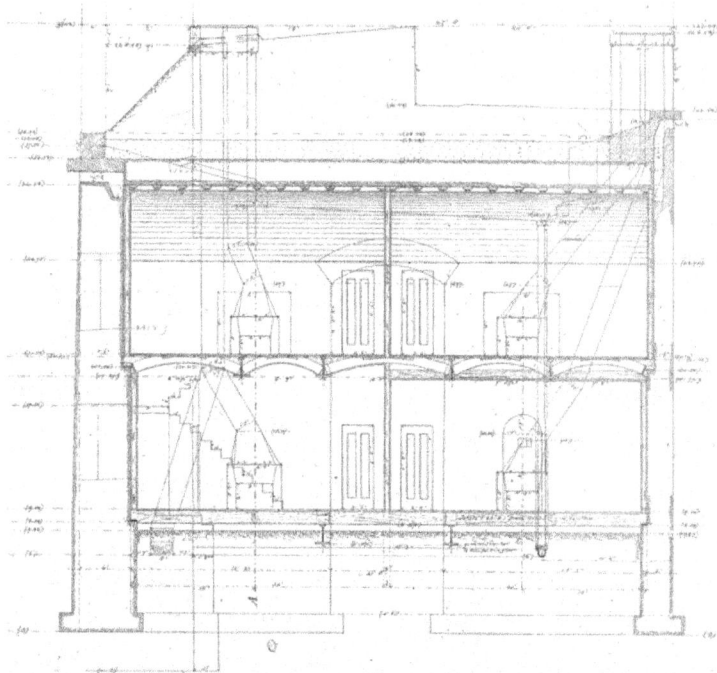

Section en 5, 6

Detail of NARA, Drawer 7, Sheet 52, 1857- Sections & Details of Casemates in the Gorge, 1857. Of particular interest here is the way the large interior arches were utilized as closet space for the Officer's Quarters, note the closet doors in center of drawing.

tioned inside the scarp wall. Of its massive length, only nine feet actually extended over the moat to meet the stationary bridge. The other eleven feet pivoted inside the postern into a twelve foot deep pit just inside. The drawbridge was nine and a half inches thick, eight inch pine topped with an inch and a half of oak. In later years the drawbridge was lowered and the opening for it was tightly framed in wood with narrow doorways that were also boarded up.

The Gorge Officer's Quarters within Curtain III did not fare well at the hands of the Weston Company demolition crews. Looking at it today, it is hard to visualize how it looked prior to the arrival of the wrecking crews. Where once were located finely finished rooms with plastered walls, windows and doors with glass and wooden frames, attractive fireplaces with custom mantles, and high ceilings with elaborate ornamentation now stand but the massive stone arches once concealed deep within the structure. Huge quantities of brick have been removed as has all of the wood except for lathe far above on what was the second tier arched ceilings. Chunks of original plaster cling to it to this day and the careful observer can note what is left of ceiling ornamentation where once hung oil lamps.

The finely finished limestone that comprised the parade wall was an easy mark for the Weston crews and every piece of it was thrown into the maw of the crusher. Despite being adjacent to the water of the moat, the scarp did not escape their attention either. Except for small segments at the north and south ends of the Curtain all was pulled down. Even these small sections were torn asunder, only the lower part of the wall remains. A walk through the gorge can be disorienting, only after studying the detailed plans can one get a real sense of how this part of the fort really looked. While the demolition crews were not willing to tackle the enormous stone arches built so well to support the massive guns on the barbette tier above, they did not hesitate to pull down even the second story floors. Only the second floor fireplaces open to nothingness and an occasional floor joist betray where the floor was located.

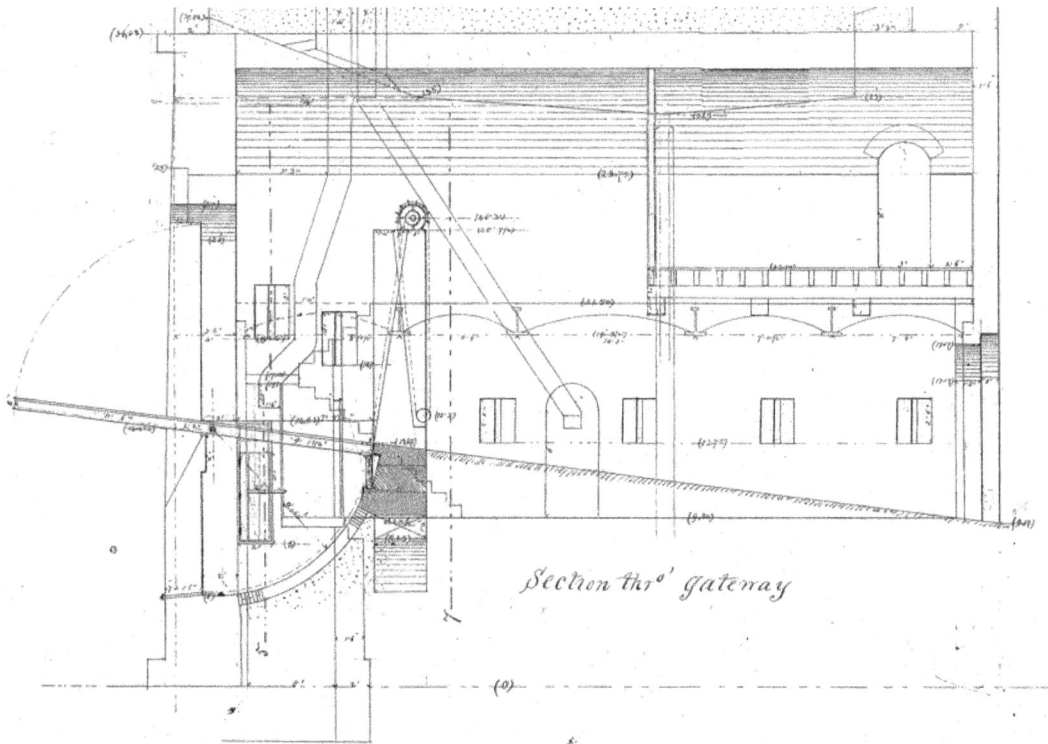

Section thro' gateway

Details of NARA, Drawer 7, Sheet 49- Plans, Elev. Sections of Postern and drawbridge in the Gorge, 1857. Of interest in the drawing at top are the drawbridge, showing how it rotates into the open/closed position, the loopholes lining each side of the postern, and the way the postern gently slopes onto the parade. Note also the pass-through for Tier II.

Left: This view of the front of the Gorge provides a good view of the massive interior arches and how the drawbridge receded into a pit in the postern when closed.

Section on 5. 6'

Details of Drawbridge in the Gorge. NARA, Drawer 7, Sheet 48, 1858. A close study of this plan will explain the operation of the main drawbridge at the gorge/postern entrance to Fort Montgomery.

The Gorge Officer's Quarters, Curtain III, circa 1920: Top, view from barbette tier of Bastion A, Bottom. View from the parade. Courtesy: Ben Arno.

Two views of the Gorge Officer's Quarters, Curtain III, from the parade. Top: This photo circa 1920 shows Curtain III largely intact. Glass remains in the windows and many doors are in place. The photo below, taken in 2004, dramatically illustrates the devastation wrought by the Weston crews to this section of the fort. Top: courtesy Ben Arrno. Bottom: author photo.

The drawbridge and stationary bridge over the wet ditch/moat. Top: This wonderful photo, believed taken by Fort Keeper Thomas Bourke, shows the gorge, bridges and cover face from the barbette tier of Bastion D. At left is a detail view of the actual drawbridge. Bottom: A very early photo, also from Bourke, showing the bridge before the addition of handrails. This bridge, probably the first of three constructed here, was evidently never intended for use by anything other than pedestrian traffic. Courtesy: Elizabeth Clark and Powertex, Inc.

Closeup photos of people on the bridge from the cover face to the postern. Clockwise from top left: Three boys playing on the bridge, postern boarded up. Author collection courtesy of Tia Hollowood. Young man on the bridge with postern open and drawbridge down. Closeup of same man. This photo provides a rare glance inside the postern and a look at the actual oak boards of the drawbridge. Courtesy: Charles Barney. Young couple on the bridge. Author collection, courtesy of Raymond Seguin.

Nothing is known about this group of well-dressed people standing on the bridge. The postern is tightly boarded up in this photo, photos of it open are very rare. Courtesy of Raymond Seguin.

FORT MONTGOMERY,   ROUSES POINT. N Y

Vintage postcard views of Fort Montgomery. Top: View from cover face south, showing early bridge with no side rails. Bottom: Later view looking northeast from cover face. This view shows the modified bridge reinforced with large piles driven into the wet ditch. Courtesy of Ben Arno.

Fort Montgomery, Rouses Point, N. Y.

CHAPTER XII

Bastions D-E and Curtains IV -V

Bastion D was the mirror image of Bastion C to the south beyond Curtain III. The primary differences were that Bastion C had the bakery and ovens while Bastion D's casemates were for guns only and that Bastion D had slightly smaller magazines, four hundred fifty six square feet. Another difference was in the staircase. While Bastions B and C's spiral staircases were round, Bastion D (and E) had stairs positioned in a semi-circle. Like the large bastion to the south, Bastion D was left largely untouched by the Weston crews. Unfortunately, that did not prevent it from considerable damage at the hand of man and nature.

Located at the northwestern "corner" of Fort Montgomery, Bastion D was largely completed by 1857. Stone from both Kings Bay in New York and Fisk Quarry in Vermont was used. Vintage photos of the exterior clearly show the lighter New York stone at the lower levels of the scarp.

Like Bastion C, this bastion was designed to mount seventeen guns. Four 24-pounder flank howitzers on tier I, another four on tier II, and four "seacoast" guns mounted *en casemate* pointed north on the second tier. The barbette tier was to mount five guns, four fore-pintle mounted and another on a center-pintle mount. All eight flank howitzers were mounted but it is likely that one of them was removed or repositioned early on since one of the flank howitzer embrasures was bricked up sometime after 1872, due, probably, to an error in construction (see pages 43-44). Two "big" guns were also mounted on the "casemate

Bastion D viewed from the cover face. This bastion collapsed into the moat in April 1980. Author collection courtesy of Tia Hollowood.

tier", a 32-pounder on a wooden carriage and a 10-inch Rodman on an iron carriage. All four of the fore-pintle mounts on Bastion D's barbette tier had 10-inch Rodman's mounted. Bastion D was the most heavily armed bastion at Fort Montgomery. As mentioned earlier, despite being left largely undamaged by the demolition crews in 1936/37, Bastion D is now mostly in a state of complete ruin. The Weston people did not cut the iron reinforcing rods placed in the 1870's to secure the separating scarp wall. Unfortunately, they did not miss the attention of someone else later on.

Two views of north-facing Front IV consisting of Bastions D, Curtain IV and Bastion E. This is the only front of Fort Montgomery to receive almost its full complement of armament. It is also the part of the fort where demolition was most extensive. Top photo courtesy Clinton County Historical Association, Bottom, author collection, courtesy of Tia Hollowood.

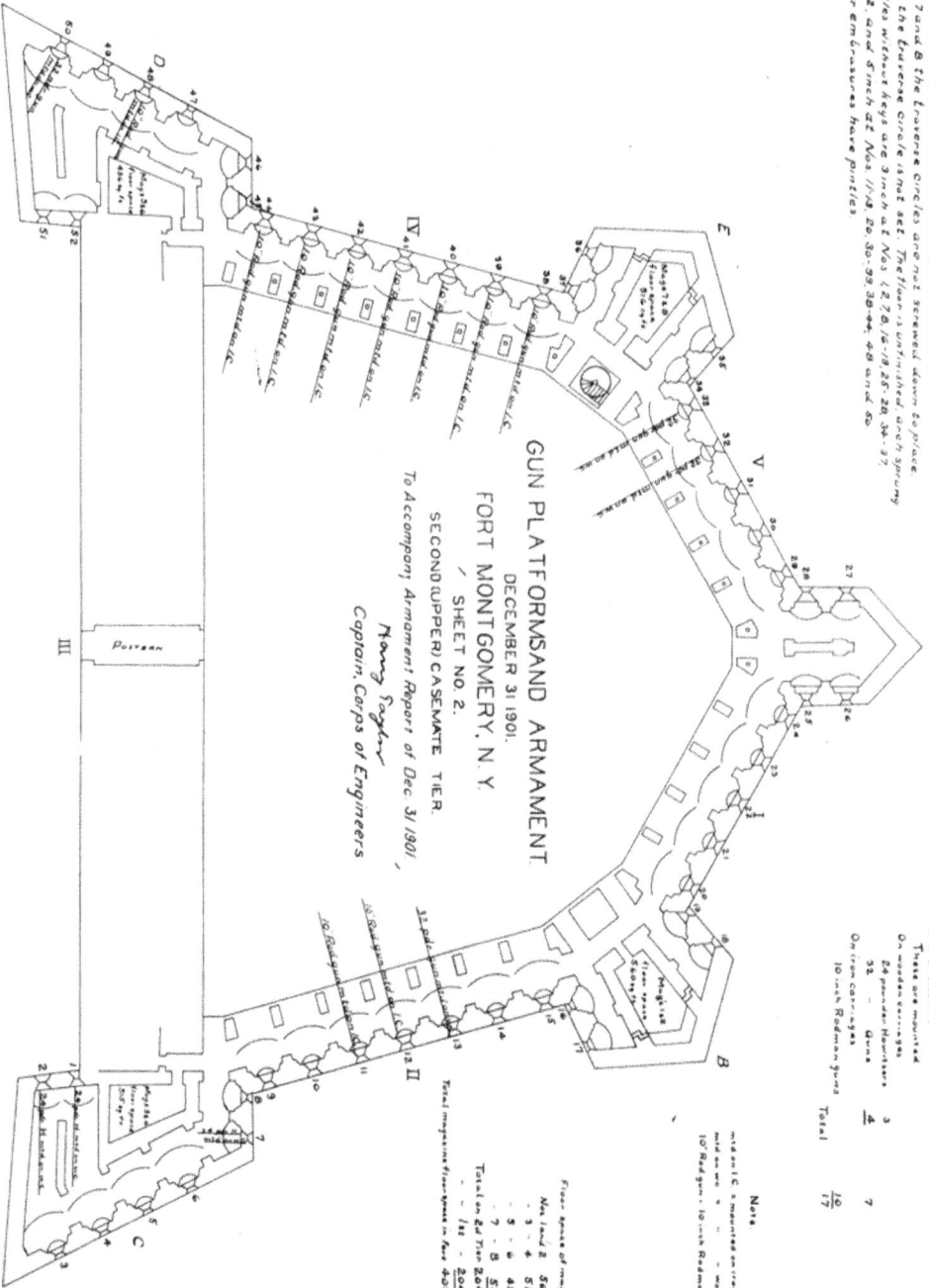

GUN PLATFORMS AND ARMAMENT
FORT MONTGOMERY, N.Y.
DECEMBER 31 1901.
SHEET NO. 2.
SECOND (UPPER) CASEMATE TIER.
To Accompany Armament Report of Dec. 31 1901,
Henry Taylor
Captain, Corps of Engineers

Platforms

Guns

Note

Sheet No. 2 Second (Upper) Casemate Tier to accompany Armament Report of Dec. 31, 1901. NARA: Drawer 246, Sheet 32-37, 1901. Note that most of the "seacoast" guns are still mounted at this late date but most of the 24-pounder flank howitzers have been removed.

Plan of Barbette Tier Fort Montgomery showing the present armament, February 1st 1872. NARA: Drawer 259, Sheet 95

Above: These two photos may look virtually identical but they are actually images of Tier II on Bastions C and D. The two bastions, nearly mirror-images of each other, have suffered dramatically different fates so far. The recent photo at top left shows Bastion C, the best preserved part of the fort. The image on the right shows Bastion D. This bastion collapsed into the moat in April 1980. Note the cut reinforcing rods that this writer believed contributed to the collapse. Left photo by the author. Right photo, author collection courtesy of Raymond Seguin.

Below: Bastion C as it appeared in May, 2004. The photo at bottom left shows the two flank howitzer embrasures facing south into the wet ditch/moat. The embrasure at right in the photo is the one shown above at top right. The photo at bottom right taken from within the moat looking north, shows the scarp wall and an embrasure for a casemate that used to house a 10-inch Rodman gun. This collapse is especially frustrating since the bastion was left undamaged by the Weston crews in 1936-37.

The semi-circular Bastion D staircase. Unlike the staircase at Bastion C, there are no stair steps remaining here. The pedestal that they rested on remains intact. Photos by the author.

It is this writer's belief that the rods were cut during the 1940's probably for scrap iron. This effectively sealed the fate of the western-facing scarp. It held itself up until April, 1980 when the scarp pan caked into the moat. This would have been bad enough. Unfortunately, despite being separate from the scarp, several of the arches came down too, taking down the entire bastion west of the magazine. The large magazine is still accessible but the rest of the bastion is in dreadful condition.

Curtain IV was the only part of Fort Montgomery to ever receive its full complement of guns. The north-facing mirror image of Curtain II, this long stretch of casemates between Bastions D and E bristled with guns. Every mount on Curtain IV, casemate and barbette tier had a formidable 10-inch Rodman gun in place. Curtain IV is distinctive for another reason— it is the only part of Fort Montgomery of which every trace is now gone.

Collapsed Bastion D as seen from the north in 2004. Author photo.

Bastion E did not fare much better than Curtain IV. Again, similar to Bastion B with the exception of different gun platform arrangements on the barbette tier, all brick embrasures, slightly smaller magazines (five hundred sixteen square feet), wooden casemate floors and a semi-circular staircase, this important, northeastern bastion was almost completely removed by the Weston crews. A small section of the right shoulder is still visible; one embrasure stands awkwardly above the ground. Even the outline of Bastion E is gone, buried under a mound of debris bulldozed to the site. Bastion E enclosed two five hundred sixty square foot magazines. Eight 24-pounder flank howitzers were mounted there on tiers I and II. The barbette tier differed from Bastion B in that it did not have a west-facing earthen parapet. Guns were to be arranged differently also. Bastion E was to mount three heavy guns on center-pintle mounts at the salient and shoulder angles and two fore-pintle mounted guns at the junctions with Curtains IV and V. One of these latter mounts received its gun, an 8-inch Rodman on an iron carriage.

Curtain V is also gone, the entire row of casemates scraped down to the level of the "water gate" drawbridge. Nothing but four courses of limestone remains.

Top: Bastion E, Curtain V, Bastion A and a small portion of Curtain I are visible in this photo. The iron braces below the casemate doors are for a catwalk. Courtesy: Clinton County Historical Association. Bottom: This photo gives us a rare glimpse of Curtain IV. Also seen are Bastion E and part of Curtain V. Courtesy of Ben Arno.

Bastion E, then and now. Top: Weston crews begin their demolition of Bastion E, 1936. Bottom: Bastion E as seen from the lake in 2005. Top photo courtesy of Clinton County Historical Association. Bottom photo by the author.

CHAPTER XIV

Ordnance at Fort Montgomery

We know for certain that three types of heavy ordnance were mounted at Fort Montgomery. Armament Reports on file at National Archives prove that there were a number of 32-pounders, both 8 and 10-inch Rodman guns and the fort's full complement of 24-pounder flank howitzers on site. I have reproduced many of those reports within this book. Solid shot (cannon balls) has been found on the site in addition to one US Army Model 1816 contract conversion musket.[1]

The fort received the first of its heavy ordnance during the early years of the Civil War, probably in 1862.[2] In December, 1861, Totten stated that the fort's full complement of heavy ordnance was to be "seventy-six 10-inch guns, ten 32-pounders, forty 24-pounder howitzers, ten mortars— 136 pieces."[3] By January, 1865 there were seven 32-pounder's mounted *en casemate* and 36 of the fort's forty 24-pounder flank howitzers were in place in the bastions.[4] The fort was far from complete when these big were mounted.

The presence of small arms is significant in that it verifies contemporary accounts by individuals such as Daniel Taylor that tell of drills in "infantry and heavy artillery tactics" by the "Fort Company."[5]

Once hostilities ceased, more modern ordnance was sent to the fort. By the summer of 1866 ten 10-inch Rodman's were mounted on iron carriages in the casemates of Curtain IV and guns were being mounted on the barbette tier where an additional eight 8-inch Rodmans were in place. Every flank howitzer embrasure had a muzzle pointing out of it.

The big Rodman guns could not be mounted within the casemates of Curtains I and V since they were constructed with wooden casemate floors that would not support their massive weight. Plans were drawn up for replacement of these floors but funding was not forthcoming.[6] These casemates mounted some 32-pounders on wooden carriages.[7]

It appears the fort had the most guns it would ever mount by 1872 with a total of 74 guns mounted. There were also two enormous 15-inch Rodmans on site but unmounted at the time.

The fort's ordnance was to be placed as follows:

Seventy-two guns *en casemate* consisting of forty flank howitzers and thirty-two "seacoast guns." Fifty-seven of those guns were actually mounted. Fifty-three guns were to be mounted *en barbette,* forty-five fore-pintle mounted guns and another eight center-pintle mounted. Seventeen of these guns were actually mounted, all on fore-pintle mounts. I have been unable to determine if any of the ten mortars ever arrived at Fort Montgomery.

While there were two, un-mounted, 15-inch guns on the parade, the largest gun mounted at Fort Montgomery was the 10-inch Rodman. This smoothbore, muzzle-loading weapon was very important in its day. The brainchild of Thomas J. Rodman, the gun was innovative in that it was cast in a way that made it much stronger than previous cannon. Together with its iron carriage the 10-inch Rodman guns weighed some 15,000 pounds each. A fifteen pound charge was required to fire either a 128 pound, 9.8 inch diameter solid shot ball or a 103 pound shell. The 10-inch Rodman could fire these heavy spherical rounds over 4,800 yards at 30 degrees elevation.

The 8-inch Rodman's mounted were somewhat smaller. Weighing in at 8,465 pounds on iron carriages, they could fire 65 pound solid shot or a 50 pound shell 3,800 yards at 30 degrees with a 10 pound powder charge.

As previously noted, the 15-inch Rodman's were never mounted on Fort Montgomery's barbette tier. Had they been these massive guns would have weighed an astounding 50,000 pounds (with carriage). They were capable of firing 400 pound solid and 352 pound shell spherical shot over 5,000 yards.

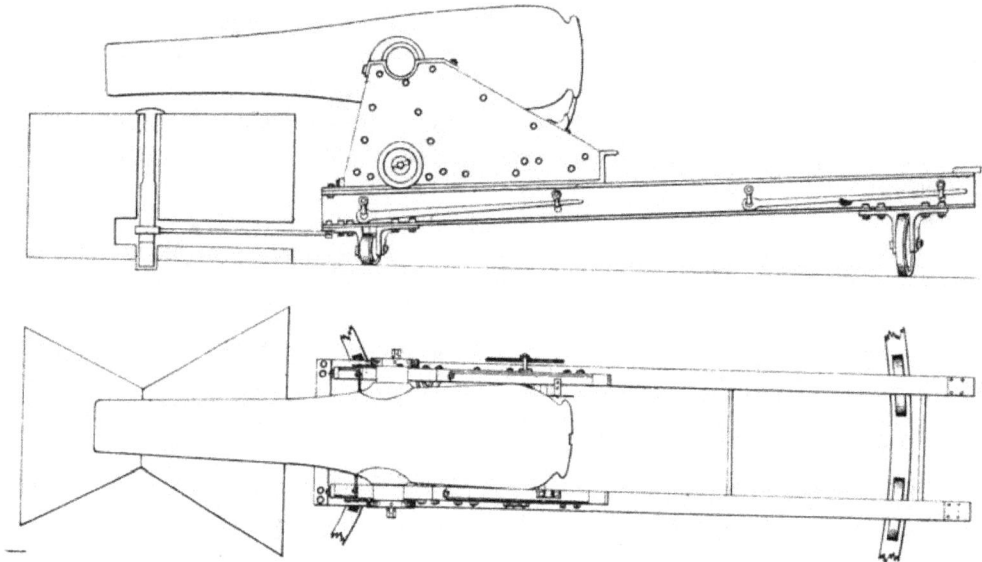

Rodman gun mounted *en casemate*. From a contemporary ordnance manual.

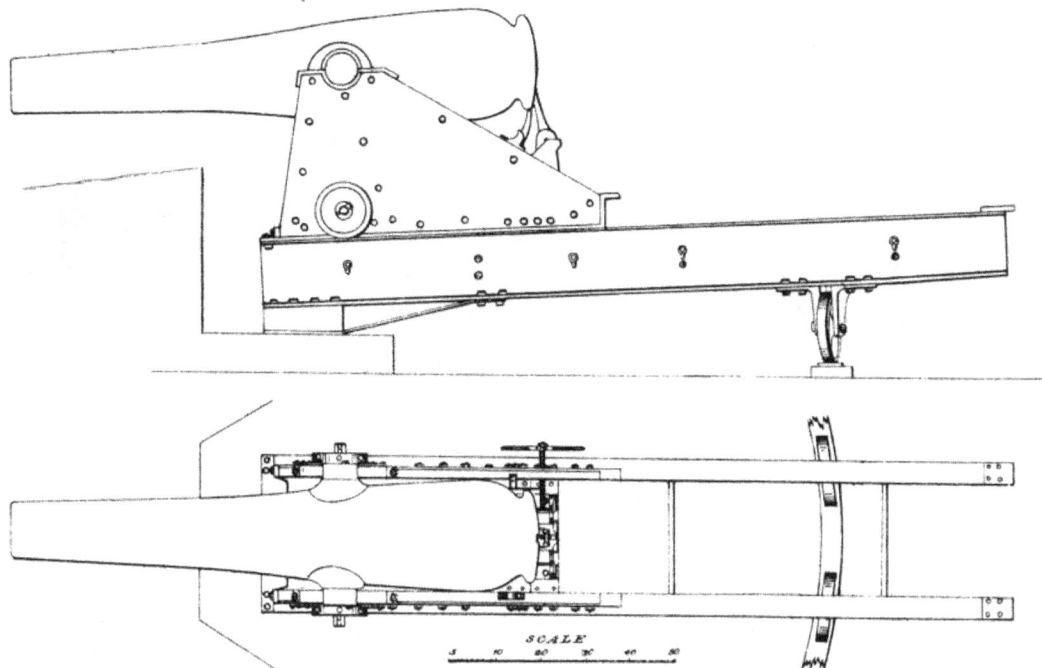

Top: Fore-pintle mounted Rodman gun, *en barbette*. Bottom: Center-pintle mounted Rodman gun, *en barbette*. From The Ordnance Manual for Use of the Officers of the United States Army, 1850.

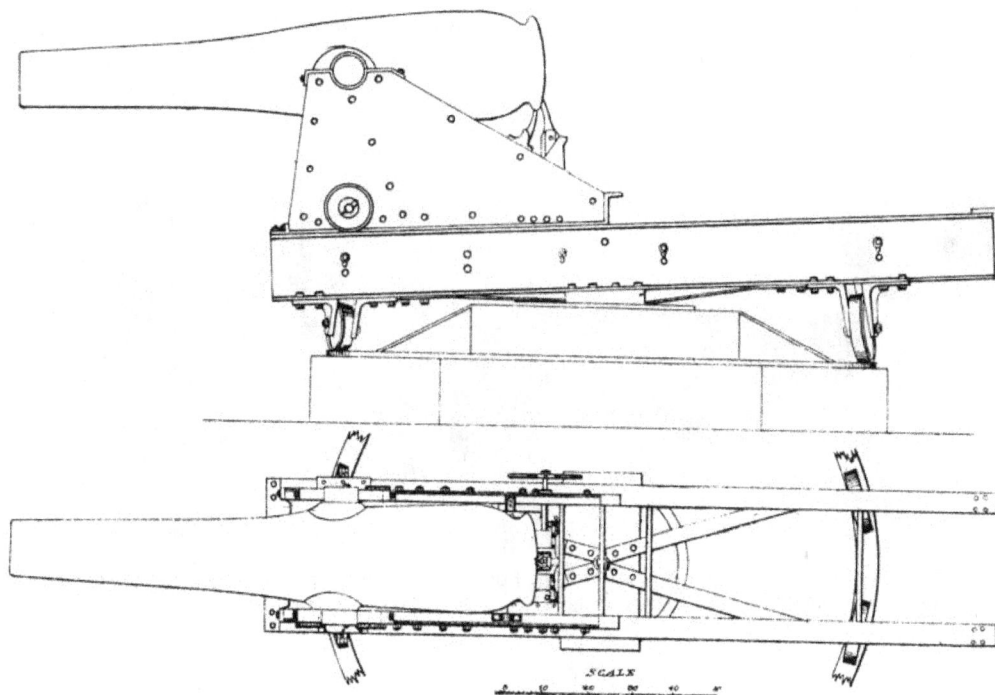

Above and below left: 10-inch Rodman mounted *en casemate* at Fort Knox, Maine. Author photos. Above and below right: 10-inch Rodman's mounted fore-pintle *en barbette*, Fort Clinch, South Carolina. Courtesy of Charles Barney. Fort Montgomery's Rodman guns, carriages, and mounts were virtually identical to this.

Above, left and right: 15-inch Rodman on center-pintle mount, Fort Knox, Maine. Fort Montgomery had two of these guns on site but they were never mounted as the mounts on the barbette tier were never finished. Two photos by the author.

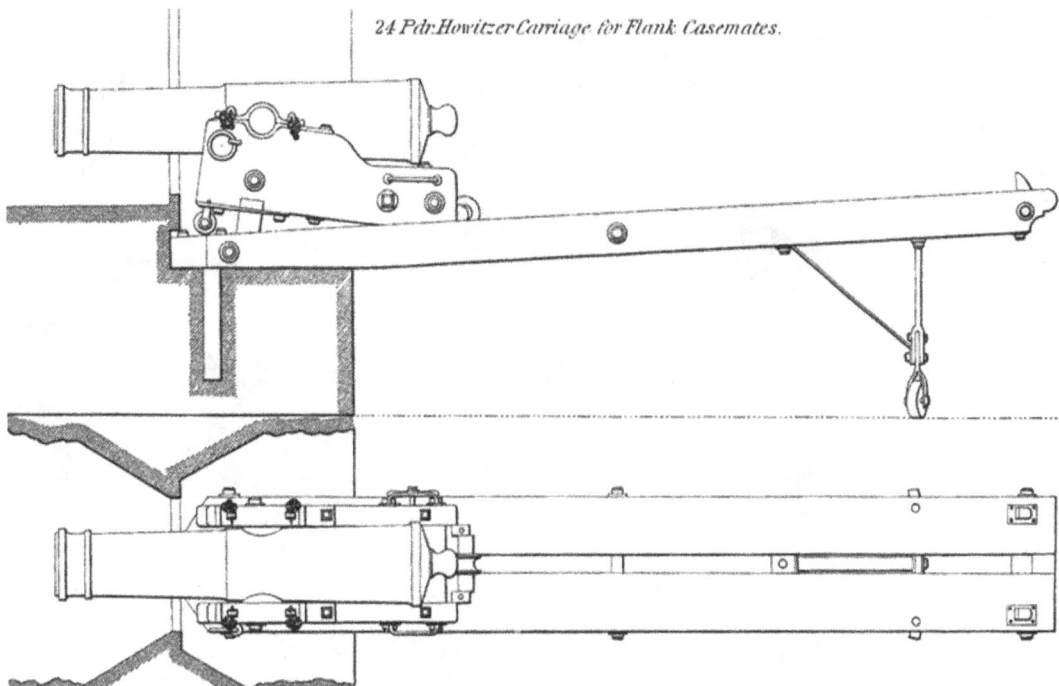

24 Pdr. Howitzer Carriage for Flank Casemates.

24-pounder flank howitzer on wooden carriage. From The Ordnance Manual for Use of the Officers of the United States Army, 1850. Fort Montgomery had a full complement of forty mounted flank howitzers.

The forty 24-pounder flank howitzers mounted in all bastions of the fort were the smallest of the heavy ordnance. An anti-personnel weapon, these guns were really the equivalent of large shotguns. These guns were specifically designed and mounted for the flanks of the bastions so that they could rake the length of the curtains with grape and canister shot should an attacker get that close to the fort walls. Weighing in at 1480 pounds, they were all mounted on wooden carriages.

Left: 24-pounder flank howitzer at Fort Moultrie. Photo courtesy of Roger Harwood.

Vestiges of Flank Howitzers at Fort Montgomery. Above, left and right. Pintles for flank howitzers still in place. This particular pintle still has part of an iron piece that was attached to the wooden carriage around the pIntle. Below: Flank howitzer from Fort Montgomery on display in Isle La Motte, Vermont. The top carriage that supports the gun was reportedly recreated by Lockwood Clark in the 1970's. Three photos by the author.

The Fort Montgomery flank howitzer at Isle La Motte. Photos by the author.

This twenty-four pounder at Fort Adams is mounted on a carriage similar to those used with the 32-pounders at Fort Montgomery. Author photos.

Fort Montgomery mounted a total of seven 32-pounders on wooden carriages. The oldest ordnance at the fort, Col. C.E. Blunt made it clear in one of his Ordnance Reports that he believed their time at Fort Montgomery was "only temporary."[8] Yet, while these seven guns were among the first mounted at the fort, they were also among the very last to be removed. Capt. Harry Taylor's Armament Report of 1901 lists four 32-pounders still mounted in casemates on tier II.[9] The workhorse of the army prior to the development of the Rodman gun, these guns would fire a 6.25 inch diameter, 33 pound solid shot or 32 pound shell.

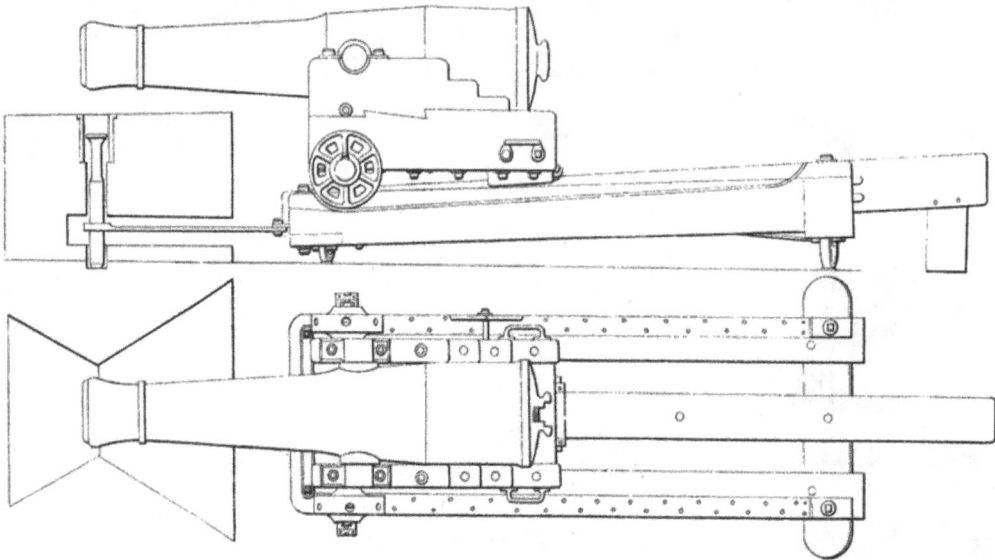

Casemate Carriage.

Early gun, possibly a 32-pounder, mounted on a wooden casemate carriage. This is the carriage that would have been used for the seven 32-pounders mounted at Fort Montgomery. From The Ordnance Manual for Use of the Officers of the United States Army, 1850.

The last of Fort Montgomery's big guns were removed in 1908.[10] According to former Rouses Point Mayor and fort enthusiast Tom Batha, all of the flank howitzers were donated to municipalities around the country. Batha believes twenty survived wartime scrap drives and are still on display. Batha also believes one of the venerable 32-pounders is on display in Mechanicville, NY. It is not known if any of the Rodman guns are still in existence.

Another photo of the 24-pounder mounted on a wooden casemate carriage at Fort Adams. Author photo.

We do know there were small arms present at Fort Montgomery. There are several accounts in this book of alerts at the fort and drilling by the "Fort Company." In addition, I have located a document that states that there was a detachment of Federal troops briefly garrisoned at the fort in 1862.[11]

Charles Barney Sr. found what is probably a Model 1816 contract conversion musket manufactured at the Harper's Ferry Armory and Arsenal, converted to percussion in the 1850's, in a dirt bank at the fort in the early 1950's. The musket and a powder horn also found at the fort are now owned by Charles Barney Jr.

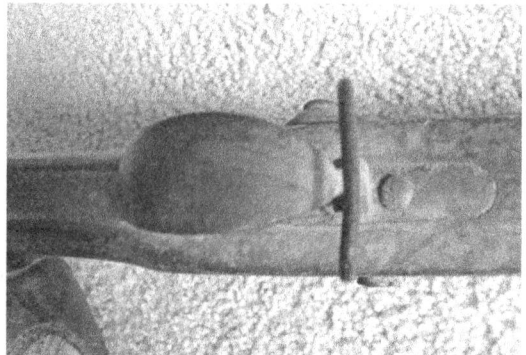

Charles Barney's Model 1816 contract conversion musket. The musket was found along with a powder horn, in a dirt bank at the Fort Montgomery ruins by Charles Barney, Sr. The musket is stamped "Harper's Ferry 18xx." Photos courtesy of Charles Barney.

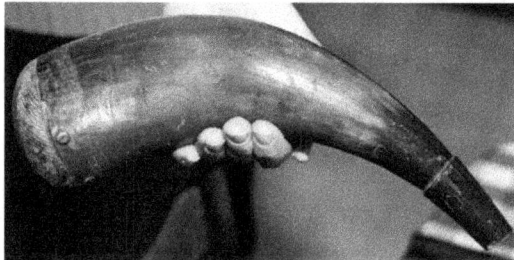

Above and left: Details of the musket and the powder horn found by Charles Barney, Sr. at Fort Montgomery. Photo courtesy of Charles Barney, Jr.

Below: Musket illustration from The Ordnance Manual for Use of the Officers of the United States Army, 1850.

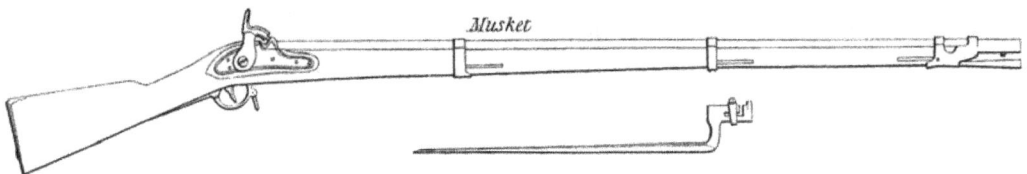

Musket

GLOSSARY

Barbette Tier: The uppermost tier or level of a fort, usually without any overhead protection.

Bastion: A projection between the straight, recessed sections of a fort known as curtains. Fort Montgomery had five bastions, labeled clockwise from the east bastion A-E.

Battery: A position for a gun or group of guns within a fort.

Canister: An anti-personnel weapon consisting of containers filled with iron balls (or shot). When fired, the container splits open filling the air with the small projectiles much like a shotgun.

Casemate: A masonry vault specifically designed to be bombproof usually constructed under the ramparts of a fort. Casemates usually housed cannon, but they were also designed to protect and enclose quarters, storerooms, kitchens and other general purpose rooms.

Cordon: An outward projection from the scarp wall near the top. The main purpose of the cordon was to help reduce weathering due to drainage. It may have also been considered an obstacle to scaling the wall.

Counterscarp: The wall of the wet ditch or moat opposite the main work. At Fort Montgomery this was the coverface wall directly opposite the gorge, or western wall.

Coverface or cover face: An earth or masonry outwork placed to protect a masonry front of a fort from siege guns. At Fort Montgomery the coverface was a huge artificial island constructed between the gorge, or western front, and the western shore.

Curtain: The straight sections of a fort that lie between two bastions. Fort Montgomery had five curtains, numbered clockwise from the southeast curtain I-V.

Embrasure: An opening in the wall through which guns are fired.

En barbette: A gun mounted on a barbette or top tier of the fort. These guns would fire over the wall rather than through an embrasure.

En casemate: A gun mounted in a casemate. Guns mounted en casemate would fire through an opening or embrasure in the scarp.

Flank howitzer: A smaller gun specially designed as an anti-personnel weapon. Flank howitzers were placed in the flanks of the bastions and were primarily designed to fire grapeshot or canister.

Front: The exterior portion of a fort between the salients of two bastions. Fort Montgomery had five fronts.

Gorge: The front of a fort facing away from the water, usually where the main entrance to the fort was located. At Fort Montgomery the gorge was the westward-facing side, toward the coverface and "commons."

Loophole: A narrow opening or embrasure designed to allow the defenders to fire small arms from within.

Magazine: Storage room for gun powder. There were two types of magazines at Fort Montgomery. Four main storage magazines deep within bastions B-E and two smaller service magazines atop the gorge barbette.

Moat, aka Wet Ditch: A low area filled with water around a scarp wall designed to prevent troops from accessing the fort wall. Not all forts had wet ditches, often they were not filled with water.

Parade: The open space within the fort, often used for barracks, drilling and assembling, etc. In Third-System forts this open area was not referred to as a parade *ground*.

Parade wall or face: The interior wall of the rampart facing the parade.

Parapet: A low earth or masonry wall along the top of the rampart over which defenders would fire their weapons.

Pintle: An upright iron pin upon which a gun chassis rotates.

Postern: The entrance from a fort toward the moat or ditch. At Fort Montgomery the postern was the entryway to the fort from the west, across the moat, through the gorge.

Rampart: The main body of fort wall from scarp to parade.

Salient: The outward-pointing angle of a bastion.

Sally Port: A postern, usually the main entrance to the fort located in the gorge.

Scarp, scarp wall: The exterior wall immediately in front of the rampart along the perimeter. Third-System scarp walls were by design unattached to the rest of the rampart.

Shell: A hollow projectile usually filled with explosives.

Shot: A solid projectile made of iron.

Traverse circle or iron: An arc of stone or iron upon which the wheels of a gun chassis rotated.

NOTES

I: The First Fort- Fort "Blunder"

[1] NARA Records of the Chief of Engineers. Record Group 77, Fortifications File. *Metes & Bounds of a tract of land transferred by his Excellency Gov. Clinton on the 17th day of Oct. 1817 from the State of New York to the U.S.*. Drawer 7, Sheet 20. 1817. Annotated Oct., Nov. 1850.

[2] H.S. Tanner: Plan of Rouses Point at the foot of Lake Champlain. 1814. Clinton County Historical Association. *See also* Robert Bouchette: The American Fort at Rouses Point. Sketch of the American Fort at Rouses Point on the River Richelieu about 20 chains south of the Old Line found erroneous, and is considerably within the New established Line or Parallel 45 North Latitude; it can mount 64 pieces of cannon and is Bomb proof with respect to its commanding position (see Plan of the Boundary Line.) This sketch was taken by Colonel Bouchette on board the Steam Boat in May 1818 - and copied by Robert Bouchette. Library and Archives Canada, Documentary Art Collection Division: LAC, e006079067 *and* H.P. Bruyeres: Sketch showing the Position of the American Works at and near Rous's Point Cantonment. 1818. Library and Archives Canada, Documentary Art Collection Division: NMC 7722. The latter two documents clearly show the structures built along this strip of land between the "mainland" and Island Point. There were so many early buildings here that Daniel Taylor referred to this strip of land as "Old Rouses Point" (The Shores of Champlain: pages 14,15)

[3] Dewitt Clinton and the State of New York to the United States. October 17, 1817 Recorded November 19, 1817 Vol. F of Deeds, at Page 9. Holcombe Abstract Corporation No.1 F-9) Courtesy of Ann Thurber, Powertex Corporation.

[4] Ibid: Vol. F of Deeds, at Page 112. Holcombe Abstract Corporation No. 4 F-112—3)

[5] This document is in the collections of the Clinton County Historical Museum at Plattsburgh, NY.

[6] A modern perch of stone equals a quantity 1 and 1/2 feet thick, 1 foot high and 16 and 1/2 feet long (24 3/4 cubic feet) A perch of stone is often computed differently in different localities. West of the Mississippi a perch equals 16 1/2 cubic feet, this is the measure apparently used by Totten.

[7] Plattsburgh Republican: March 15, 1817, April 7, 1817.

[8] Warder H. Cadbury. *The Men Who Built Fort Blunder.* The Antiquarian- Clinton County Historical Association. Fall 1989. 10

[9] Plattsburgh Republican: August 2, 1817

[10] Cadbury. 11

[11] NARA Records of the Chief of Engineers. Record Group 77. Drawer 7, Sheet 5. Profile and Elevations for a Castle for Island Point. Rouse's Point, Lake Champlain. Undated, probably 1816

[12] NARA Records of the Chief of Engineers. Record Group 77. Fortifications File. *Profile and Elevations of a Castle for Island Point.* Drawer 7, sheet 5 and *Fortifications, _____ New York. Plan and Sections of Fort _____, Rouses Point.* Drawer 7, Sheet 15. This document shows the construction of Fort Montgomery in its earliest stages (1844). The plan of the original fort on Island Point is drawn out to scale, making this an especially useful document for researchers of both structures.

[13] American State Papers, Military Affairs I: *Estimates for 1819*. 812

[14] H.P. Bruyeres: Sketch showing the Position of the American Works at and near Rous's Point Cantonment. 1818. Library and Archives Canada, Documentary Art Collection Division: NMC 7722. This bridge is referred to in the recollections of Harold Bourke, son of the last caretaker of Fort Montgomery. There were still traces of this original bridge around the time of the First World War. Bourke, writing about the road to the fort through the swamp, notes "The road continued through a swamp of alders to the lake and then made a slight left turn on a causeway to the fort. The roadway was always under water in the spring floods and *there were the remains of pilings that supported a bridge in earlier times.* The annual ice floes probably destroyed the bridge." Harold Bourke Papers: Sgt. Thomas Bourke. Courtesy of his granddaughter, Elizabeth Clark. Personal correspondence with author, October 2007.

[15] John and Mary Warford to the United States of America. November 18, 1817. Recorded November 19, 1817. Vol. F of Deeds, at Page 13. Holcombe Abstract Corporation No. 2 F-13. Courtesy of Ann Thurber, Powertex Corporation.

[16] André Charbonneau "The Fortifications of Île aux Noix" (Ottawa, Parks Canada 1994) 165

[17] Ibid. 170-173

[18] Cadbury. 11

[19] Plattsburgh Republican: August 22, 1818.

[20] Rev. Daniel Taylor: *The Shores of Champlain*. 1892. Sect. 15: 38.

II: The Border Controversy and Fort "Blunder"

[1] John T. Faris: *The Romance of Boundaries*. 1926. New York: Harper & Brothers. 48-49

[2] Lawrence Shaw Mayo. *The Forty-Fifth Parallel: A Detail of the Unguarded Boundary*. Geographical Review: April 1923. Vol. 13, No. 2. pp. 255-265. JSTOR: < http://links.jstor.org/sici?sici=0016-7428%28192304%2913%3A2%3C255%3ATFPADO%3E2.0.CO%3B2-9> (Accessed October 16, 2007)

[3] Joint Report of Upon the Survey and Demarcation of the Boundary Between the United States and Canada, From the Source of the St. Croix River to the St. Lawrence River. 1925: International Boundary Commission. Washington. Government Printing Office

[4] James Trager: *People's Chronology*. 1992. New York: Henry Holt. 382

[5] Lawrence J. Burpee: *The Vicissitudes of Fort Montgomery*. 1941. Ottawa: Royal Society of Canada. 59 See also Warder H. Cadbury. *The Men Who Built Fort Blunder*. The Antiquarian- Clinton County Historical Association. Fall 1989. 12

[6] Montreal Herald: November 21, 1818.

[7] American State Papers, Military Affairs I: *Estimates for 1819*. 810

[8] Ibid. III. 252. This amount is roughly equivalent to $2,281,000 in 2008 dollars according to the web site "Measuring Worth." Figure determined using the GDP deflator which is best for comparing "project" costs. Measuring Worth. 2009. "Six Ways to Compute the Relative Value of a U.S. Dollar Amount, 1774 to Present." <http://www.measuringworth.com/calculators/uscompare/result.php#> (accessed June 29, 2009)

[9] Plattsburgh Republican: October 19, 1819

[10] Edward P. Alexander: "Rouse's Point Boundary Controversy" Dict. Am. History, Rev Ed. Vol. VI New York: Charles Scribner's Sons. 165

[11] Burpee: 60

[12] Library and Archives Canada: H.P. Bruyères, Sketch showing the Position of the American Works at and near Rous's Point Cantonment. 1818. NMC-7722. This plan is featured in Charbonneau: *The Fortifications of Ile aux Noix. Parks Canada: 1994. 172*

[13] Taylor. Sect. 14, p. 38, Sect. 19, p. 39

[1] Andre Charbonneau: *The fortifications of Ile aux Noix.* Ottawa:Parks Canada. 1994.187, 191

[2] American State Papers, Military Affairs VI. 1836. Page 391

[3] Albert B. Corey: *The Crisis of 1830-1842 in Canadian-American Relations.* 1941: New Haven, Yale University Press. 61. Colborne and Fox comments from Public Archives of Canada (now LAC), Series Q: Transcripts from Colonial Office Records.

[4] Encyclopædia Britannica. 2005. "Aroostook War." Encyclopædia Britannica Premium Service. <http://www.britannica.com/eb/article-9009595> (accessed December 28, 2005) also see Wikipedia contributors, "Aroostook War," *Wikipedia, The Free Encyclopedia,* <http://en.wikipedia.org/w/index.php?title=Aroostook_War&oldid=32617182> (accessed December 28, 2005).

[5] Report of the Secretary of War, November 30, 1839. Congressional Globe, 26th Congress, 1st Session. Page 23.

[6] NARA Records of the Chief of Engineers. Record Group 77, Fortifications File. Lake Champlain, Project for the defense of Rouse's Point. No.1. Board of Engineers 1840, Drawn under the direction of Lt. Col. Thayer by M.C. Meigs. Drawer 7, Sheets 8-11

[7] National Archives of Canada at Ottawa: *American plan for permanent fortifications at Stony Point and Windmill Point.* 1840. NMC-51426. This plan is featured in Charbonneau: *The Fortifications of Ile aux Noix.* Parks Canada: 1994. 267

IV: We will protect the lake- The massive new fort at Stony Point

[1] Charles R. Tuttle: Tuttle's popular history of the Dominion of Canada. Boston: Tuttle & Downie. 1877. 382

[2] Andre Charbonneau: The fortifications of Ile aux Noix. Ottawa: Parks Canada. 1994. 251, 253

[3] Plattsburgh Republican: January 30, 1841

[4] John F. Ross: This happened here: The story of the Lake Champlain territory. Rouses Point, NY: Northern Publishing Company.1955.

[5] NARA Records of the Chief of Engineers. Record Group 77, Fortifications File. Lake Champlain, Project for the defense of Rouse's Point. No.1. and No. 2 Board of Engineers 1840, Drawn under the direction of Lt. Col. Thayer by M.C. Meigs Sheets 8, 9, 10 and 11.

[1] NARA Records of the Chief of Engineers. Record Group 77. Metes & Bounds of a tract of Land transferred by His Excellency Gov. Clinton on the 17th day of Oct. 1817 from the State of New York to the U.S. (Rec'd with ltr. Of Lt. Meigs of Nov. 2, 1850 (M 2082) Drawer 7, sheet 20

[2] Though a good example of third-system design and construction, Fort Montgomery is "technically" not a Third-System fort, since this term was applied primarily to *coastal* defense forts, not forts along the northern frontier. See John R. Weaver II, "A LEGACY IN BRICK AND STONE- American Coastal Defense Forts of the Third System, 1816-1867." Pictorial Histories Publishing Company, Missoula, MT 2001 66,67

[3] NARA Records of the Chief of Engineers. Record Group 77. Plans, Sections & Elevations Fort Rouse's Point Project for the Defense of the Outlet of Lake Champlain. Drawn under the direction of H. Brewster. (Proj. apprvd. By S/W in 1844) Oct. 15, 1843 Drawer 7, sheet 14.

[4] NARA Records of the Chief of Engineers. Record Group 77. Fortification File. Study of Block House or Redoubt. (Plan of Cover Face). Col. Mason. Oct. 22, 1850. Drawer 7, Sheet 28. See also Drawer 7, sheet A, 1886, Drawer 7, sheet 14, 1844 and Drawer 7, sheet 16, 1845- Sketch of the altered cover face for the new fort at Rouse's Point, N.Y. Each of the terms are used- Block House, Redoubt and Guard House.

[5] NARA Records of the Chief of Engineers. Record Group 77. Fortifications _____ New-York, Out-let of Lake Champlain", and subtitled "Plan and Sections of Fort _____, Rouse's Point; exhibiting the condition of the work on the 30th of September 1844 Drawer 7, Sheet15.

[6] John F. Ross, *Sidelight on History.* 1978 Publisher unknown.

[7] Brevet Lt. Col. James L. Mason: An analytical investigation of the resistance of piles to superincumbent pressure, deduced from the force of driving; with an application of the formula to the foundations at Fort Montgomery, Rouses Point, N.Y. 1850. Washington: Robert A Waters. 5-8

[8] Ibid. 7, 8

[9] Rev. Daniel T. Taylor: The Shores of Champlain. 1892. The Champlain Counselor. Reprinted 1979 Champlain, N.Y.: Moorsfield Press. 42

[10] NARA Records of the Chief of Engineers. Record Group 77. *Plan & Sections of Fort- Rouse's Point Exhibiting the Condition of the Work on the 30th Sept. 1844.* Drawer 7, Sheet 15

[11] Senate Executive Document No. 1, 28th Congress, 2nd Session, 1844. Also quoted in "The Vicissitudes of Fort Montgomery by Lawrence J. Burpee. 1941. Royal Society of Canada. 66

[12] Champlain Journal August 4, 1869. The Hamelin source is a personal email correspondence to the author from Joe Hamelin (great grandson) , June 8, 2005.

[13] Champlain Journal August 4, 1869

[14] Roll of Honor: US casualties of the Battle of Molino del Ray-
<http://www.dmwv.org/honoring/molino.htm> Accessed March 16, 2008

[15] Plattsburgh Republican September 5, 1846, see also Arthur B. Cohn: Lake Champlain's Sailing Canal Boats: 2003. Basin Harbor Vermont: Lake Champlain Maritime Museum. 116

[16] Plattsburgh Republican April 21, 1846

[17] Mason. 14

[18] War of the Rebellion: Official Records- Series III, Vol. I. Totten to New York Governor Morgan: December 30: 1861. 773-774.

[19] NARA Records of the Chief of Engineers. Record Group 77. *CURTAIN IV GUN ROOM IV TO VII.* 1851: M.C. Meigs. Drawer 7, sheet 39

[20] John R. Weaver II, "A LEGACY IN BRICK AND STONE- American Coastal Defense Forts of the Third System, 1816-1867." 2001. Pictorial Histories Publishing Company, Missoula, MT. 12, 13

[21] Personal conversation, July 2005: Vermont author and historian John Duffy. Mr. Duffy maintains that many of the lovely stone structures on both sides of the lake and into Quebec were built by men temporarily freed from their duties at Fort Montgomery.

[22] NARA Records of the Chief of Engineers. Record Group 77. *Sketch of Bastion D & adjoining Gorge casemates made in Engr. Dept. & sent to Lt. Blunt with the reqst. To finish and put in ink, making such corrections as are nec. To make it conform to the work as actually construcd. and return it to Engr. Dept.* 1857: Drawer 7, sheet 54

[23] Annual Report of the Engineer Bureau: November 14, 1860, cited in C.P. Stacey, The Myth of the Unguarded Frontier 1815-1871. The American Historical Review, Vol. LVI, No. 1. October 1950. 16

[24] Champlain Journal: August 4, 1869

[25] War of the Rebellion- Official Records: Series III, Vol. I. 49

[26] Taylor: Sect. 17, p. 43

[27] War of the Rebellion: Series III- Volume I. p. 685. It is hard to reconcile Blunt's statements with those of Rev. Taylor. Taylor talks of great progress on the fort during the summer/fall of 1861 while Blunt states not much has been done due to lack of funds. Obviously, Blunts report to Totten holds more weight. It is clear that some work on Curtain II was carried out in 1861 under David White. However, it was not until 1862, after the Congressional appropriations of February 20 that work was greatly accelerated. It is my belief that Taylor, writing in 1892, erred and got the year wrong. There is no documentation to prove that the summer of 1861 was when work on the fort accelerated dramatically. There is plenty of evidence to show that it did happen in 1862, after the appropriations of February 20, 1861 and the Trent Affair. Accordingly, I have used 1862 as the year of "acceleration" rather than 1861.

[28] Taylor: Sect. 17, p. 43. I have not found anything to verify Taylor's claim that Lincoln personally intervened and diverted funds for Fort Montgomery.

[29] U.S. Department of State. 2005. "The Trent Affair." Bureau of Public Affairs, Office of the Historian, Timeline of U.S. Diplomatic History, 1861-1865. <http://www.state.gov/r/pa/ho/time/cw/17612.htm> (accessed December 29, 2005)

[30] War of the Rebellion: Official Records- Series III, Vol. I. 773-774

[31] Stacy: 17

[32] Taylor: Sect. 17, p. 44

[33] Ibid: 44. I have not been able to verify this. The earliest Armament Report I have located is C.E. Blunt's report of January 31, 1865.

[34] NARA Record Group 153, Records of the Adjutant General. U.S. Reservation, Rouses Point, NY. Sheet 1, undated. The legend reads, in part, "The reservation is north of and adjoining the Village of Rouses Point, Clinton County, N.Y. on the northwestern bank of Lake Champlain. It was deeded to the U.S. by the State of N.Y. Nov. 19, 1817, for the purposed of establishing a military post for the protection of the country. The area of the reservation is about four hundred and eighty acres. The original boundaries have not been changed. The fort is a bastioned work built of stone. It was begun in 1844, and is essentially finished. Cost about $2,250,000. *It was garrisoned for about three months in 1862 by a detachment of fifteen men from the 14th Infty...* " [Italics added].

[35] Plattsburgh Sentinel: September 14, 1926 "Old Fort at Rouses Point to be Sold"

[36] Taylor: 45

[37] Champlain Journal: August 4, 1869

[38] Library of Congress: A Century of Lawmaking for a New Nation: U.S. Congressional Documents and Debates, 1774-1875. Journal of the House of Representatives of the United States, 1863-1864-Wed., March 2, 1864 <http://memory.loc.gov/cgi-bin/query/r?ammem/hlaw:@field(DOCID+@lit(hj06154))> (accessed December 29, 2005)

[39] Taylor: Sect. 19, pg. 46, 49

[40] New York Times: November 23, 1864. Proquest Historical Newspapers: The New York Times (1851-2001) pg. 1

[41] Taylor: Sect. 19, pg. 48, 49

[42] NARA Records of the Chief of Engineers. Record Group 77. Fort Montgomery Armament Sheet. January 31, 1865. Drawer 246, sheet 32-1

† Clinton County Historical Society: January 1964. North Country Notes, No. 16. Extracts from a translation by Hulda B. McLellan from "Zouaviana" by Gustave A. Drolet. First published in French in Montreal, 1893. This story, while entertaining, has much to make it suspect. Drolet repeats common, latter-day inaccuracies about the fort- referring to it as "the remains of an old fort, which the government had lately ordered restored... a dismantled fort...." In 1865, when these events purportedly took place, Fort Montgomery was still being finished, hundreds of workers each day were at the site just the year before, it had recently received one-third of its guns. An argument could be made that it was a new fort.

[43] William H. Powell.: A History of the Organization and Movements of the Fourth Regiment of Infantry, United States Army, from May 30, 1796 to December 31, 1870" 1871. M'Gill &Witherow: Washington City. 64, 65.

[44] Plattsburgh Sentinel: January 18, 1866. "The death of Col. Judah"

[45] Powell: 65

[46] Champlain Journal: August 4, 1869 Reese is only there for "a few months" See also Taylor, P. 49

[47] Analytical and Topical Index to The Reports of the Chief of Engineers and Officers of the Corps of Engineers, United States Army, 1866-1900. Volume III. 1903. 1418 [refers to Reports of 1866, page 3]

[48] Powell: 64

[49] NARA Records of the Chief of Engineers. Record Group 77. Fort Montgomery Armament Sheet. Drawer 246, Sheet 32-2

[50] Report of the Chief of Engineers (Secretary of War). October 21, 1867. P. 4

[51] NARA Records of the Chief of Engineers. Record Group 77. Drawer 7, Sheet 66. Note: Drawer 7, Sheet O-3 report dates this as 1870, I believe this date is erroneous.

[52] Champlain Journal August 4, 1869

[53] Report of the Chief of Engineers (Sec. of War) 18 October 25, 1869 p. 7

[54] Plattsburgh Sentinel: September 30, 1870

[55] Analytical and Topical Index to The Reports of the Chief of Engineers and Officers of the Corps of Engineers, United States Army, 1866-1900. Volume III. 1903. 1418 [refers to Report of 1870, page 12]. "The old style of armament"- meaning 32-pounders. In addition to replacing the wooden floors of Fronts I and V, alterations to the pintles was necessary for adapting them "to the Iron Carriages for 10 & 8" Rodman guns." See Drawer 76, Sheet 82, 1868. [Fort Jefferson]

[56] Analytical and Topical Index to The Reports of the Chief of Engineers and Officers of the Corps of Engineers, United States Army, 1866-1900. Volume III. 1903. 1418 [refers to Reports of 1871, page 7]

VI: The Treaty of Washington, 1871 to Private Sale, 1926

[1] Global Policy Forum. *Fear of Annexation by the United States*: Library and Archives Canada- February 19, 2002.
< http://www.globalpolicy.org/empire/history/2002/0219annexcanada.htm> (Accessed October 13, 2008)

[2] Plattsburgh Republican: "Ancient ruins on Lake Champlain" February 4, 1871

[3] Library of Congress. *American Memory- A Century of Lawmaking for a New Nation: U.S. Congressional Documents and Debates, 1774-1875*: < http://memory.loc.gov/cgi-bin/ampage?collId=llhb&fileName=039/llhb039.db&recNum=4308> (Accessed October 13, 2008)

[4] Analytical and Topical Index to The Reports of the Chief of Engineers and Officers of the Corps of Engineers, United States Army, 1866-1900. Volume III. 1903. 1418 [refers to Report of 1872, page 4]

[5] 1872 Armament Report NARA Records of the Chief of Engineers. Record Group 77 Drawer 259, Sheet 95

[6] Analytical and Topical Index to The Reports of the Chief of Engineers and Officers of the Corps of Engineers, United States Army, 1866-1900. Volume III. 1903. 1418 [refers to Report of 1873, page 5] and Report of the Chief of Engineers: 1874, page 6.

[7] Plattsburgh Sentinel December 19, 1873

[8] John F. Ross, *Sidelight on History*. March 16, 1978 Publisher unknown: See also NARA Records of the Chief of Engineers. Record Group 77. Drawer 246, Sheet 32-33 and 32-34

[9] Analytical and Topical Index to The Reports of the Chief of Engineers and Officers of the Corps of Engineers, United States Army, 1866-1900. Volume III. 1903. 1418 [refers to Reports of 1875, page 6]

[10] Report of the Chief of Engineers: 1876. Part I, page 7

[11] Report of the Chief of Engineers (Sec. of War) October 28, 1886, page 7

[12] John R. Weaver II, "A LEGACY IN BRICK AND STONE- American Coastal Defense Forts of the Third System, 1816-1867." 2001. Pictorial Histories Publishing Company, Missoula, MT. 23, footnote, page 46.

[13] Report of the Chief of Engineers: 1877, page 5

[14] Report of the Chief of Engineers: 1878, page 7

[15] Plattsburgh Sentinel: May 4, 1877

[16] Analytical and Topical Index to The Reports of the Chief of Engineers and Officers of the Corps of Engineers, United States Army, 1866-1900. Volume III. 1903. 1419 [refers to Reports of 1879, page 9]

[17] Plattsburgh Sentinel "The Plattsburgh U.S. Reservation" April-June 1882. See also Report of Hawley, Committee on Military Affairs [to accompany bill S.1843] 47th Congress, 2nd Session, March 2, 1883

[18] Analytical and Topical Index to The Reports of the Chief of Engineers and Officers of the Corps of Engineers, United States Army, 1866-1900. Volume III. 1903. 1419 [refers to Reports of 1880, page 19]

[19] Washington Post Aug. 31, 1880 "Rotting Coast Defenses"

[20] Report of the Secretary of War: December 1881- Condition of the Fortifications. Pages 22, 24

[21] Report of the Chief of Engineers: 1882, Part I, pages 11,12

[22] New York Times May 3, 1880. See also Ciborski "Patriotic Fervor or Capitalist Pawn- The Expansion of Plattsburgh Barracks 1892-1897" Clinton County Historical Association: Antiquarian 1996.

[23] Plattsburgh Sentinel June 2, 1882

[24] Report to the Secretary of War, Estimates for Buildings at Military Posts. October 16, 1882

[25] Plattsburgh Sentinel March 23, 1883

[26] Plattsburgh Sentinel November 23 and November 30, 1883

[27] Report of the Chief of Engineers: 1884, Part I, page 13

[28] Plattsburgh Sentinel "The Macdonough Park Bill" February 15, 1884

[29] Plattsburgh Sentinel November 14, 1884

[30] James R. Ciborski "Patriotic Fervor or Capitalist Pawn- The Expansion of Plattsburgh Barracks 1892-1897" Clinton County Historical Society: Antiquarian 1996

[31] Analytical and Topical Index to The Reports of the Chief of Engineers and Officers of the Corps of Engineers, United States Army, 1866-1900. Volume III. 1903. 1419 [refers to Reports of 1885, page 7

[32] NARA Records of the Chief of Engineers. Record Group 77. Drawer 7, Sheet O-3. January 1886.

[33] J.E. and H.W. Kaufmann. "Fortress America." 2004. Cambridge, MA: Da Capo Press. 311

[34] Plattsburgh Sentinel May 20, 1885

[35] Report of the Chief of Engineers: 1886. Vol. II, Part I, page 7

[36] Plattsburgh Sentinel June 11, 1886, August 28, 1896. Annual Report of the Chief of Engineers: 1886. Appendix 3 (Endicott Report), January 16, 1886

[37] Reports of the Chief of Engineers (Sec. of War) October 28, 1886, page 7

[38] Fort Covington Sun: February 26, 1891

[39] Plattsburgh Sentinel Sept. 15, 1893 "Military Post at Plattsburgh- Noteworthy Improvements which are being made- Progress of the work."

[40] Plattsburgh Sentinel November 15, 1895

[41] Plattsburgh Sentinel, August 28, 1896

[42] Analytical and Topical Index to The Reports of the Chief of Engineers and Officers of the Corps of Engineers, United States Army, 1866-1900. Volume III. 1903. 1419 [refers to Reports of 1897, page 744]

[43] Report of the Chief of Engineers: 1898: Part I, page 774

[44] Analytical and Topical Index to The Reports of the Chief of Engineers and Officers of the Corps of Engineers, United States Army, 1866-1900. Volume III. 1903. 1419 [refers to Reports of 1898, page 774. 1899, page 975, and 1900, page 973]

[45] Plattsburgh Sentinel August 24, 1900

[46] NARA Records of the Chief of Engineers. Record Group 77. Drawer 246, Sheet 32-33 and 32-34. Ross: Sidelight on History. March 16, 1978.

[47] Report of the Chief of Engineers: 1901.; Part I, page 855

[48] NARA Records of the Chief of Engineers. Record Group 77. Drawer 246, Sheet 32-39.

[49] Former Rouses Point Mayor and fort enthusiast Thomas Batha: Personal email correspondence to author. May 4, 2008. Batha stated: "… all 40 of the 24-pdr flank howitzers were donated to municipalities all over the country. To date 20 have been found to survive but we do not know where all 40 originally went. It is important to understand that while the approval dates were in 1900, some did not actually leave the fort until a few years later." I do not have documentation for the Batha remarks.

[50] Plattsburgh Sentinel May 8, 1908

[51] Ibid. May 15, 1908

[52] John Ross: Sidelight on History March/April 1978

[53] Plattsburgh Sentinel April 11, 1916

[54] Plattsburgh Sentinel July 30, 1926

[55] Plattsburgh Sentinel "Old fort at Rouses Point to be sold" Sept. 14, 1926

[56] Quit Claim Deed: United States of America to Champlain and Saint Lawrence Railroad Company, No. 5. November 22, 1926, Vol. 150 of Deeds, page 67; Quit Claim Deed: United States of America to The Delaware and Hudson Company, No. 6. December 23, 1926, Vol. 150 of Deeds, page 273; Contract of Sale and Purchase: United States of America to The Fort Montgomery Development Co. Inc. No. 7. September 23, 1926, Vol. 163 of Deeds, page 114. Holcombe Abstracts provided to the author by Ann Thurber, Powertex, Inc. See also Plattsburgh Sentinel "Fort Montgomery at Rouses Point Sold" Sept. 17, 1926 and Adirondack Record-Elizabethtown Post: "Fort Blunder" at Rouses Point Sold. September 23, 1926

[57] New York Times: "Fort Blunder, Near Border, Becomes Camp for Tourists" November 7, 1926

VII: Fort Keepers: Sgt. William McComb to Sgt. Thomas Bourke

[1] Regulations for the Army of the United States. 1857. New York: Harper & Brothers. 5-8

[2] Report of the Chief of Engineers: 1857. The report for Fort Preble reads, in part: "The grassed surfaces of the work have been mowed by a fort-keeper…and who has also attended to the ventilation of the buildings…" 275.

[3] Regulations for the Army of the United States. 1857. New York: Harper & Brothers. 5-8

[4] Charles Barney, formerly of Rouses Point, has a Model 1816 Musket that was converted to percussion in the 1850's in his possession. The musket was found protruding from a large dirt bank by his father at the fort in the 1930's shortly after a large part of the fort was demolished.

[5] Report of the Chief of Engineers: 1900. Part I, Page 973.

[6] Plattsburgh Sentinel: May 4, 1877

[7] Supplement to the Annual Report of the State Engineer and Surveyor of the State of New York, for the fiscal year ended September 30, 1912. Albany: 1913. J.B. Lyon Company. Page 9

[8] Ibid. April 17, 1885. See also the Official Register of the United States, Officers, and Employes [sic] in the Civil, Military and Naval Service, on the First of July, 1885. Volume I. Washington: Government Printing Office.

[9] Daniel Taylor, John Ross and Carolyn Severino all state that McComb was on the job as late as 1893.

[10] Taylor: P.49

[11] Plattsburgh Sentinel July 13, 1883. See also http://archiver.rootsweb.com/th/read/IRL-CLARE/2006-03/1142087434 for details about the Canavan family from the 1880 census.

[12] Plattsburgh Sentinel August 17, September 21, 1883

[13] Plattsburgh Sentinel October 8, 1886

[14] Report of the Chief of Engineers: 1900. Part I, Page 973. Note that both a fort keeper and an ordnance sergeant were employed at this late date.

[15] Plattsburgh Sentinel September 3, 1886

[16] Plattsburgh Sentinel October 8, 1886

[17] Plattsburgh Sentinel November 5, 1886

[18] Plattsburgh Sentinel August 19, 1887

[19] Plattsburgh Sentinel June 7, 1889

[20] Plattsburgh Sentinel November 16, 1923

[21] According to the Plattsburgh Sentinel of November 16,1923 Sergeant Robert Moore retired from his "fort keeper" job in 1906. Thomas apparently took on the job in 1914. I can't explain the discrepancy at this point.

[22] This remark about the pilings solves a mystery from a very early map of the first fort [H.P. Bruyeres: Sketch showing the Position of the American Works at and near Rous's Point Cantonment. 1818. Library and Archives Canada, Documentary Art Collection Division: NMC 7722.] That map actually shows this "bridge in earlier times" that they saw the "remains of pilings" for. It was built back in 1816-1818. The area where the bridge was has now largely been filled in due to eutrophication and filling in of the wetland.

[23] This area now is completely grown up and gone to new, scrubby, very dense forest.

[24] The first bridge, apparently the one built by the army, was supported only by sawed boards at the fort end. Printed in this book is a wonderful photo of it, taken by Thomas himself. This bridge is the one that was "dangerous" and replaced by Elisha Goodsell in the 1920's. Goodsell reinforced his bridge with large wooden piles driven into the moat.

[25] According to the February 21, 1916 Report of the Chief of Engineers the watchman at Fort Montgomery was paid $540 a year and took in $340 a year in "pasturage rent".

[26] Care of Fortifications regulations did not allow burning of the grass for this very reason. Winds can become very strong here, particularly atop the barbette tier. The "two wooden buildings" that burned were almost certainly the rooftops of the service magazines. They were never finished and had wooden covers instead of brick and stone.

[27] The government auction of the property was on September 16, 1926.

[28] Harold W. Bourke memoirs. Courtesy of Elizabeth Clark, great granddaughter of Sergeant Thomas Bourke. Published by permission of the family.

VIII: Fort Montgomery in private hands, 1926-2009

[1] New York Times: "Fort Blunder, Near Border, Becomes Camp for Tourists" November 7, 1926

[2] Plattsburgh Daily Press: "Town unable to collect any taxes" August 2, 1932.

[3] Plattsburgh Press Republican, "Common's Tract, Where Lithium Plant will be built, Has interesting History" November 23, 1957

[4] John R. Ross, "Sidelight on History," *The North Countryman*, May 11, 1978.

[5] Harold W. Bourke, Memoirs. Courtesy of Caroline and Elizabeth Clark, granddaughter and great granddaughter of Sergeant Thomas Bourke. Published by permission of the family.

[6] Quit Claim Deed: United States of America to The Lake Champlain Bridge Commission. Holcombe Abstract No. 15. February 19, 1936. Vol. 179 of Deeds, page 277.

[7] Land Contract: George Bierman, Seller, to Mott Creek Corporation. Abstract No. 19. April 21, 1936. Vol. 179 of Deeds, page 389. Quit Claim Deed: George Bierman to Mott Creek Corporation. Abstract

No. 20. May 22, 1936. Vol. 179 of Deeds, page 436. Agreement: George Bierman and Mott Creek Corporation. Abstract No. 21. May 22, 1936. Vol. 179 of Deeds, page 440. Quit Claim Deed: Fort Montgomery Development Co., Inc., George Bierman, President to Mott Creek Corporation. Abstract No. 22. May 22, 1936. Vol. 179 of Deeds, page 438.

[8] See various Agreements, Quit Claim Deeds, Tax Deeds, etc. included in Holcombe Abstracts Nos. 17-32 recorded at Clinton County Clerk's office.

[9] I have heard much about this auction and the items sold. Evidently there is a list of the items sold at the auction that day but I have not been able to locate it. Nor have I been able to determine the final disposition of these historical artifacts sold that day.

[10] The North Countryman, "Historic Fort Montgomery to be Demolished." May 7, 1936.

[11] Plattsburgh Daily Press, "Thousands view opening of lake bridge" July 17, 1937

[12] The North Countryman, "Weston signs bridge contract" May 7, 1936

[13] Plattsburgh Daily Press, "Fort Blunder Falls Before Onslaught of Blasts & Drills…" August 29, 1936. Plattsburgh Daily Press: "Operation on Rouses Pt. Bridge held up" July 15, 1936

[14] Plattsburgh Daily Press, January 27, 1940. Advertisement

[15] Ibid, [blurb] April 21, 1942

[16] Plattsburgh Press-Republican, "Fort Montgomery in state of collapse" September 9. 1980

[17] New York Times, May 6, 1947

[18] Executors Deed: Vivian C. Weston, Donald McLean and Harry M. Goldblatt, As executors of the Last Will and Testament of Andrew Weston, Deceased, to William Castine and Belle Castine, his wife as tenants by the entirety. Holcombe Abstract No. 35. February 15, 1948. Vol. 255 of Deeds, page 109.

[19] Plattsburgh Press Republican, Nov. 22, 1957. Warranty Deed: William Castine, to Quebec Lithium Corporation (N.P.L), Holcombe Abstract No. 39, December 23, 1957. Vol. 394 of Deeds, page 593. Note that the Abstract uses Dec.1, 1957 and lists the amount as $1.00. This is not uncommon.

[20] Plattsburgh Press Republican, Nov. 22, 1957

[21] Ibid, "Construction of Lithium Plant Facilities Set to Begin" December 2, 1957

[22] Ibid, "Rouses Point Wants Beach-Campsite Set Up" September 6, 1961

[23] Harold Otley, "Rouses Point C of C to Step Up Drive to Develop Beach —Campsite," *Plattsburgh Press-Republican,* October 5, 1961

[24] Plattsburgh Press-Republican, "Canadian Firm Willing to Dispose of 400-Acre Site in Rouses Point" November 30[?], 1961

[25] The "Banner" was a weekly shopper's guide published in Rouses Point. Ryan was the editor.

[26] Plattsburgh Press Republican, "Champlain Town Board Seeks Meeting With Area Legislators on Campsite Aid" December 7, 1961

[27] Ibid, "Lag in Getting Right of Way Stalls Housing Development" June 15, 1962 Remarks are contained within blurb

[28] Mary Bolich, "Rouses Point Must Move Soon on Campsite Plans," *Plattsburgh Press-Republican,* August 4, 1962. See also Roy Southworth, "Rouses Point Mayor Confused About Campsite Plan," *Plattsburgh Press-Republican,* August 8, 1962

[29] Roy Southworth, "Rouses Point C of C Asks Backing for Campsite Plan," *Plattsburgh Press-Republican*, August 13, 1962

[30] Plattsburgh Press-Republican, Letters to the Editor- "Rouses Point Citizens Asked to Back Plan for Campsite" August 16, 1962

[31] Ibid, "Rouses Point Developer Takes Option on 400 Acres" February 13, 1963

[32] Roy Southworth, "Point au Roche, 7 sites seen as County Park System," *Plattsburgh Press-Republican*, April 23, 1963

[33] Plattsburgh Press-Republican, "Polino to seek planning board help in restoring fort" July 22, 1966

[34] Al Ryan, "Whatever happened to Fort Montgomery idea?" *Plattsburgh Press Republican*. October 19. 1966

[35] Plattsburgh Press-Republican, "Fort Plan awaiting funds" November 5, 1966

[36] Al Ryan, "Rouses Point's Fort Montgomery for sale," *Plattsburgh Press-Republican*. December 1, 1966

[37] Plattsburgh Press-Republican, "Lake front recreation urged by planner" February 14, 1974

[38] Steve Adamek, "Rouses Point bridgework expected by summer," *Plattsburgh Press-Republican*. May 19, 1976

[39] Plattsburgh Press-Republican, "Fort Montgomery is added to "register of historic places'" September 30, 1977. See also National Register of Historical Places - NEW YORK (NY), Clinton County: <http://www.nationalregisterofhistoricplaces.com/ny/Clinton/state.html> Accessed October 26, 2008.

[40] Steve Manor, "Aid ok'd for Fort Montgomery," *Plattsburgh Press-Republican,* October 27, 1977

[41] Jim Plateau, "Bridge repair unlikely, audit eyes replacement," *Plattsburgh Press-Republican*. January 17, 1980

[42] Report of the Chief of Engineers: 1877, page 5, Report of the Chief of Engineers: 1878, page 7, Report of the Chief of Engineers: 1882, Part I, pages 11,12. See also John R. Weaver II, "A LEGACY IN BRICK AND STONE- American Coastal Defense Forts of the Third System, 1816-1867." 2001. Pictorial Histories Publishing Company, Missoula, MT. 23, footnote, page 46.

[43] Plattsburgh Press-Republican, "Fort Montgomery in state of collapse," September 9. 1980

[44] Steve Manor, "Planned bridge is seen as environmentally safe," *Plattsburgh Press-Republican*. July 22, 1982

[45] Sullivan Mining Group, Ltd. to Fort Montgomery Estates, Holcombe Abstract No. 41, April 29, 1983. Actual purchase price unknown (not stated in deed). Steve Manor, "The Commons' bought by Montreal developer," *Plattsburgh Press-Republican,* May 4, 1983

[46] Steve Manor, "Hearing on "Commons' plan set," *Plattsburgh Press-Republican,* May 11, 1983

[47] Ken Klepper, "Rouses Point eyes 3 new firms, 200 jobs," *Plattsburgh Press-Republican,* June 4, 1983

[48] Steve Manor, "Rouse got the last laugh," *Plattsburgh Press-Republican,* July 9, 1983

[49] Manor, "Vandalism at Commons reported by developer," *Plattsburgh Press-Republican,* August 3, 1983

[50] Manor, "Hearing set for Monday on Commons annexation, *Plattsburgh Press-Republican,*" January 21, 1984

[51] Manor, "Podd's Development Plans Extensive" and "Fort may have a better future," *Plattsburgh Press-Republican,* February 21, 1984

[52] Manor, "Commons annexation gets board approval," *Plattsburgh Press-Republican,* March 31, 1984

[53] Manor, "Pact restricts, directs Commons development" and "Village has option to buy fort," *Plattsburgh Press-Republican,* May 3, 1984. See also "Beach included in annexation pact", "Commons development restricted", August 1, 1984. There is a map of the proposed development and beach to be built along the southwest bank of the cover face in the May 29, 1987 edition of the Press-Republican.

[54] Manor, "1st IDA project may be bonds for Podd plant," *Plattsburgh Press-Republican*, August 25, 1984

[55] Ibid.

[56] Plattsburgh Press-Republican, "Local fort's history reviewed," September 14, 1984

[57] Manor, "Fort Montgomery Restoration Proposed" and "Podd reveals more plans in talk with Village," *Plattsburgh Press-Republican*, September 24, 1984 P. 17

[58] Plattsburgh Press-Republican, Classified Ad, February 5, 1985, Page 21

[59] Manor, "Re-Fortification may be hidden in old bridge," *Plattsburgh Press-Republican*, February 8, 1985

[60] Manor, "Maine company to build Rouses Point bridge," *Plattsburgh Press-Republican*, May 8, 1985, P. 13. See also "Rouses Point bridge to be finished Sept. 22," September 8, 1987

[61] Plattsburgh Press-Republican, "Fort Montgomery studied" July 18, 1985

[62] Manor, "Trip attracts 100 to Fort Montgomery," July 26, 1985 and "Tourists storm fort to support restoration," *Plattsburgh Press-Republican*, July 30, 1985

[63] Manor, "$133,000 sought to study fort" and "Restoration Project has wide backing," *Plattsburgh Press-Republican*, August 1, 1985.

[64] Ibid, of note is that CAMP National Secretary Hart cites the erroneous border fallacy as a key argument for preservation.

[65] Manor, "2 million Fort Montgomery addition means up to 75 jobs," *Plattsburgh Press-Republican*, August 9, 1985

[66] Manor, "Grassroots campaign at work to save fort," *Plattsburgh Press-Republican*, August 19, 1985 (part I of 4). In this series Manor erroneously continues to merge the two forts into one, referring to what should have been the first structure as "Fort Montgomery" and the second as "Fort Blunder."

[67] Manor, *Plattsburgh Press-Republican*, Four-part series running August 19-22, 1985 and "Waterfront development would help support fort" August 22, 1985

[68] Manor, "LDC, DEC at odds over industrial park," *Plattsburgh Press-Republican*, March 26, 1986, Part 1 of 2 parts

[69] Manor, "DEC sets conditions on development," *Plattsburgh Press-Republican*, March 27, 1986 Part 2 of 2. See also "LDC votes to accept half of industrial park," March 27, 1986

[70] Manor, "DEC: Industrial park will not affect wetlands," *Plattsburgh Press-Republican*, July 30, 1986

[71] Manor, "Some original Fort Montgomery stone found in bridge causeway," *Plattsburgh Press-Republican*, May 30, 1986

[72] Manor, "Podd offers to give Fort to State," *Plattsburgh Press-Republican*, September 18, 1986

[73] Ibid.

[74] Manor, "Rouses Point supports giving fort to state," *Plattsburgh Press-Republican*, September 24, 1986

[75] Millard, James P. "The Secrets of Crab Island," America's Historic Lakes: South Hero, VT. 2004. 74,77

[76] Manor, "Jakubowski, Podd to discuss fort's future," *Plattsburgh Press-Republican*, October 21, 1986

[77] Manor, "Podd, state to discuss fort offer," *Plattsburgh Press-Republican*, October 21, 1986

[78] Manor, "State parks official tours Fort Montgomery," *Plattsburgh Press-Republican*, October 24, 1986

[79] *Plattsburgh Press-Republican,* October 25 and October 27, 1986

[80] Ibid. December 9, 1986

[81] Manor, "Podd offers to donate beach, Fort Montgomery," *Plattsburgh Press-Republican,* May 14, 1987

X: Bastion A and Curtain I

[1] NA, Records of the Chief of Engineers, Record Group 77, Fortification File, Drawer 259, Sheet 94. 1872. Armament Report of C.E. Blunt, Drawer 246, Sheet 32-3, Guns mounted, June 30, 1867.

[2] NA, Records of the Chief of Engineers, Record Group 77, Fortification File, Drawer 246, Sheet 32-34. J.W. Barlow. Gun platforms and armament. December 31, 1900 at Fort Montgomery, N.Y. Sheet No. 3 Barbette tier 19249/54

[3] "Water gate" is the term used on the plans. See NA, Records of the Chief of Engineers, Record Group 77, Fortifications File, Drawer 7, Sheet 26. 1850. Barracks Curtain No. I, Plan of, (1st floor)

[4] NA, Records of the Chief of Engineers, Record Group 77, Fortification File, Drawer 7, Sheet 47-1857. Plans, sections, & elevations of Gateway to Drawbridge on Front No. 1. July 27, 1857.

[5] Supplement to the Annual Report of the State Engineer and Surveyor of the State of New York, for the Fiscal Year ended September 30, 1912. 1913. Albany: J.B. Lyon. 9. The report goes on to state that "On windy days the depth is taken in a well within the fort inclosure by measuring the depth on a flagstone in the bottom of the well."

[6] NA, Records of the Chief of Engineers, Record Group 77, Fortification File, Drawer 259, Sheet 94. Plan of Casemate Tier Fort Montgomery showing its present armament February 1st 1872.

[7] NA, Records of the Chief of Engineers, Record Group 77, Fortification File, Drawer 7, Sheet 66. Sketch showing arrangement & dimensions of the existing masonry floors in Curtain IV & proposed modifications in 1st and 2nd floors of Fronts I & V. September 21, 1867. See also Drawer 7, Sheet 0-3, January 1886.

[8] NA, Records of the Chief of Engineers, Record Group 77, Fortification File, Drawer 7, Sheet 24. Barracks Curtain No. 1, Plan of, (1st floor). Rec'd from Col. Mason 22 Oct. 1850

XI: Bastion B and Curtain II

[1] NA, Records of the Chief of Engineers, Record Group 77, Fortification File, Drawer 246, Sheet 32-36. Gun Platforms and Armament December 31, 1902 Fort Montgomery, NY. Sheet No. 1 Lower (first) tier of guns (casemate).

[2] NA, Records of the Chief of Engineers, Record Group 77, Fortification File, Drawer 259, Sheet 95. Plan of Barbette tier Fort Montgomery showing the present armament, February 1st 1872.

XII: Bastion C and Curtain III, the Gorge

[1] NA. Records of the Chief of Engineers, Record Group 77, Fortification File, Drawer 7, Sheet 56. Plan of Barbette Tier. July 31, 1861

XIII: Bastions D-E and Curtains IV–V

XIV: Ordnance at Fort Montgomery

[1] Found by Charles Barney Sr. in 1951-52.

[2] Taylor: Sect. 17, p. 43

[3] War of the Rebellion: Official Records- Series III, Vol. 1 P. 773-774

[4] NA, Records of the Chief of Engineers, Record Group 77, Fortification File, Drawer 246, Sheet 32-1. January 31, 1865

[5] Taylor: P. 46, 49.

[6] NA, Records of the Chief of Engineers, Record Group 77, Fortification File, Drawer 7, Sheet 66. 1867.

[7] NA, Records of the Chief of Engineers, Record Group 77, Fortification File, Drawer 246, Sheet 32-37. 1901.

[8] NA, Records of the Chief of Engineers. Record Group 77. Fort Montgomery Armament Sheet. January 31, 1865. Drawer 246, sheet 32-1

[9] NA, Records of the Chief of Engineers. Record Group 77. Drawer 246, Sheet 32-37. December 31, 1901.

[10] Plattsburgh Sentinel May 8, 1908

[11] NA, Record Group 153, Records of the Adjutant General, Sheet 1, undated. Clinton County Historical Association Collection.

www.ingramcontent.com/pod-product-compliance
Lightning Source LLC
Chambersburg PA
CBHW080502110426
42742CB00017B/2974